THE SCHOOL-TO-WORK MOVEMENT

THE SCHOOL-TO-WORK MOVEMENT

Origins and Destinations

Edited by
William J. Stull and Nicholas M. Sanders

Simon Hakim, Advisory Editor

PRAEGER

Westport, Connecticut
London

Library of Congress Cataloging-in-Publication Data

The school-to-work movement: origins and destinations / edited by William J. Stull and Nicholas M. Sanders.
p. cm.
Includes bibliographical references and index.
ISBN 0–275–97016–7 (alk. paper)
1. School-to-work transition—Congresses. 2. Career education—Congresses. I. Stull, William J. II. Sanders, Nicholas M., 1939–
LC1037.S35 2003
370.11′3—dc21 2002029873

British Library Cataloguing in Publication Data is available.

Library of Congress Catalog Card Number: 2002029873
ISBN: 0–275–97016–7

First published in 2003

Praeger Publishers, 88 Post Road West, Westport, CT 06881
An imprint of Greenwood Publishing Group, Inc.
www.praeger.com

Printed in the United States of America

The paper used in this book complies with the Permanent Paper Standard issued by the National Information Standards Organization (Z39.48-1984).

10 9 8 7 6 5 4 3 2 1

Contents

Figures and Tables

FIGURES

TABLES

Preface and Acknowledgments

The chapters in this book provide an overview of academic and policy research on the school-to-work (STW) movement and the many program initiatives associated with it. The original versions of all chapters except the first two were presented and discussed at a national invitational conference held in Philadelphia, PA, during December 2000. The conference, attended by STW professionals from across the nation, was sponsored by the Mid-Atlantic Regional Educational Laboratory, the Laboratory for Student Success (LSS), at the Temple University Center for Research in Human Development and Education (CRHDE).

At the conference, nineteen papers were presented by leading researchers and practitioners in the STW field. The fourteen of them that dealt with the STW movement in general have been revised for this volume. The five that described specific STW programs were not included because of space constraints. They are summarized, however, in a September 2001 issue of *The CEIC Review*—a publication of CRHDE. That issue of the *Review* (available upon request) also contains a series of next-step recommendations that arose out of the conference deliberations.

The goal of the conference was to provide a national forum for assessing the past, present, and future of the STW movement on the basis of the findings of the most current research. To achieve this, the conference consisted of both presentations of papers and small-group discussion sessions, with the latter including the members of the audience as well as presenters. Because of the high degree of interaction throughout the conference and the broad diversity of opinions expressed, the chapter authors had many opportunities to refine and extend their ideas. Subsequently, all authors revised their work for the present volume in response to the questions and comments of their colleagues.

The book is divided into five sections, with the first serving as an introduction. It contains an essay by William Stull giving an overview of the STW movement and linking the volume's chapters to the larger STW literature. It also includes a chapter prepared by Mark Rohland, an editor in the LSS Outreach and Dissemination Unit, summarizing the individual contributions.

The second section contains chapters focusing on the economic context within which the STW movement evolved during the 1990s. The movement grew out of a specific set of economic conditions in the 1980s, and these changed markedly in the following decade. Michael Leeds and Elizabeth Wheaton, Leonard Nakamura, and William Dunkelberg describe different dimensions of these altered circumstances and draw out implications for work-based education in general and the STW movement in particular.

The third section provides an overview of the growth of the STW movement with particular emphasis on the impact of the School-to-Work Opportunities Act of 1994. Alan Hershey, Bari Anhalt Erlichson, Mark Schug and Richard Western, and Robert Zemsky examine this evolutionary process from a diversity of perspectives: local, state, federal, and international.

The chapters in the fourth section examine important individual topics in the STW literature: pedagogy (David Thornton Moore and Katherine Hughes), minority involvement (Francisco Rivera-Batiz), labor-market impacts (John Bishop and Ferran Mañe), and the college-for-all movement (James Rosenbaum). In each case, the authors make specific recommendations for educational policy and practice.

The last section focuses on the future of the STW movement in an economic and political environment that is very different from the one in which it began. There are currently great differences of opinion among researchers and practitioners as to the direction the movement should take in this new setting. Robert Lerman, David Stern, and Richard Kazis and Hilary Pennington offer alternative strategies for preserving the accomplishments of the movement and maintaining it as a viable force for educational reform in the future.

The conference on which this volume was based was one of a series of education research conferences sponsored over the past five years by LSS. Margaret Wang, the founding director of the laboratory, was unwavering in her support of STW research, and strongly encouraged us to organize a conference that focused explicitly on the status and policy implications of the most current work in the area. We are extraordinarily grateful for the energy and enthusiasm she brought to this project despite failing health and, more generally, for her superb leadership during the laboratory's formative years. We are also deeply appreciative of the continuing support provided by the current LSS director, JoAnn Manning. LSS is funded by the Institute of Education Sciences (IES) of the U.S. Department of Education. The opinions expressed in this volume do not, of course, necessarily reflect those of LSS or its funding agency.

Finally, we would like to thank the LSS staff members who assisted us in the arduous work of organizing the conference and preparing this volume. We are particularly grateful to Kim Kendall for making the conference arrangements and to Tina Caldwell and Veronica Young (and their staff) for their assistance in preparing mailings and materials. Senior Research Associates

Judith Stull and Ronald Taylor provided advice and encouragement at crucial junctures. Most of all, we want to express our appreciation for the skill and hard work of our LSS editor, Mark Rohland. Almost single-handedly, he converted a disheveled pile of academic papers into an internally consistent, unified final product. His attention to detail, command of the English language, and knowledge of manuscript architecture were critical to the completion of this project.

W. J. S.
N. M. S.

Part I
Introduction

1

School-to-Work in Schools: An Overview

William J. Stull

The transition from school to the workplace is one of the central life passages in modern society. Over the past fifteen years, schools across the country have established new programs to facilitate this transition for their students. These programs are the products of an education reform effort—now generally referred to as the school-to-work (STW) movement—that came together socially and politically in the late 1980s and early 1990s, reached a peak in the mid-1990s, and is now in steep decline.

This introductory chapter describes the movement's origins, develops a framework for assessing its educational impact, links the chapters in the volume and other research efforts to this framework, and concludes with discussions of the movement's decline and legacy. Throughout, the focus is on STW programming at the level of the individual school and its students. Because of space constraints, little attention is paid to federal and state STW policy issues, though these are addressed by several chapters in the volume. In addition, this chapter confines its attention to programming in public high schools. Some efforts were made to establish STW activities in elementary and middle schools and to provide linkages to community colleges, but these were peripheral to the main thrust of the movement. Little is known about STW programming in private schools.

ECONOMIC CONDITIONS IN THE 1980s

The origins of the STW movement can be traced to increased national concern in the 1980s about several long-term trends in the U.S. economy. The first was the sharp drop in U.S. productivity growth that began in the early 1970s and the resulting decline in the growth rates of real wages (Research and Policy Committee of the Committee for Economic Development, 1996). The low rate of productivity growth in the U.S. relative to other industrialized countries raised serious questions about the nation's long-term international competitiveness. The second trend was the large wage gap that opened up between those with and without college degrees after 1980, the joint result of higher real wages for skilled workers and lower real wages for unskilled workers (Gottschalk, 1997; Murphy & Welch, 1989). The third trend, largely the result of the first two, was a long-term increase in family income inequality (Gottschalk, 1997).

A variety of explanations were offered for these phenomena. But a common refrain—voiced by business people as well as intellectuals and policymakers—was the inability of many young workers, mainly those lacking a four-year college degree, to add significant value in a technology-driven and increasingly competitive global economy. A series of national research reports beginning in the late 1980s publicized these problems and raised doubts about the ability of the American education system to provide the required skills without substantial reform (Commission on the Skills of the American Workforce, 1990; Secretary's Commission on Achieving Necessary Skills, 1991; William T. Grant Foundation Commission on Work, Family, and Citizenship, 1988). According to these and other studies (Gardecki & Neumark, 1995; Holzer, 1996; Klerman & Karoly, 1995; Leeds & Wheaton, this volume; Zemsky, 1994), too few students left school in the 1980s with the academic knowledge, personal qualities, and job-specific competencies needed to establish themselves quickly in stable, full-time employment with reasonable earning potential. Young people without these skills frequently floundered for years before finding careers that suited them, and too often those they found had limited long-run prospects (Rivera-Batiz, this volume).

THE SCHOOL-TO-WORK MOVEMENT AND THE SCHOOL-TO-WORK OPPORTUNITIES ACT

The STW movement is best understood as the education system's response to these reports and the economic problems they addressed. There is a long tradition of work-based education in America, beginning with the manual-training movement in the latter part of the nineteenth century (Kliebard, 1999). In particular, vocational education has been a well-established aspect of public schooling since the passage of the Smith-Hughes Act in 1917, and probably earlier. Other approaches like cooperative education and career academies (Stern, this volume) also have lengthy histories. For reasons that are not clear (but certainly warrant investigation by historians of education), the STW movement did not seem to emerge out of any of these earlier initiatives (except perhaps in reaction to them). Instead, it arrived on the American political scene substantially free of connections to earlier reform or policy efforts.

The movement is made up of individuals and organizations seeking to improve the school experience and STW transition for young people by making their secondary education more work-based. It became an important force for change in the late 1980s when many communities, states, and nonprofit organizations began establishing STW programs. (For the Wisconsin experience, see Schug & Western in this volume). The growth of the movement appears to have been rapid. W. Stull, Sanders, and J. Stull (2000) found that most of the high schools in their nationwide sample had a variety of STW offerings by 1992. At the same time, many educators, politicians, and researchers began serious investigations of STW systems in other countries, usually to learn what aspects of these systems might be successfully exported to America (Lerman & Pouncy, 1990; Rosenbaum & Takehiko, 1989; Rosenbaum, Takehiko, Settersen, & Maier, 1990). Zemsky's chapter in this volume continues this tradition.

These early initiatives were reinforced by a series of federal actions in the early 1990s. First were the Carl D. Perkins Vocational and Applied Technology Education Act Amendments of 1990, a response to two interrelated trends that had adversely affected vocational enrollments in the 1980s. The first was the steady rise in the percentage of high-school students who pursued postsecondary education immediately after graduation (U.S. Department of Education, 1996). The second was the cumulative impact of research, showing that most vocational-education students did not benefit much from the occupationally specific training they received in high school (Boesel, Hudson, Deich, & Masten, 1994; Kantor & Tyack, 1982; McCormick, Tuma, & Houser, 1995). The amendments required federally supported vocational-education programs to "integrate academic and vocational education . . . through coherent sequences of courses" as a way of providing vocational-education students with both "academic and vocational competencies."

A second relevant piece of federal legislation was the 1994 Goals 2000: Educate America Act (Jennings, 1995), which enacted the National Education Goals announced at the National Education Summit five years earlier. The act encouraged the establishment of high standards and proposed focusing systemwide reform on their achievement by all students. Its passage reinforced the rapidly growing standards-based reform movement that was soon to overtake the STW movement in terms of influence on education policy at all levels. Two of the act's goals, however, did address the concerns of the STW movement and to that extent enhanced its strength. One (Student Achievement and Citizenship) specified that all American students would leave school prepared for "productive employment." Another (Adult Literacy and Lifelong Learning) specified that every adult American would possess "the knowledge and skills necessary to compete in a global economy."

The most important federal action (and the culmination of the STW movement in many respects) was the passage of the School-to-Work Opportunities Act (STWOA) of 1994. The purpose of this legislation was to create a state-based national workforce development system by providing seed money to states and localities to develop STW programs meeting their particular educational needs (Jennings, 1995). Under the STWOA, states received grants after they established governance systems and statewide STW partnerships with broad stakeholder representation. States were given considerable latitude in establishing these structures and followed a variety of administrative models according to their education goals (Erlichson, this volume). Once formed, the statewide governing bodies then made substate grants to local partnerships, which typically spanned a number of school districts and included local education, business, government, and union leaders on their boards.

After receiving funds, local partnerships worked to establish STW programs in individual schools and districts. The STWOA did not specify in detail what such programs should look like except that (a) they had to consist of school-based learning, work-based learning, and connecting activities; and (b) they had to be sufficiently structured so that students could choose among one or more "career majors": linked school- and work-based learning paths to defined postsecondary education or employment opportunities. For students not attending a baccalaureate institution, it was hoped that successful completion of such a program would lead to a high-school diploma, a certificate or diploma from a postsecondary institution when appropriate, and an industry-recognized occupational skill certificate. Overall, the decentralized nature of the funding process was designed to encourage experimentation at both the state and local levels.

By the end of 1998, all fifty states plus Puerto Rico and the District of Columbia had qualified for the STWOA development and implementation grants. Total funding over the life of the legislation will be perhaps two billion dollars, with the largest annual appropriations occurring in fiscal years 1997 and 1998 (Kazis & Pennington, this volume). As a result of the substate grants, approximately half of U.S. school districts will receive funds from the STWOA (Hershey, this volume). Appropriations ceased in 2001, although previously approved monies may flow to some states after that date.

THE MODEL STW PROGRAM

As a result of the passage of the STWOA, mainstream advocates of the STW movement came to general agreement by the mid-1990s about what the model STW program at the level of the individual school should look like and what it should accomplish. The essence of this "consensus" program may be summarized as follows:

> A coherent combination of linked school-based learning, work-based learning, and connecting activities for a broad range of students leading to higher academic achievement and improved labor-market outcomes.

This statement is a synthesis of what many advocates hoped (and still hope) the movement would achieve at the school level, and thus does not necessarily reflect the exact views of any single advocate or researcher. Despite the end of federal funding, it continues to be the dominant paradigm, though some writers (including several in this volume) are beginning to consider alternative approaches.

The model is described broadly to accommodate the diversity of real-world school STW programs—most of which are complex combinations of cooperative education, vocational education, school-based enterprises, tech-prep, youth apprenticeships, school-to-apprenticeship, mentorships, internships, job shadowing, workplace visits, entrepreneurship training, dual enrollment, career development, career majors, and career academies (Charner, Fraser, Hubbard, Rogers, & Horne, 1995; Stern, Finkelstein, Stone, Latting, & Dornsife, 1995). Also, it is important to note that the model includes both input components (structure, type, and scale of activities) and output components (student outcomes). It is not enough that students engage in integrated work-related activities in school and school-related activities at work. These activities must also have real impact on students' skills and opportunities.

PRELIMINARY ASSESSMENT OF THE MODEL PROGRAM

Creating STW programs consistent with this model in a significant number of schools was an ambitious undertaking for a variety of reasons. First, such programs represent a significant deviation from the "shopping mall" approach taken by the typical comprehensive public high school with its rigid separation of academic and vocational tracks (Powell, Farrar, & Cohen, 1985). Second, they require strong school–employer partnerships that have never existed in most school districts. Third, work-based education programs have historically served only the weaker students (Kliebard, 1999; Ravitch, 2000), making it difficult to build a broad constituency for STW programs. And fourth, the resources necessary for full implementation are far greater than those provided by the STWOA. The legislation had a short lifespan and limited funding (Grubb, 1996a), and because it lost its political support in the mid-1990s, there never was much likelihood of its continuation (Kazis & Pennington, this volume; Lerman, this volume).

There was also no guarantee that programs with the characteristics stressed by STW advocates could produce the desired student outcomes. The theory of learning that underlies STW programming (often more implied than explicit) asserts that combining school-based with work-based learning will produce a substantial increase in both academic knowledge and career-relevant skill acquisition. Unfortunately, these ambitious claims have been only partly substantiated by research (discussed throughout the rest of this chapter). It has thus always been uncertain whether STW programs, no matter how well-designed and funded, can deliver on the promise of raising academic and career performance for large numbers of students.

These considerations suggest that, despite federal funding and the enthusiasm of STW advocates, it was never very likely that the model program would be widely established in American high schools—or, if implemented, that it would have an important effect on both the academic and career outcomes of students. We should be realistic in our overall assessment of the STW movement, however. It should not be judged a failure just because it will not achieve its most optimistic objectives. A balanced appraisal suggests that the movement has effected some broad changes in secondary education that are likely to have enduring value. I return to these issues in the final section of the chapter.

RESEARCH ON SCHOOL-TO-WORK

I turn now to an overview of the STW research literature, organized in terms of the characteristics of the model program previously described. This literature is still evolving in important ways because programs and the research on them, particularly in the area of student outcomes, are ongoing. Consequently, the conclusions I reach are necessarily tentative.

There are three important strands to the STW literature. The first seeks to determine the extent of school-level implementation. Much of this work is anecdotal, focusing on the programs of individual schools and districts. However, a major research grant was awarded to Mathematica Policy Research, Inc. by the U.S. Department of Education to assess (among other things) implementation of the STWOA in local partnerships across the country. Many results from this project, the National Evaluation of School-to-Work Implementation, have already been published and will be cited extensively throughout this chapter (Hershey, Hudis, Silverberg, & Haimson, 1997; Hershey, Silverberg, Haimson, Hudis, & Jackson, 1999; Silverberg, Haimson, & Hershey, 1998). In addition, Hershey's chapter in this volume summarizes the most important findings. A potential limitation of the Mathematica study from the point of view of the entire STW movement is that it provides no information about STW activities in the 50% of American school districts not part of a local STWOA partnership. This problem is not as serious as it might appear, however, because a disproportionate share of public high-school students attends partnership schools. Additional information on implementation (and student outcomes) is also becoming available from the 1997 National Longitudinal Survey of Youth (NLSY97) and several special STW surveys associated with it (Rivera-Batiz, this volume).

A second strand of literature is concerned with what might be called "process" outcomes. This research looks at schools or local partnerships with established STW programs, and seeks to identify the elements that work insofar as they have significantly engaged the students, teachers, and employers who participate in them (Olson, 1997; Urquiola et al., 1997). Most of these studies tend to be anecdotal and emphasize student participation, satisfaction, and retention.

The third strand seeks to measure the educational and occupational outcomes for students who participate in STW programs. Because the STW movement has existed for little more than a decade, and because it takes time for students to pass through the education system into the labor force, many studies of the impact of STW programming on educational achievement and labor-market success are still in progress. Nonetheless, what is available—including several studies in this volume—will be reported on later in this chapter. Some findings from an older literature concerned with the effectiveness of vocational and cooperative education will also be discussed.

In the analysis that follows, research from all three strands will be incorporated into a framework organized in terms of the input and output elements of the model program. The purpose of the inquiry will be to determine the extent to which the model has been put in place around the country and is yielding the student-outcome results hoped for by its advocates. The chapters in this volume will be positioned within this framework so the reader can see how they relate to the larger STW literature.

School-Based Learning Activities

School-based learning activities are classroom and other activities in the school that link the traditional academic curriculum to the world of work. As envisioned by STW and STWOA advocates, school-based learning activities encompass two interrelated groups of program components. The first consists of career-development activities. They help students become aware of career options, set realistic long-run personal and career goals, begin the process of career selection, and prepare themselves for entry into the labor force. The second group, building on the first, consists of curricular elements—course units, entire courses, or sequences of courses (which may lead to career majors)—that are explicitly connected to particular sectors, industries, or occupations. These elements may be offered in traditional comprehensive high schools, in schools-within-schools (e.g., career academies), or in specialized career-oriented schools. A subset of STW writers emphasizes the importance of using applied, contextual pedagogy to deliver these elements.

All research on STW implementation shows that career development is the most widely established program element around the country (Hershey, this volume; Hershey et al., 1997; Hershey et al., 1999; Olson, 1997; Silverberg et al., 1998). Mathematica's surveys show that career-development activities are widely offered by partnership schools and that their availability has increased in recent years. For example, the percentage of partnership schools offering individual career planning increased from about 45% in 1996–1997 to nearly 55% in 1999–2000 (Hershey, this volume). Further, Mathematica's student-survey data show that many students participate in these activities. Approximately 80% of surveyed students in the class of 1998, for example, attended a work-readiness class. A variety of reasons explain the success of career development as a STW focus. In many cases, schools built on preexisting career programs that had proven popular with students, parents, and school staff.

Moreover, career-development activities can often be launched quickly, because they do not require substantial resources or collaboration with outsiders. Overall, it is clear that this aspect of STW programming has been well received.

Perhaps not surprisingly, career-focused curriculum elements and curricula are less commonly found in schools, and forward movement in establishing them has been slower. More specifically, the Mathematica study found that career majors and integrated curriculum elements were somewhat less available in partnership schools than career-development activities and were increasing at a more modest pace. For example, written career-course sequences with at least some student clustering (one form of career major identified by the study) were offered by 33% of the schools in 1996 and 40% of the schools in 1999 (Hershey, this volume). More intensive, career-based programs of study were offered by 25% of the schools in 1996 and 27% in 1999. Student involvement in these activities presents a more mixed pattern. A very high percentage of the surveyed students reported having at least one career-related assignment in an academic class (87% in 1996, 83% in 1998), but many fewer took a class explicitly designed to satisfy their career interest (17% in 1996, 24% in 1998).

The overall picture presented by these data is fairly clear. In the second half of the 1990s, a substantial proportion of high schools offered school-based learning activities, with career development somewhat more popular than integrated curricula, and with both groups of activities showing modest increases over time. Student participation, however, was largely confined to those activities that could be undertaken with the least effort on the part of both the school and its students. Relatively few students participated in structured programs in which students were clustered together by career interest. Schools thus made in-depth programming available, but student involvement was limited.

In part, the slow progress in developing the more intense forms of school-based learning is a consequence of the difficulty of the task. Building career-focused courses and curricula that truly integrate academic and vocational components requires a significant commitment of time and energy on the part of teachers, administrators, and other school personnel. In addition to the hours of work involved, developing an integrated curriculum requires school staff to be creative, flexible, and willing to experiment. It also obliges them to work intensively with each other and with potential partners in business and post-secondary education. Obtaining this level of commitment in support of education reform is always a major challenge for school leadership—particularly because in most districts, resources available for professional development are limited.

Perhaps an even more important barrier to the widespread creation of integrated curricula appears to be their low priority in most schools when compared to career development. Cost differences may partially explain this disparity, but a deeper reason appears to be the widespread doubts of students, parents, and school staff that secondary education should be organized around careers (Zemsky, this volume). Given the breadth and depth of this concern (reported by many researchers), it seems unlikely that participation in in-depth, career-focused curricula will ever approach a majority of secondary students. This, of course, is not to say that "education through occupations" (Grubb, 1996b) could not be a valuable approach for certain students and in certain settings.

Work-Based Learning Activities

Work-based learning activities are designed to give students significant real-world work experience and skills, and reinforce and motivate their academic studies at the same time. They represent a way outside of conventional school settings to inform students about careers, encourage them to persevere in their education, and help them develop skills that will enable them to succeed in the labor market (Hughes, Moore, & Bailey, 1999). Examples of such activities (in roughly increasing order of engagement) are worksite visits, job shadowing, unpaid internships, community service projects, school-based enterprises, workplace mentorships, cooperative education, jobs linked to career majors, and apprenticeships. The first two of these might best be classified as career-development activities because they involve little time commitment on the part of students or employers. The remainder are much more likely to provide both career development and genuine job skills.

Many advocates regard the work-based learning component of the STW model to be its important element. As a result, work-based learning activities were a high priority in many local STW efforts from the movement's beginning (Bailey, 1995b; Hershey et al., 1997). Since that time, schools have continually attempted to expand the breadth of such activities by increasing the number of participating students and employers. They have also tried to increase activity depth by developing more intensive workplace experiences that include paid employment, on-the-job mentoring, and close linkages with academic courses. Often, they built on preexisting programs and employer relationships in these efforts.

In general, schools have been successful in making connections with local businesses. According to one study (Zemsky, Shapiro, Iannozzi, Cappelli, & Bailey, 1998), approximately one-quarter of U.S. firms participate in a STW partnership, and one-third provide some form of work-based learning activity. Data from Mathematica's research provide comparable evidence from the point of view of schools rather than employers. The percentage of partnership high schools offering a variety of work-based learning activities increased, sometimes significantly, from school year 1995–1996 to 1998–1999. As one might expect from the discussion in the previous subsection, schools were more likely to offer activities that were not necessarily related to a student's career major than activities that were related, and the former grew more quickly than the latter. Also, pure career-development activities were most common and increased most rapidly. To illustrate, Mathematica found that paid, school-year jobs related to career majors were offered by 28% of the partnership schools in 1995–1996 and 31% in 1998–1999 (Hershey, this volume). Worksite visits or job shadowing not necessarily related to career majors were offered by 49% of the schools in 1995–1996 and 58% in 1998–1999.

Schools also made some advances in broadening student participation in work-based learning activities, but mainly in those not requiring significant student time and employer involvement. Mathematica found, for instance, that student participation in either job shadowing or worksite visits increased from 66% in 1996 to 70% in 1998 (Hershey, this volume). Progress in developing more in-depth workplace activities, particularly those involving paid positions with structured training and significant hours, has been more difficult. For example, the proportion of students in partnership schools obtaining jobs through their schools remained constant (at 28%) through the second half of the 1990s.

Part of the problem lies with low student demand for more intensive work-based options. Many students are already devoting significant effort to after-school jobs or extracurricular activities that they are reluctant to give up. They therefore have neither the time nor inclination to involve themselves in intense work-based learning activities outside of school. In addition, the widespread doubts about career-centered education will limit the number of youth who will seek such opportunities. Equally important, it is often difficult to increase the supply of positions because of their high cost and limited benefit to most employers (Bassi, Feeley, Hillmeyer, & Ludwig, 1997; Osterman, 1995). The employer incentives identified by Bailey (1995a) do not appear to be strong enough to permit significant scaling up from existing levels. Finally, most schools do not have the resources or expertise to engage in job-development activities on a large scale.

Although some research has shown that adequate planning and organization can overcome these obstacles to employer and student recruitment (Hughes, 1998), it is doubtful that many students will ever be engaged in work-based learning activities requiring significant time away from school and extensive coordination with classroom teachers. It does seem likely, however, that less-intrusive work-based learning activities, mainly those whose main purpose is career development, will become a permanent part of the high-school experience for many students.

Connecting Activities

The model STW program requires substantial administrative support, mostly in the form of staff time. Much of this is needed to establish and then maintain linkages between the school and employers on the one hand, and between the school and institutions of postsecondary education on the other—the latter potentially including baccalaureate institutions, junior colleges

(Dougherty, 1994; Grubb, 1996b), and noncollege training programs (Hansen, 1994). Connecting activities are the administrative functions, typically taking place in the school, that provide these links. They include recruitment of employers and mentors, job development, student placement and monitoring, organization of job shadowing and worksite visits, coordination of school–employer curriculum development, curriculum coordination with institutions of higher learning, data collection on program participants, and assistance to program completers who seek employment or further education.

Despite their importance, relatively little has been explicitly written about connecting activities. One reason perhaps is that such "nuts-and-bolts" functions do not capture the imagination of education researchers and reformers the way school-based and work-based learning activities do. In general, STW writers and advocates have always implicitly assumed that connecting activities would be carried out by the existing staff of teachers and guidance counselors in a school with a small amount of support and direction from the school's central administration. The Mathematica study presents some anecdotal evidence from the early years of STWOA, suggesting that this view is accurate (Hershey et al., 1997). Teachers in its study schools were encouraged through both moral and material incentives to become more aware of career opportunities for their students, to help students make choices among the options available, and to work with employers on curricula. At the same time, the role of guidance counselors was redefined to increase their involvement in career awareness, job development, and curriculum. STWOA funds were evidently used to support these activities, but no permanent changes in staffing or funding were mentioned.

It is clear from the research findings previously reported that some connecting activities were successfully undertaken over the past decade. Otherwise, the observed links between schools and employers (and between schools and postsecondary education institutions) would not have come into existence. The dearth of empirical research on these activities is unfortunate, however, because it means that little is known about how they were carried out, what they cost, and which were successful and which were not. Nonetheless, it seems beyond dispute that maintaining a set of school–employer and school–college collaborations that provide integrated work- and school-based learning experiences for many students is likely to be an expensive undertaking. Among other things, it requires a staff of trained professionals who will devote their full time to these tasks. It is unreasonable to expect a school's existing teachers and administrators to carry them out as additional duties over the long run with only minimal extra compensation. An additional problem is that few school personnel, initially at least, have the necessary skills or experience. Given the tightness of local education budgets, it is hard to escape the conclusion that connecting activities will always be underfunded in most schools. This will in turn seriously limit the expansion of STW activities that require external collaborators.

Coherent Combination of Linked Activities

For students to get the full benefit of a STW program, it is not enough that they participate in a set of school-based and work-based activities. These activities must build on one another and establish a direction in which the student wants to go. A central requirement of the STW model program, therefore, is that it must have an integrated sequence of school- and work-based activities linked to each other, to the academic curriculum, and to the diverse long-term goals of students. Most advocates believe the sequence should begin in the freshman year (if not sooner) with low-intensity activities and build progressively through the senior year (Charner et al., 1995). Such a structure enables the program to have a real impact on the long-run learning and decision making of students and encourages potential dropouts to stay in school.

STW-program supporters also repeatedly emphasize the importance of substantive, mutually reinforcing links between the student's work and school experiences (Osterman & Iannozzi, 1993; Research and Policy Committee of the Committee for Economic Development, 1996). Students find it easy to compartmentalize their in-school and out-of-school lives, so the full benefit of STW programming will occur only when many points of contact exist between what they are experiencing in the classroom and the workplace (Charner et al., 1995). Moore and Hughes (this volume) extend this idea by advocating that academic teachers encourage students to take a more critical perspective of their work experiences. In their view, students should acquire from these experiences not only job-relevant "skills," but also a deeper understanding of the social structure of work in the United States and the ability to see deficiencies in that structure.

All evidence indicates that many schools during the 1990s committed themselves to establishing STW programs that provide the coherent, linked sequence of activities specified by the model program. For example, the Mathematica study (as previously noted) found that the proportion of partnership schools offering some form of career major has increased over time (Hershey, this volume). The number of career academies nationwide has increased also. Stern (this volume) notes that membership in the three largest academy networks grew from 100 in 1990 to more than 700 in 2000. It is one thing to develop a program on paper, however, and another to have it work out in practice. Schools may structure programs so that activities build on one another if taken in order, but because of scheduling conflicts or other factors, students may not follow the prescribed sequence. More seriously, because of its inflexibility and time demands, only a small number of students may choose to participate in a highly integrated program.

Mathematica's surveys provide some evidence on the extent to which students in the late 1990s engaged in a diversity of STW activities—a necessary condition for participation in a truly integrated program (Hershey, this volume). A substantial majority of students in partnership schools (approximately

65% in 1998) reported participating in at least four different types of career-development activities while in high school, and the proportion seems to be increasing slightly with time. There was also a noticeable increase in the percentage of students (from 12% in 1996 to 18% in 1998) who moved beyond career development to a career-related academic program. However, there appeared to be no increase in the number of students reporting significant links between their work and school experiences. Most tellingly of all, Mathematica's surveys indicated that the percentage of students that could reasonably be viewed as participating in a comprehensive STW program with both school-based and work-based elements was only 2% in 1996 and 3% in 1998.

Taken together, these data suggest strongly that the STW movement has failed to draw even a sizable minority of students into career-based programs of study with the breadth and integration specified by the consensus model. Many students have participated in multiple career-development activities (though not necessarily in any logical order), but most have chosen not to move beyond career exploration to more intensive forms of STW programming. In part, this lack of engagement is attributable to the modest funding and short time horizon of the STWOA, but as noted earlier, other factors were at work as well. Perhaps participation in integrated STW programs will increase in the future, but this must be considered unlikely, given their high cost from the point of view of both students and schools.

Broad Range of Students

The STW movement arose out of a generalized national concern in the late 1980s about the future employability of young people who do not graduate from a four-year college or university. As a result, the movement in its early years focused most of its attention on this target group. By the mid-1990s, however, the consensus view had changed fundamentally: The STW movement became a reform effort aimed at all students, including those destined to earn a baccalaureate degree. (See Lerman's chapter in this volume for more details on this change.) The language of the STWOA both contributed to and reflected this change.

The reasons for this fairly radical shift in perspective appear to be threefold. First, many STW advocates came to believe that all students, even those going to baccalaureate institutions, could benefit from activities focusing on workplace skills and career opportunities (Bailey & Merritt, 1997). The popularity of such activities in many schools probably contributed to this view. Second, advocates became increasingly worried that if STW programs lacked a college-preparatory track, they would become stigmatized as "dumping grounds" and not attract able students or adequate resources. Undoubtedly, the spread of "college-for-all" policies (discussed at length by Rosenbaum in this volume) provided a strong impetus for this position. A third factor was concern about creating programs that too rigidly tracked individuals on the basis of decisions made in their early high-school years. Osterman and Iannozzi (1993), for example, have argued that STW programs must allow students to change their minds about long-term education and career goals without penalty. Anecdotal research findings focusing on process outcomes support their view. The most successful programs seem to be those providing channels to a variety of postsecondary options, including immediate employment, advanced training, junior college, and baccalaureate higher education (Charner et al., 1995; Stern et al., 1995).

Research on STW implementation shows that schools have achieved considerable success in engaging all types of students in STW activities. Student response data from NLSY97 indicate that approximately 50% of all U.S. high-school students had participated in at least one STW activity by 1998 (Rivera-Batiz, this volume). Also, unlike in traditional vocational education, female students appear to be participating at approximately the same rate as male students. Other studies suggest that students in college-preparatory programs are frequent participants in STW programming—although usually in less-intensive career-awareness and work-based learning activities (Hershey et al., 1997; Olson, 1997). More-intensive programs that combine career-related academic courses, work experiences linked to school, and comprehensive career development have tended to attract students from the general and vocational tracks who do not plan extensive postsecondary education (Silverberg et al., 1998).

The experience of minority students in STW programming is mixed. Black students seem to be engaged in STW activities in disproportionate numbers. Rivera-Batiz (this volume) found that non-Hispanic blacks in the late 1990s had higher rates of participation in both career-major programs and what he called STW-preparatory programs than non-Hispanic whites. Hispanic students, on the other hand, had participation rates consistently lower than either of the other two groups. A study by Joyce and Neumark (2000), also using NLSY97 data, produced similar results. Rivera-Batiz's research suggests that the black–Hispanic participation differential can be attributed to the weak English language skills and recent immigrant status of many Hispanic students.

Overall, the breadth of STW participation is one of the major accomplishments of the movement. The high participation rates of female, college-preparatory, and black students are particularly noteworthy. The lower rates of Hispanic participation, on the other hand, are cause for some concern and should probably be addressed programmatically in the years ahead.

Higher Academic Achievement

The goal of enhancing student academic achievement became a priority of the STW movement as it evolved through the 1990s. In part, this change was a response to the movement's own internal efforts to expand STW programming to prebaccalaureate students. It also was in part a response to external forces—notably, the rise of the standards movement and the emergence of college-for-all policies in the nation's schools.

The educational theory underlying the STW movement suggests that STW programming will enhance student academic achievement three different ways: through more effective in-class instruction, workplace reinforcement of school learning, and greater student motivation. (For further discussion of this theory, see Schug & Western, this volume.) Empirical verification of the theory is not easy, however. Typically, students participating in STW programs engage in a variety of activities at different times and with differing degrees of involvement. This makes it difficult to identify the specific STW "treatment" that a student receives. Further, opinions diverge about the proper outcomes to be measured. Should they be test scores, grades, attendance, academic self-concept, educational aspirations, graduation rate, college attendance, college completion, or something else? Finally, there are the usual selection and control issues. How can researchers be sure that they have effectively controlled for all non-STW influences on student achievement, including difficult-to-measure factors such as prior motivation?

Despite these difficulties, there is now a fairly substantial literature on the academic impact of STW programming. Stern et al. (1995) and Urquiola et al. (1997) review early research on the topic. Several chapters in this volume (Hershey, Rivera-Batiz, and Stern) summarize more recent efforts. A significant portion of the most careful STW research has focused on the effects of career academies (in particular, see Stern, this volume). As one would expect, given differences in study objective, research methodology, and type of program evaluated, the findings are mixed. However, a rough consensus has emerged concerning the impact of STW participation on two important areas of student performance: school engagement and test scores. With regard to the first, a substantial number of studies show that STW participation increases student engagement in school, as measured by attendance, grades, retention, educational aspirations, and enrollment in math and science courses. These results suggest strongly that work-based education structured according to the STW model motivates at least some students (often those most at risk) to take their education more seriously. Rivera-Batiz's original research reported here confirms some of these findings. Unfortunately, however, no studies have shown that this greater level of engagement translates into increased learning, as measured by higher standardized test scores. Even the Manpower Demonstration Research Corporation random assignment study of career academies was unable to find test-score gains for participating students (Stern, this volume).

Certainly, increasing student engagement in school is an important accomplishment—particularly when (as appears to be the case) the strongest effects are on the students most at risk of dropping out. The failure of research to demonstrate positive test-score effects, however, raises serious questions about STW programs' capability to increase learning in comparison with other interventions. It has also seriously handicapped the movement in its struggle to maintain relevance in an educational environment increasingly focused on achievement of education standards as measured by standardized tests. Further research may show that STW participation enhances test scores, but these results will have to become available fairly soon to keep the movement from becoming completely marginalized.

Improved Labor-Market Outcomes

Although the relative priority of workforce preparation has fallen over the history of the STW movement, it remains an important objective for both advocates and participants. Thus, in addition to increasing academic achievement, the model STW program must contribute to the future labor-market success of participating students through provision of skills valued by employers (and also possibly through improved employer–employee matching; see Bishop & Mañe, this volume). Most students get involved in STW programs because they believe they will enhance their employment prospects. For such programming to be sustained in the long run, these expectations must be fulfilled. If they are not, students and schools are likely to abandon the STW concept, even if it succeeds in raising academic achievement.

Unfortunately, it is even more difficult to measure the labor-market impact of STW programs than to assess their effect on academic achievement. All of the general problems of treatment isolation, outcome measurement, and adequate controls discussed in the previous subsection apply. In addition, students acquire work skills in after-school and summer jobs that are difficult to separate from those acquired through STW participation. Finally, and perhaps most importantly, labor-market effects can take a long time to manifest themselves (Bishop & Mañe, this volume; Rosenbaum, this volume).

Studies prior to the STW movement do not provide much evidence that work-based education enhances students' labor-market skills or outcomes (Rivera-Batiz, this volume; Stern et al., 1995). The preponderance of this research seems to indicate what does not work rather than what does. Perhaps this is one reason why STW advocates have kept their distance from traditional vocational-education and cooperative-education programming. Stasz, McArthur, Lewis, and Ramsey (1990), for example, found that programs that focus only on provision of general skills without attempting to motivate students to acquire and use them are unlikely to succeed. Other studies (see Osterman & Iannozzi, 1993) have reached a similar conclusion with respect to programs that provide "training" for low-quality jobs—i.e., those that pay only the minimum wage and have limited promotion potential. Research on cooperative education suggests that the absence of skill certification limits the ability of co-op students to capitalize on their education in the marketplace (Stern & Stevens, 1992). Finally, work on vocational and cooperative education has tended to show that these programs provide economic gains only to students whose subsequent employment is in the area of their high-school occupational concentration (Bishop, 1989, 1994; Campbell, Elliot, Laughlin, & Seusy, 1987; Rumberger & Daymont, 1984).

The results of more recent studies that focus explicitly on labor-market effects of STW programming are also quite mixed. The findings reported in this volume appear to be illustrative. For example, according to Stern's comprehensive survey of career-academy research, participation in an academy has no effect on wages and only a small positive effect on hours in the first few years after graduation. Bishop and Mañe, on the other hand, find that students graduating from schools with school–business partnerships have lower unemployment rates and higher wages two years after graduation than those graduating from schools that lack these partnerships. They also find that both high- and low-GPA students benefit from such partnerships. It should be noted however, that Bishop and Mañe attribute their results more to improved information and employer–employee matching than to enhanced student skills. Under this interpretation, their results do not provide support for STW programs as a curriculum component.

Overall, there is still not enough evidence to support strong conclusions about the labor-market benefits of STW participation. It is unfortunate (and ironic) that a movement that had its origin in deeply felt concerns about the employability of young people has, at this late date, been unable to demonstrate that at least some of its proposed interventions have positive impacts in this area.

THE DECLINE OF THE SCHOOL-TO-WORK MOVEMENT

Despite its early promise and the accomplishments noted previously, the STW movement is no longer a significant force for educational reform in the U.S. It is thus highly improbable that anything like the ideal STW system will ever be permanently established in a significant number of American high schools. There are a variety of reasons for the movement's swift reversal of fortune, many of which were touched on earlier and are addressed in more depth by authors in this volume. In my judgment, the most important are the following.

Changed Economic Conditions

The economic circumstances that spawned the STW movement in the late 1980s have changed significantly. The performance of the U.S. economy over the past decade has been extremely strong, driven by a technology-based investment boom that has only recently subsided (Dunkelberg, this volume; Nakamura, this volume). During this period, unemployment fell, inflation remained low, the stock market soared, and the productivity growth rate returned to the levels of the 1950s and 1960s. Fears that the U.S. would be unable to compete internationally with its closest rivals dissipated as well. Finally, the wage gap between the college- and noncollege-educated stabilized (Leeds & Wheaton, this volume). Some of these trends have been at least temporarily reversed by the current recession, but this change is unlikely to lead to renewed concern about either the competitiveness of the U.S. labor force or the wage gap. The economic success of the 1990s demonstrated to most economists and policymakers that nothing is structurally wrong with the U.S. labor markets.

Diminished National Political Support

National political support for STW programs diminished very rapidly after the STWOA was passed in 1994. This occurred even though there was large and probably growing support for the movement at the state and local levels. Both the Lerman and the Kazis and Pennington chapters in this volume provide some explanation for Washington's unexpectedly quick loss of interest in the concept. The most important consequence of this reversal for the movement was the drying up of federal funding. The implementation research on STW programs shows that states and school districts made reasonable use of STWOA monies in establishing STW programming and that much of this programming was well received by students and schools. Another five years of funding at the same level as the STWOA would have led to institutionalization of the best of these practices. Although some states will continue support of STW programs after federal funding ceases, it will likely be at a fairly low level, so that most of the gains in STW programming during the second half of the 1990s are likely to be lost.

Overselling by Its Proponents

The STW movement quickly evolved from a movement aimed at improving the employment prospects for noncollege youth after they leave high school to a movement essentially promising to be all things to all students. By the mid-1990s, its proponents were arguing that extensive STW programming was as appropriate for students destined to graduate from a baccalaureate institution as for those whose terminal degree was a high-school diploma. Further, they argued that such an education would not only facilitate the transition from school to work for all students but also enhance their academic skills. Unfortunately, these claims could not be fully supported by research, which made it difficult to sell the STW concept to those educational constituencies that traditionally have been suspicious of work-based education. Moreover, movement proponents often underestimated or ignored the high costs of establishing the model STW system in a school. Both these habits of discourse—overstatement of benefits and understatement of costs—also weakened the movement's capability to compete successfully with the standards movement for scarce resources when the latter became a strong force in the education-reform community.

THE LEGACY OF THE SCHOOL-TO-WORK MOVEMENT

Even though its lifespan as a major force for reform was relatively short, the STW movement effected some important changes in educational practice nationwide. It is unlikely that the superstructure of STW programs erected by the STWOA will survive the termination of federal funds. As Hershey and other authors in this volume point out, a number of states have committed themselves to the continuation of STW programs using their own resources. In most cases, however, these efforts will not be as broad-based as those funded under the STWOA, and they will also almost certainly not build upon the state and local partnership structures required by that legislation. Nonetheless, at the level of the individual school where education actually takes place, there have been some positive changes attributable to the movement that are likely to be enduring. The future is uncertain, of course, but the corpus of STW research suggests that the following are likely to be the movement's most important legacies.

Increased Career Development for All Students

The STW movement substantially strengthened a preexisting trend among secondary schools to make career awareness and planning more significant parts of the high school experience. All studies of STW implementation show that career awareness and planning activities have become very popular with students, parents, and school staff—and further, that they engage all students, including those planning to attend four-year colleges and universities. Given the difficulty that many students, including those with baccalaureate degrees, have in making the transition from school to work (and given the increased complexity of the working world), this enhanced career emphasis seems very appropriate. The STW movement deserves considerable credit for working hard to establish it in the nation's schools.

Improved Connections to Employers for Students Entering the Workforce

Before the STW movement, linkages between high schools and employers were weak. Firms were not much involved in local school activities; few students got jobs after graduation through their schools; personnel officers distrusted the value of high-school diplomas and transcripts; and schools seemed uninterested in providing student information to prospective employers (Bishop & Mañe, this volume). The STW movement in general, and the

STWOA in particular, sought to make a fundamental change in this state of affairs by actively connecting employers to education systems in two ways: first, through participation in local partnerships; and second (more importantly), through direct involvement in work-based education and school activities more generally. Research on employer–school interaction shows that it grew rapidly in the 1990s. Employers are now much more engaged with their local schools through activities such as school sponsorship, job shadowing, career days, and internships than they were a decade ago. High schools in turn are making a greater effort to prepare their noncollege graduates for future employment, to provide employers with timely information about them, and to place them in appropriate positions. Clearly, these changes represent a major accomplishment of the movement.

Enhanced Credibility of Work-Based Curricula for Nonbaccalaureate Students

Before the emergence of the STW movement, work-based education was on the decline in America's schools despite some success stories like career academies. Students were abandoning the vocational approach to learning because increasingly they felt that it was a dead end—preparing them neither for higher education nor a good job after graduation. One of the most important consequences of the STW movement was reestablishing the appropriateness of work- or career-based curricula for a broad range of students, including both those contemplating some form of postsecondary education and those at risk of dropping out. The movement accomplished this in several ways. First, it proposed imaginative curricula designed to strengthen academic as well as work skills. Second, it expanded the range of careers that students could prepare for beyond those typically included in traditional vocation and cooperative education programs. And third, the movement legitimated the idea that work-based education programs can be appropriate preparation for at least some form of college degree.

It is my belief that these accomplishments provide a solid foundation on which to rebuild the STW movement into a stronger force than it is today. Several of the authors in this volume share this conviction. The STW approach to secondary education can never be (and should never have been promoted as) appropriate for everyone. Nearly all students, however, can derive benefits from individual STW activities. Furthermore, and more importantly, there are many students for whom a comprehensive STW program represents an approach to secondary education that is genuinely superior to alternatives in terms of its capability to engage them in their studies and prepare them for the working world. Let us hope that in our mad rush to establish academic standards and high-stakes testing for everyone that these fundamental truths are not forgotten.

REFERENCES

Bailey, T. (1995a). Incentives for employer participation in school-to-work programs. In T. Bailey (Ed.), *Learning to work: Employer involvement in school-to-work transition programs* (pp. 14–25). Washington, DC: The Brookings Institution.

Bailey, T. (1995b). Summary, discussion, and recommendations. In T. Bailey (Ed.), *Learning to work: Employer involvement in school-to-work transition programs* (pp. 88–104). Washington, DC: The Brookings Institution.

Bailey, T., & Merritt, D. (1997, October 29). School-to-work for the college-bound. *Education Week, 17*(9), 32, 37.

Bassi, L., Feeley, T., Hillmeyer, J., & Ludwig, J. (1997). *Learning and earning: An employer's look at school-to-work investments.* Alexandria, VA: American Society for Training and Development.

Bishop, J. (1989). Occupational training in high school: When does it pay off? *Economics of Education Review, 8*(1), 1–15.

Bishop, J. (1994). *The payoff to schooling and learning in the United States.* Ithaca, NY: School of Industrial and Labor Relations.

Boesel, D., Hudson, L., Deich, S., & Masten, C. (1994). *National assessment of vocational education, final report to Congress. Volume II: Participation in and quality of vocational education.* Washington, DC: U.S. Department of Education.

Campbell, P., Elliot, J., Laughlin S., & Seusy, E. (1987). *The dynamics of vocational education efforts on labor market outcomes.* Columbus, OH: Ohio State University, National Center for Research in Vocational Education.

Charner, I., Fraser, B., Hubbard, S., Rogers, A., & Horne, R. (1995). Reforms of the school-to-work transition: Findings, implications, and challenges. *Phi Delta Kappan, 77*(1), 40, 58–60.

Commission on the Skills of the American Workforce. (1990). *America's choice: High skills or low wages!* Rochester, NY: National Center on Education and the Economy.

Dougherty, K. J. (1994). *The contradictory college: The conflicting origins, impacts, and futures of the community college.* Albany, NY: State University of New York Press.

Gardecki, R., & Neumark, D. (1995). *Early labor market experiences and their consequences for adult labor market outcomes.* Washington, DC: Office of Technology and Assessment.

Gottschalk, P. (1997). Inequality, income growth, and mobility: The basic facts. *Journal of Economic Perspectives, 11*(2), 21–40.

Grubb, W. N. (1996a). The "new vocationalism" in the United States: Returning to John Dewey. *Educational Philosophy and Theory, 28*(1), 1–23.

Grubb, W. N. (1996b). *Working in the middle: Strengthening education and training for the mid-skilled labor force.* San Francisco: Jossey-Bass.

Hansen, J. (Ed.). (1994). *Preparing for the workplace: Charting a course for federal postsecondary training policy.* Washington, DC: National Academy Press.

Hershey, A. M., Hudis, P., Silverberg, M. K., & Haimson, J. (1997). *Partners in progress: Early steps in creating school-to-work systems.* Princeton, NJ: Mathematica Policy Research, Inc.

Hershey, A. M., Silverberg, M. K., Haimson, J., Hudis, P., & Jackson, R. (1999). *Expanding options for students: Report to Congress on the National Evaluation of School-to-Work Implementation.* Princeton, NJ: Mathematica Policy Research, Inc.

Holzer, H. (1996). *What employers want: Job prospects for less-educated workers.* New York: Russell Sage Foundation.

Hughes, K. (1998). *Employer recruitment is not the problem: A study of school-to-work transition problems.* New York: Columbia University, Teachers College, Institute on Education and the Economy.

Hughes, K. L., Moore, D. T., & Bailey, T. R (1999). *Work-based learning and academic skills.* New York: Columbia University, Teachers College, Institute on Education and the Economy.

Jennings, J. (Ed.). (1995). *National issues in education: Goals 2000 and school-to-work.* Bloomington, IN, & Washington, DC: Phi Delta Kappa International & The Institute for Educational Leadership.

Joyce, M., & Neumark, D. (2000). *An introduction to school-to-work programs in the NLSY97: How prevalent are they, and which youths do they serve?* (NBER Working Paper No. 7733). Cambridge, MA: National Bureau of Economic Research.

Kantor, H., & Tyack, D. (1982). Introduction: Historical perspectives on vocationalism in American education. In H. Kantor & D. Tyack (Eds.), *Work, youth, and schooling: Historical perspectives on vocationalism in American education* (pp. 1–13). Stanford, CA: Stanford University Press.

Klerman, J., & Karoly, L. (1995). *The transition to stable employment: The experience of youth in their early labor market career.* Berkeley, CA: University of California at Berkeley, National Center for Research in Vocational Education.

Kliebard, H. (1999). *Schooled to work: Vocationalism and the American curriculum, 1876–1946.* New York: Teachers College Press.

Lerman, R. I., & Pouncy, H. (1990). The compelling case for youth apprenticeships. *The Public Interest, 101,* 62–77.

McCormick, A., Tuma, J., & Houser, J. (1995). *Vocational course taking and achievement: An analysis of high school transcripts and 1990 NAEP assessment scores.* Washington, DC: National Center for Education Statistics, U.S. Department of Education.

Murphy, K., & Welch, F. (1989). Wage premiums for college graduates: Recent growth and possible explanations. *Educational Researcher, 18*(4), 17–26.

Olson, L. (1997). *The school-to-work revolution: How employers and educators are joining forces to prepare tomorrow's skilled workforce.* Reading, MA: Addison-Wesley.

Osterman, P. (1995). Involving employers in school-to-work programs. In T. Bailey (Ed.), *Learning to work: Employer involvement in school-to-work transition programs* (pp. 75–87). Washington, DC: The Brookings Institution.

Osterman, P., & Iannozzi, M. (1993). *Youth apprenticeships and school-to-work transitions: Current knowledge and legislative strategy* (Working Paper No. 14). Philadelphia: University of Pennsylvania, National Center on the Educational Quality of the Workforce.

Powell, A., Farrar, E., & Cohen, D. (1985). *The shopping mall high school.* Boston: Houghton Mifflin.

Ravitch, D. (2000). *Left back: A century of battles over school reform.* New York: Simon & Schuster.

Research and Policy Committee of the Committee for Economic Development. (1996). *American workers and economic change.* New York: Committee for Economic Development.

Rosenbaum, J., & Takehiko, K. (1989). From high school to work: Market and institutional mechanisms in Japan. *American Journal of Sociology, 94*(6), 1334–1365.

Rosenbaum, J., Takehiko, K., Settersen, R., & Maier, T. (1990). Market and network theories of the transition from school to work: Their application to industrial societies. *Annual Review of Sociology, 16*, 263–299.

Rumberger, R., & Daymont, T. (1984). The economic value of academic and vocational training acquired in high school. In M. Borus (Ed.), *Youth and the labor market: Analyses of the national longitudinal survey* (pp. 157–192). Kalamazoo, MI: Upjohn Institute.

Secretary's Commission on Achieving Necessary Skills. (1991). *What work requires of schools: A SCANS report for America 2000.* Washington, DC: U.S. Department of Labor.

Silverberg, M. K., Haimson, J., & Hershey, A.M. (1998). *Building blocks for a future school-to-work system: Early national implementation results.* Princeton, NJ: Mathematica Policy Research, Inc.

Stasz, C., McArthur, D., Lewis, M., & Ramsey, K. (1990). *Teaching and learning generic skills in the workplace.* Santa Monica, CA: RAND Corporation for University of California at Berkeley, National Center for Research in Vocational Education.

Stern, D., Finkelstein, N., Stone, J., Latting, J., & Dornsife, C. (1995). *School-to-work: Research on programs in the United States.* Washington, DC: Falmer Press.

Stern, D., & Stevens, D. W. (1992). *Analysis of unemployment insurance data on the relationship between high school cooperative education and subsequent employment.* Washington, DC: U.S. Department of Education, Office of Educational Research and Improvement, Office of Research, National Assessment of Vocational Education.

Stull, W., Sanders, N., & Stull, J. (2000). The effects of school size and leadership on participation in the school-to-work movement. *The Journal of Vocational Education Research, 25*(4), 472–502.

Urquiola, M., Stern, D., Horn, I., Dornsife, C., Chi, B., Williams, L., et al. (1997). *School-to-work, college, and career: A review of policy, practice, and results 1993–1997.* Berkeley, CA: National Center for Research in Vocational Education.

U.S. Department of Education, National Center for Education Statistics. (1996). *Findings from the condition of education 1996: Preparation for work* (No. 8). Washington, DC: U.S. Government Printing Office.

William T. Grant Foundation Commission on Work, Family, and Citizenship. (1988). *The Forgotten half: Pathways to success for America's youth and young families. Final report on Youth and America's Future.* Washington, DC: William T. Grant Foundation Commission on Work, Family, and Citizenship.

Zemsky, R. (1994). *What employers want: Employer perspectives on youth, the youth labor market, and prospects for a national system of youth apprenticeships* (Working Paper No. 22). Philadelphia: University of Pennsylvania, National Center on the Educational Quality of the Workforce.

Zemsky, R., Shapiro, D., Iannozzi, M., Cappelli, P., & Bailey, T. R. (1998). *The transition from initial employment to working life in the United States.* Washington, DC: National Center for Postsecondary Improvement.

2

Summary of Chapters

Mark Rohland

THE ECONOMIC CONTEXT

Chapter 3, by Michael A. Leeds and Elizabeth Wheaton, puts STW programs in the context of the youth labor market in the 1990s. Economic inequality between men and women, whites and blacks, and more- and less-educated workers diminished in the 1970s and grew in the 1980s. The authors examine whether changes in inequality have continued, focusing on youth labor trends in the past decade. Besides gains for college-educated black workers, the 1990s showed no significant divergence or convergence, although causes proposed for earlier trends like declining labor-union membership continued to affect youth. Wages and employment were, predictably, related to education, with the greatest wage gains for college graduates. Economic differences between whites and blacks and between men and women remained fairly constant over this decade, unlike the 1980s, when inequality for black college graduates grew and the gender gap narrowed. However, young workers, especially blacks, shifted to a lower educational level over the 1990s. The reasons for this shift are too poorly understood to suggest specific educational policies, but the decline gives cause for concern to those interested in providing youth with a smooth transition from school to work.

Borrowing Joseph Schumpeter's term, Leonard I. Nakamura views the economic era facing today's youth as one of *creative destruction.* Examining the last twenty-five years of economic change in historical context, he offers suggestions for coping with educational challenges resulting from an economy transformed by technological advances. These advances are causing jobs to evolve so quickly that schools struggle to train workers adequately. As new products and services are created and old ones destroyed rapidly, workers must prepare for continuous job change and reeducation. Today's economy contrasts strongly with the stable, managed economy it replaces. Because technology reduces the costs of selling new products, small innovative companies can compete with large corporations. Thus, demand for creative workers—from computer programmers to entrepreneurs—has risen while that for industrial, sales, and clerical workers has fallen. In turn, demand for college graduates exceeds supply, boosting the wage premium for college degrees and fostering economic inequality. Meanwhile, schools struggle to train students in the interdisciplinary skills the creative economy needs. Nakamura recommends that computers provide basic teaching, so that educators can assimilate technology and inculcate the soft skills such as creativity and cooperation that leaders in the school-to-work (STW) movement advocate.

In Chapter 5, William C. Dunkelberg maintains that what the media terms *the new economy* is new in only a limited sense. Although technological innovation in the 1990s has spurred an investment boom and more efficient business practices, it has created only an improved, computerized version of the economy of earlier decades. Reviewing changes such as growth in business-to-business transactions, high-technological production, and stock investment, Dunkelberg shows how today's economy relies on computer chips to improve product value. Such value-added changes have characterized earlier technologically driven booms. New is the rapidity of change as well as the relative invisibility of its causes. Like earlier booms, this one has created demand for skilled technical workers that the educational system cannot immediately meet. However, opportunities for low-skilled workers have increased as computerization has made academic skills such as math less essential to many service-industry jobs. A worrisome development is the weak performance on financial-knowledge tests of high-school seniors, who must manage the capital that today's investment boom generates. Dunkelberg suggests that schools model themselves on successful enterprises in order to motivate financial learning and efficient acquisition of technical skills.

THE SCHOOL-TO-WORK MOVEMENT

Mathematica Policy Research, Inc. has extensively investigated implementation of the STW movement. Mathematica Senior Fellow Alan M. Hershey reports on how well the movement has met the goals of the 1994 School-to-Work Opportunities Act (STWOA), which envisioned progress in school–business partnerships, career learning, academic outcomes, and lasting policy change. Hershey shows that partnerships have grown, providing work experiences such as job shadowing for students, that secondary schools have added more career-learning components to curricula, and that students appreciate these opportunities. However, participation in intensive career curricula and work-based learning (WBL) linked to academic courses has not flourished, largely because of cost and training obstacles. Effects of STW activities on achievement are unclear because valid comparison groups have been hard to define. School–business partnerships and some state STW agencies are likely to continue, Hershey predicts, but the end of the STWOA funding leaves it uncertain whether the STW movement can be broadly sustained.

In Chapter 7, Bari Anhalt Erlichson surveys the results of a thirty-seven-state study on state systems created to use STWOA funds. The act allowed states to decide how to govern and implement WBL, school activities, and connections between the two. Governance structures typically combined state-agency and private-sector representation. Assessing effects of governance on implementation, Erlichson observes that state and local policy contexts determined the extent of reform. Some states chose *comprehensive* goals such as statewide school reform, as in Oregon, where legislation established career-learning standards in all schools. Some states chose *intermediate* goals such as improving vocational education, as in North Carolina's JobReady partnerships. In these states, private-sector leadership and poor coordination with departments of education tended to restrict school participation. Other states were restricted to *programmatic* goals, as in Nebraska, where a preponderance of rural, low-income districts limited activities to modest programs such as skills assessments and career fairs. The potential for sustaining STW programs depends on the degree of existing state implementation and of coordination among governing agencies.

Mark C. Schug and Richard D. Western focus on one state, Wisconsin, which began STW initiatives before the STWOA in response to industrial decline and low high-school achievement. A 1990 state commission recommended school–business partnerships, a technical-prep program, and apprenticeships. Support from the STWOA inspired increased efforts to implement the recommendations, but progress was hampered by a complex administrative scheme making accountability unclear. The authors surveyed district curriculum directors about STW implementation. Participation has grown, but not in WBL, which was hard to structure, fund, and schedule. Faculty involvement in STW programs was low, especially in work-based components. Little impact on curriculum or student outcomes was reported. Overall, though student and employer satisfaction has been high, the impact of STW programs in Wisconsin has been minimal, and economic recovery has removed the rationale for STW programs as a comprehensive reform. The authors discuss lessons learned from implementation, including the need for curricular integration, demonstration of results, and focused programs.

In Chapter 9, Robert Zemsky considers international experiences in moving students from school to work. He observes that the 1980s' crisis in workforce preparation caused American educational leaders to look abroad for better methods, such as nationwide apprenticeship. The 1990s' economic boom has weakened the need for such methods, and most American youth find satisfying careers without the aid of occupational programs. Meanwhile, other countries have begun to question their workforce training and to undertake multinational studies in search of answers. Zemsky reports on one such study that investigated companies, providers of vocational-technical education (VTE), and secondary schools at representative sites in four countries grappling with college-for-all attitudes and with the need to adapt vocational education in the wake of rapid economic change. In the *United States,* manufacturing decline has led VTE to shift focus from industrial to service skills. In high schools, VTE students face stigmatization, as college becomes the postgraduation norm. In *Singapore,* vocational students face the same stigma, and without the informal work opportunities American students have, the country's best students enter careers without essential work skills. *Switzerland* boasts a successful apprenticeship system, but the tracking of immigrant children into apprenticeships and corporate requirements for college-level skills has stigmatized apprenticeships and spurred college mania. In *Japan,* too, VTE is an increasingly weak alternative, and students are more concerned with personal advancement than with the academic competition and company loyalty essential to Japan's former economic success. All nations would do well to learn from one another's workforce-training problems and solutions.

ISSUES, OBSTACLES, AND OPPORTUNITIES IN SCHOOL-TO-WORK PROGRAMS

Chapter 10 probes the pedagogical principles underlying WBL. David Thornton Moore and Katherine L. Hughes argue that pedagogy needs to be more broadly defined to include school practices and the shared knowledge, social relations, and resources of those involved in learning. Moreover, WBL pedagogy includes not only classroom, but also workplace learning, which can influence student workers just as strongly. Educators implementing WBL should distinguish between two different (but not mutually exclusive) pedagogical models: *functionalist* pedagogy, which prepares students to work in a context of stable knowledge, skills, and social relations, and *critical* pedagogy, which trains students to understand their socially constructed, possibly flawed work context as open to questioning. The authors provide a case study and guidelines for professional development of critical pedagogy for WBL. They also stress key critical-pedagogy principles. Essential principles include *learning opportunities analysis* to determine the degree of access students have to workplace knowledge, *reflection* on work organization and roles, *connecting academic knowledge to workplace learning* to analyze contradictions, *helping students construct knowledge* through dialogue, *and making school instructors responsible* for critical pedagogy. The authors conclude that critical pedagogy can help students, particularly disadvantaged ones, understand workplace cultures and thus increase their chances for success in work and self-development.

Francisco L. Rivera-Batiz explores effects of STW participation on minority students, asking whether programs to ease the economic plight of black and Hispanic youth in the past decade have succeeded. Noting the perception that vocational programs have tracked minority students into unchallenging courses and low-skill jobs, he investigates whether modifications in those programs after the STWOA give reason to change that perception. His controlled analysis of longitudinal data on STW participation, academic performance, and work outcomes suggests that modifications have succeeded. Black and Hispanic participation in STW programs has increased. These groups participate more than white youth in intensive technical-prep and apprenticeship programs, so they are not being channeled toward low-skill opportunities. However, Hispanic involvement is generally lower than black or white. Immigrant status explains this problem; limited English proficiency may hamper immigrant students' participation. Nevertheless, black and Hispanic youth show positive outcomes from STW involvement. Participation in STW programs tends to motivate minority students to take math and science courses, and it increases their chances of retention, even as it increases their work hours. Thus, STW programs improve both the academic motivation and economic conditions of minority youth.

John H. Bishop and Ferran Mañe investigate the success of school–business partnerships in signaling student achievement. In Chapter 12, they show that high-school achievement has been irrelevant in hiring decisions, keeping many qualified graduates out of the primary, skilled labor market and hindering motivation for high-school achievement. To solve this problem, the STW movement has fostered partnerships to improve employer knowledge of and rewards to high-achieving graduates. Research on school–business collaboration suggests that signaling achievement to employers improves job quality and strengthens learning incentives. Participation in WBL does not lower academic performance, and it leads to more working hours. Further, well-controlled analysis of longitudinal data shows that school–business collaboration tends to reduce unemployment and increase employment, wages, and earnings for graduates two years after high school. Both low- and high-performing students benefit. Scored minimum competency exams aid in signaling achievement to employers and increase economic benefits for better students. Such benefits, which can clarify incentives for students, justify sustaining school–business partnerships now, after the end of the STWOA funding.

Examining today's college-for-all policies, James E. Rosenbaum contends that high schools mistakenly recommend college entry for all, although most students, especially those with weak academic skills, will not graduate college. Counselors fail to help students unprepared for college to explore well-paid careers not requiring bachelor's degrees. High schools also fail to inculcate the soft skills, such as dependability, that employers value. Students misunderstand incentives for achievement because schools lack mechanisms for communicating the value of academic achievement for college and career goals and because colleges' open-admission policies discourage excellence. In contrast, countries such as Germany and Japan clearly link school performance to career outcomes, providing incentives for achieving and for adjusting goals to abilities. To motivate American students, Rosenbaum proposes European-style apprenticeships, more rigorous college admission, informing students that grades and soft skills relate to higher earnings, and encouraging trustworthy school–business partnerships that involve teachers extensively. Colleges can increase incentives by developing technical-prep programs in high schools and instituting college-readiness tests.

THE FUTURE OF SCHOOL-TO-WORK

Robert I. Lerman argues that the STW movement strayed from the original goals of the STWOA proponents. The act represented a rapid transformation of problem to policy, responding to a pressing need to help America's underskilled high-school students learn through WBL opportunities such as apprenticeships that could improve career and earnings potentials. Proponents envisioned these advantages flowing from systemic change and intensive student involvement. However, it was feared that such extensive policy would limit college opportunities, yield too few employer openings, and give federal government too strong a role. The act's final wording stressed career majors, not apprenticeships, and left WBL decisions to the states. The act articulated too many goals at various governance levels, and initial implementation, attempting to reach all students, focused on career exploration instead of the career experience central to the legislation. Lerman shows that WBL activities, confronted with resistance to tracking, have been largely low-intensity ones such as job shadowing. He proposes that an apprenticeship-style system could more effectively equalize educational opportunity and increase productivity. To initiate that system, lead industries and governments could model training and standards and promote regional and national skill certification.

In Chapter 15, David Stern examines the reconfiguration of high schools to combine vocational and academic paths, focusing on the career academy, an established structure within larger schools. Stern reviews the history of academies and identifies their basic features as small learning communities that share teachers and classes, combine an academic curriculum with a career theme, and partner with community employers. Studies of California academies show academy students outperforming similar students in their schools. Despite recruiting a majority of disadvantaged students, academies enroll as many students in college as the rest of their schools do. A random-assignment study by the Manpower Demonstration Research Corporation confirms academies' advantages. However, the Manpower study shows no benefits for academy students over controls on standardized-test scores, and it could not rule out teacher self-selection. Stern surveys other small high-school structures, concluding that career academies have been a successful model, but that results do not warrant large-scale implementation of smaller structures. Nevertheless, by heightening awareness of the benefits of integrated career development, smaller structures, and school–business partnerships, career academies may constitute the STW movement's chief legacy.

In the final chapter, Richard Kazis and Hilary Pennington review the efforts of the school-to-career (STC) reform culminating in the STWOA, drawing on research from their organization: Jobs for the Future. Progress has been slow and uneven, but successes include increases in employer engagement with schools, community partnerships, the number and satisfaction of students involved, college attendance among disadvantaged youth, and motivation to study (though standardized-test score progress has not appeared). Challenges have included political resistance to reform as an obstacle to equal opportunity, complex ambitions that slowed implementation, excessive emphasis on quantity not quality, and isolation from standards-driven reform. As the STWOA funding ends, optimism seems warranted. Enthusiasm for school–career links is growing, retention crises make alternatives such as career academies attractive, and employers increasingly demand certifiable, work-based competency. The authors suggest strategies to help STC reform return to the mainstream: focusing on high schools and postsecondary connections, promoting STC principles within other reform movements, funding long-term community partnerships locally, and supporting research to improve design and implementation.

Part II

The Economic Context

3

The Youth Labor Market in the 1990s

Michael A. Leeds
Elizabeth Wheaton

INTRODUCTION

The school-to-work (STW) movement sparked one of the major educational initiatives of the 1990s: the School-to-Work Opportunities Act (STWOA) of 1994. The STWOA brought federal funds to numerous local programs, all of which shared two goals. As the name implies, STW programs were intended to ease the transition from school to the labor force. The STW movement, however, was never meant as a purely vocational initiative. It also sought to enhance the academic experience of all students taking part in it, regardless of their future academic plans.

With funding from the STWOA ending in 2001, policymakers need adequate information to assess the impact of STW programs. Specifically, one must judge these programs by asking two questions:

- Did STW programs lead students to stay in school longer?
- Did STW programs make students more employable, thus reducing unemployment rates?

The latter half of the 1990s did not provide the optimal setting for controlled experiments to test the effectiveness of STW programs. It was a period of prolonged prosperity in which other social initiatives (e.g., higher minimum wages and welfare reform) also took place, making it difficult to assess the impact of STW programs.

This chapter provides a background against which one can evaluate the success or failure of STW programs.[1] Although our data set does not allow us to draw conclusions regarding STW programs, we can present the setting in which STW programs operated in the 1990s. Specifically, we examine how education affected the unemployment rates and wages of young workers during the 1990s.

Using wage rates has several drawbacks in a study of this type. The most severe problem is the failure to account for other sources of income. The dramatic rise of the stock market in the 1990s greatly augmented the nonlabor income of some Americans and made incomes far less equally distributed than wages. Using wages, however, also provides advantages. Most significantly, wages "are more closely related to market prices for human capital components" (Juhn, Murphy, & Pierce, 1993, p. 411). Wages thus reflect the market value of the skills that workers acquire. Because STW programs are intended to increase the skills that an individual brings to the marketplace, real wages allow us to measure the effectiveness of these programs.

The remainder of this chapter shows how unemployment and real wages changed in the 1990s. The next section briefly describes the labor market of the 1970s and 1980s and presents explanations for inequality declining in the 1970s and rising in the 1980s. Next, we show how labor-market conditions changed over the 1990s for all young workers and for young workers with different levels of education. Finally, we present our conclusions and suggest how future studies of STW programs might build on our results.

THE 1970s AND 1980s: DECADES OF CONVERGENCE AND DIVERGENCE

Before discussing the youth labor market in the 1990s, we first consider the 1970s and 1980s. The experiences of American youth (aged nineteen to twenty-four)—and of the entire American labor force—through the 1970s and 1980s constituted a study in contrasts. The contrary experiences of those two decades suggest that one should be wary about drawing general lessons from any single decade. One should thus be cautious about the impact of STW programs because labor market conditions have changed dramatically over the last three decades.

The 1970s might best be termed a decade of compression. During the 1970s, wage gaps between blacks and whites, between men and women, and between highly and less-educated workers fell dramatically, leading some economists to ask whether too many people were pursuing higher education.[2] In contrast, the 1980s saw growing inequality. The hourly pay of highly educated workers grew dramatically, while the real wages of less-educated workers fell. The gains that blacks had experienced in the 1960s and 1970s disappeared, and gains by women fell dramatically. The popular literature used the growing inequality of the 1980s to lament the disappearance of America's middle class.[3]

Economists have offered many theories for the different experiences of the 1970s and 1980s. One can divide these theories into four basic categories: supply and demand, technology, trade, and government policy.[4] Freeman (1976) cited the rising supply of educated workers as a cause of the declining returns to education in the 1970s. Katz and Murphy (1992) explained the growing returns to such workers in the 1980s through the declining supply of highly educated workers. Acemoglu (1999) combined the Freeman and the Katz and Murphy explanations to claim that the growing supply of skilled workers in the 1970s and 1980s eventually created a critical mass of skilled workers. With a sufficient pool of skilled workers, employers switched to more skill-intensive methods of production by replacing less-skilled with highly skilled workers.

Other demand factors, such as the advent of what has been called the new economy and of the technological divide between those with and without access to the appropriate skills, have also been cited as the source of the growing inequality. Juhn et al. (1993) claim that the demand for such skills grew rapidly in the 1980s, accounting for the increased inequality.

Some researchers point to market factors outside our immediate control. Borjas and Ramey (1994) and Wood (1995), among others, suggest that trade patterns may have determined employment and pay in the 1970s and 1980s. In particular, workers who produced goods or services easily replaced by imports fell behind as the economy became more open to trade. The researchers claim that growing trade deficits increased unemployment among workers competing with low-wage, low-skill workers in developing nations.

Still other researchers feel that changing government policy caused inequality to grow in the 1980s. Freeman (1973) and Donohue and Heckman (1991) feel that enforcement of civil rights laws spurred the gains made by blacks in the 1960s and 1970s. Leonard (1990) sees affirmative action as crucial in closing the gap between highly educated blacks and whites, although he questions its value otherwise. The declining enforcement of these laws could reverse previous gains. Lee (1999) claims that the growing inequality of the 1980s came from the government's allowing the real value of the minimum wage to fall.

THE LABOR MARKET FOR YOUNG WORKERS IN THE 1990s

Overview

In this study, we focus on young workers, defined as individuals aged nineteen to twenty-four, who no longer attend high school or college. When computing real hourly wages, we include those who reported positive weekly wages.

In contrast to the previous two decades, wages neither converged nor diverged in the 1990s. Table 3.1 uses data[5] from the Current Population Survey (CPS) to show the real hourly pay of the 90th and 10th percentiles of the wage distribution.[6] The ratio of the two showed no clear trend over the decade, rising as high as 4.20 and falling as low as 3.85. In contrast, Juhn et al. (1993) found that income inequality grew steadily in the 1980s. Table 3.1 suggests that the 1990s consisted of two distinct subperiods. During the recession of the early 1990s, real wages stagnated and unemployment rates rose for all workers. During the recovery that followed, unemployment rates fell and real wages rose.

Table 3.1
Real Hourly Pay of the 90th and 10th Percentiles of Wage Distribution in the 1990s

Year	Hourly Pay of 90th Percentile ($)	Hourly Pay of 10th Percentile ($)	Ratio of 90th and 10th Percentiles
1990	11.54	2.78	4.15
1991	11.54	2.84	4.06
1992	11.54	3.00	3.85
1993	12.02	2.97	4.05
1994	12.02	2.88	4.17
1995	12.50	3.21	3.89
1996	13.14	3.13	4.20
1997	13.46	3.33	4.04
1998	13.89	3.37	4.12
1999	14.83	3.72	3.99

In fact, unemployment and real wages for young workers and prime-age workers moved in tandem over the course of the decade, although as expected, young workers consistently had higher unemployment rates and lower real wages than prime-age workers. The unemployment gap between young and prime-age workers stayed roughly constant, averaging about 5.4 percentage points. Greater unemployment among young workers reflects their ignorance of labor-market opportunities and their lack of job-specific skills. Young workers' lack of labor-market information causes them to spend more time seeking employment. Their lack of job-specific skills means that employers do not lose an investment if young workers go elsewhere. Young workers are thus more likely to be let go by employers.

Real wages (or the hourly equivalent) fell for young and prime-age workers early in the decade and then rose to new highs by its end.[7] The wages of prime-age workers began to rise somewhat earlier and returned to their 1990 level a year earlier, in 1994, than those of young workers. As a result, the wage differential between young and prime-age workers was slightly greater during the last four years of the decade than during the first six years.

Explaining the 1990s

Although not conclusive, data from the CPS (available upon request) suggest that none of the factors used to explain movements in unemployment and real wages in the 1980s—neither changing trade patterns nor declines in the real minimum wage and unionization—fully explains the experience of the 1990s. If, for example, rising imports displace young workers, unemployment rates should rise, and real wages should fall as imports rise. Evidence from the 1990s shows just the opposite. Although the decline of unions in the economy appears to track declining unemployment among young workers in the 1990s, one cannot conclude that falling unionization has helped young workers because unionization has steadily declined for several decades.

Finally, the minimum wage shows no clear impact on either unemployment or hourly pay. The nominal minimum wage increased in both 1991 and 1997. Although unemployment rose with the 1991 increase, it fell with the 1997 increase. Similarly, there is no obvious impact on hourly pay, as it fell in 1991 and rose in 1997.[8]

THE IMPACT OF EDUCATION ON UNEMPLOYMENT AND HOURLY PAY OF YOUNG WORKERS

Overview

The 1970s and 1980s showed no consistent pattern in the returns on education for young workers. Between 1963 and 1971, college graduates had the greatest increase in real wages (25.5%) followed by high-school dropouts (17.1%) and high-school graduates (16.7%). In the 1970s, the average real weekly wage level decreased for college graduates (−10.1%). The wages of high-school dropouts and high-school graduates continued to increase, though at slower rates (0.3% and 1.4%).[9] During the 1980s, the real pay of college graduates increased by 7.7%, while high-school dropouts and high-school graduates experienced decreases of −6.6% and −4.0%.

Freeman (1976) explained the movements in the 1970s by appealing to the cobweb model of earnings. He claimed that the shortage of highly skilled workers in the late 1960s and early 1970s led many youths to attend college. This increased the number of skilled workers in the market, placing downward pressure on their pay and making college less valuable. Combined with the baby bust, this led to a shortage of educated workers in the 1980s, starting the cycle again. By contrast, Acemoglu (1999) claimed that the rapid pace of technological advance over the last generation made it difficult for firms to find enough workers with the skills they wanted. As a result, firms delayed hiring workers with the appropriate skills until an adequate pool of appropriate workers existed. According to Acemoglu (1999), the buildup of skilled workers in the 1970s made the high returns to education in the 1980s both possible and irreversible.

The Experience of the 1990s

Table 3.2 shows unemployment for different levels of education among young workers in the 1990s. It shows that college graduates experienced the lowest unemployment, seldom exceeding 5%. High-school dropouts experienced the greatest unemployment, with rates ranging from 13.6% to 19.7%. Again, young workers with some college fared slightly better than those with only a high-school diploma, with both groups lying between the extremes.

Differences between all groups grew during the economic downturn of the early 1990s, but fell later in the decade, so that unemployment rates were slightly more compressed at the end of the decade than at the beginning. Overall, unemployment was slightly lower at the end of the decade for all groups except college graduates, who were roughly unchanged.

Table 3.3 shows movements in real hourly wages by educational group in the 1990s. Again, the data show neither the convergence of the 1970s nor the divergence of the 1980s. Real hourly pay declined through 1992. It then rose fairly steadily for most groups. High-school dropouts are an exception to this pattern because their real wages were insensitive to the overall movement of the economy.

As expected, college graduates earned significantly more than all other groups, and high-school dropouts earned less. By contrast, the earnings of

Table 3.2
Unemployment Rates for Young Workers in the 1990s (Percentage)

Year	Dropouts	High-School Graduates	Some College	College Graduates
1990	15.6	9.2	8.3	3.0
1991	19.3	12.0	11.0	4.1
1992	19.9	12.6	11.3	4.5
1993	19.3	11.2	9.7	4.4
1994	19.7	11.4	9.9	2.8
1995	15.9	10.4	8.8	3.3
1996	16.8	9.8	8.4	5.5
1997	15.4	8.8	8.0	2.4
1998	13.6	9.5	8.1	1.6
1999	14.9	8.5	7.8	3.0

Table 3.3
Real Hourly Pay for Young Workers in the 1990s by Education Level (in Dollars)

Year	Dropouts	High-School Graduates	Some College	College Graduates
1990	5.66	6.44	6.71	9.65
1991	5.43	6.33	6.47	9.05
1992	5.90	6.28	6.46	8.80
1993	5.72	6.31	6.51	8.82
1994	5.53	6.46	6.59	8.91
1995	5.82	6.90	6.82	9.00
1996	5.39	6.32	6.57	9.17
1997	5.65	6.54	6.76	10.94
1998	5.29	6.50	6.70	10.38
1999	5.90	7.08	7.22	9.65

high-school graduates were indistinguishable from those young workers who had some college but no degree. The hourly pay of young college graduates lost ground slightly to less-educated groups over the 1990s. One should not read too much into this compression because the relative gains by young workers without a college degree were slight, and almost all of it occurred in 1999, when college graduates experienced a significant decline, while the other groups registered solid gains.[10]

RACE AND EDUCATION IN THE YOUTH LABOR MARKET OF THE 1990s

The general impact of education on the youth labor market masks the fact that education had dramatically different impacts for young blacks and whites. In this section, we examine the interaction of race and education for young workers.

Background

Something went drastically wrong for black youth in the 1980s. After steady progress for more than a decade had effectively erased racial wage differentials for young men with the same level of schooling, gaps reappeared in the late 1970s and grew significantly in the 1980s (Bound & Freeman, 1992, p. 201). Using CPS data, Bound and Freeman have shown that the overall weekly wage gap for black and white youth rose from about 13.6% in 1980 to 17.9% in 1989.

Decomposing the sample by education level reveals that the 1980s were cruelest to the group that benefited the most in an earlier era. Bound and Freeman (1992) indicate that the differential for black and white high-school dropouts stayed relatively constant through the 1980s, as did the gap for youths with high-school degrees. Moreover, black youth had roughly the same disadvantage in both groups.[11] The racial wage differential for students with a college degree, however, rose dramatically during the 1980s. Starting from near-zero, the differential grew to almost 17% by the end of the decade, roughly the same as the other groups.[12]

The declining relative position of black college graduates in the 1980s is particularly puzzling because one cannot readily attribute it to the usual explanations. Black college graduates are less likely to be hurt by declining job opportunities in inner cities or the shift of manufacturing jobs overseas. Declining union membership in the 1980s is unlikely to apply here because black college graduates tend to belong to white-collar and public-sector unions, whose unions did not decline so significantly in the 1980s. Similarly, declines in the real value of the minimum wage would have little impact on the pay of most college graduates.

The Experience of the 1990s

In contrast to the 1980s, racial differences in both hourly pay and unemployment fell during the 1990s. Table 3.4 shows how unemployment rates varied for blacks and whites with different levels of education in the 1990s. It shows that education clearly mattered for blacks and whites in the 1990s. Young black and white college graduates had by far the lowest unemployment rates, while high-school dropouts had the highest rates. High-school graduates and those with some college were roughly equal between the two extremes. The impact of both race and education, however, changed significantly during the 1990s.

Young black dropouts were roughly 2 to 2.5 times more likely to be unemployed than young high-school graduates, while young white dropouts were generally 1.7 to 2 times more likely to be unemployed. For those without college, black unemployment rates worsened relative to whites over the early, recessionary part of the decade and improved thereafter. By the end of the decade, blacks' dropout rates had improved slightly in comparison to whites, while the differential for those high-school degrees or some college remained largely unchanged.

Young black college graduates saw the greatest changes in unemployment rates.[13] From 1990 through 1993, the unemployment rates of black college graduates far exceeded those of white college graduates and closely resembled those of white high-school graduates. Starting in 1994, however, the unemployment rates of black college graduates fell dramatically. For the remainder of the decade, their unemployment rates closely resembled those of white college graduates and actually fell below those of whites in 1996 and 1998.

Table 3.5 shows that the real hourly pay of young whites rose with education levels in the 1990s. The outcome was cloudier for young blacks. The hourly

Table 3.4
Unemployment Rates for Young Blacks and Whites by Education Group in the 1990s (Percentage)

Year	Dropouts		High-School Graduates		Some College		College Graduates	
	Blacks	Whites	Blacks	Whites	Blacks	Whites	Blacks	Whites
1990	32.5	16.7	19.7	9.2	18.6	8.3	11.1	3.6
1991	40.0	20.6	20.6	12.0	20.2	10.9	11.1	4.2
1992	41.3	20.4	24.6	12.8	22.1	11.4	12.5	5.5
1993	48.3	21.2	28.2	11.5	25.2	9.6	13.8	5.2
1994	43.5	22.1	24.3	12.0	20.8	10.5	6.0	3.3
1995	41.6	16.2	23.4	10.6	18.6	9.0	4.7	3.9
1996	34.7	17.4	20.4	10.7	18.8	9.0	3.3	5.9
1997	42.5	15.0	20.7	8.6	20.3	7.8	7.9	1.9
1998	34.4	14.7	17.1	9.7	14.1	8.3	0.0	2.1
1999	26.9	15.7	18.5	8.4	15.3	7.0	5.0	2.5

Table 3.5
Real Hourly Pay in the 1990s for Young Blacks and Whites by Educational Level (in Dollars)

Year	Dropouts		High-School Graduates		Some College		College Graduates	
	Blacks	Whites	Blacks	Whites	Blacks	Whites	Blacks	Whites
1990	6.41	5.46	6.20	6.47	6.34	6.69	9.36	9.65
1991	5.46	5.64	6.38	6.64	6.28	6.80	7.81	9.52
1992	7.72	6.18	6.34	6.81	6.34	7.02	8.38	9.45
1993	5.44	6.31	6.37	7.07	6.75	7.26	8.32	9.68
1994	6.87	6.23	7.89	7.31	7.70	7.46	7.64	10.26
1995	7.04	6.87	7.63	8.16	7.44	8.04	12.25	10.20
1996	5.86	6.59	7.55	7.60	7.51	7.92	10.20	10.83
1997	8.38	6.78	7.84	8.09	8.19	8.34	10.74	13.80
1998	6.82	6.60	7.27	8.19	7.77	8.40	14.34	12.88
1999	6.68	7.61	8.00	9.14	8.61	9.26	14.79	11.90

pay of young black high-school dropouts was essentially equal to that of young high-school graduates and close to that of young workers with some college. Only black college graduates had clearly higher pay.

Unlike unemployment rates, real hourly pay did not weaken early in the decade. Only young black college graduates saw a noticeable decline in real wages from 1990 and 1994, continuing the decline documented by Bound and Freeman (1992), with the differential between whites and blacks growing to 30% in 1994. Over the last five years of the decade, however, the average pay of young black college graduates exceeded that of young white college graduates in three years.

Despite the clear advantages of a college education, young blacks and whites were less likely to have a college degree and more likely to have dropped out of high school at the end of the 1990s than at the beginning of the decade. Part of the decline in schooling may be a statistical artifact because the CPS altered its measure of educational attainment in 1992. Beginning in 1992, the CPS measured schooling more precisely, accounting for those who had completed twelve years of schooling but did not receive a high-school degree. It also measured postsecondary schooling more precisely, explicitly accounting for degrees. Before 1992, one had to impute a college degree for those with sixteen years of schooling.

Even so, the trends since the change are disturbing. As black college graduates experienced dramatic gains in employment and real hourly pay over the 1990s, the percentage of young black workers with college degrees rose only slightly from 1992 to 1999,[14] while the percentage of blacks who did not complete high school continued to rise after the survey was changed in 1992. The shift to educational groups with much higher unemployment and lower pay helps to explain why blacks as a whole did not benefit significantly in the 1990s.

CONCLUSION AND SUGGESTIONS FOR FUTURE WORK ON STW PROGRAMS

The youth labor market suggests several groups that might benefit from STW programs. Young workers generally benefit from increased schooling. Completing more years of schooling leads to lower unemployment and higher pay. If STW programs increase the likelihood of completing high school and obtaining higher education, then some of the benefits of greater education are due to STW involvement. These programs will be particularly valuable to African-American youth if the programs increase the likelihood that they complete high school. Young black dropouts generally had the lowest pay and the highest unemployment of any of the groups we considered. Moreover, black youth were generally less likely to finish high school and far less likely to complete college than white youth.

Still, one must be careful about using the experiences of the 1990s to justify the use of STW programs. The large and poorly understood changes in the distribution of income by education and race in the 1970s, 1980s, and 1990s show the dangers of appealing to current labor-market conditions. But the continuing gaps between highly educated and less-educated workers and between blacks and whites suggest a role for STW and related programs.

As students who have taken part in STW programs enter the labor force, one should be able to test for effects of these programs. One can, for example, test whether the unemployment rates of youth who have participated in STW programs are lower than the rates of those who have not. One can perform similar tests to determine whether STW participants receive higher pay. The impact of STW programs, however, may not be directly measurable. Instead, they may affect employment and compensation indirectly by increasing the likelihood of completing high school and college. One should thus test whether STW participants have received more schooling than otherwise identical individuals who have not participated in STW programs. Other studies in this volume, such as those by Bishop and Mañe and by Rivera-Batiz, take significant steps toward such assessment.

NOTES

1. We thank Irina Pistolet for her outstanding research assistance.

2. Freeman (1976) is the most popular source of this claim, though his findings have been borne out by Katz and Murphy (1992).

3. See, for example, Cassidy (1995).

4. This is only a partial list, though many other factors stem from those listed. For example, the decline of unions can be attributed to the impact of changing trade patterns and increasingly hostile government policy.

5. All tables use data drawn from the Annual Demographic Files of the Current Population Survey.

6. The wages of the lowest 10% lie below the minimum because many of the lowest-paid workers are not covered by minimum-wage laws.

7. We computed the wage as workers' annual wage and salary income divided by the product of their average hours per week and weeks worked. We also discarded individuals for whom we computed hourly wages greater than $500. We computed the real wage by using the CPI deflator from the Bureau of Labor Statistics (2000).

8. The same basic result holds when one restricts one's attention to the bottom 10% of wage earners or to high-school dropouts.

9. Specific data come from Katz and Murphy (1992).

10. Recall that, by construction, 16.6% of the sample turns over every year. This, combined with relatively small sample sizes for the subgroups, leads to volatility in measures. Overall, we are surprised at the stability of most of our measures.

11. Bound and Freeman (1992) did not consider high-school graduates with some college.

12. Our figures show a smaller gap in hourly pay than Bound and Freeman (1992) for several reasons. First, Bound and Freeman considered only young men, for whom studies have repeatedly shown a larger gap than for women. Second, Bound and Freeman impute wages to individuals who did not report any, whereas we do not.

13. A portion of the volatility can be attributed to the small sample size of black college graduates. There were only 31 black college graduates in the sample for 1998, when the unemployment rate for this group was 0.0%.

14. This was still better than for whites, for whom the percentage with a college degree fell.

REFERENCES

Acemoglu, D. (1999). Changes in unemployment and wage inequality: An alternative theory and some evidence. *American Economic Review, 89,* 1259–1278.

Borjas, G., & Ramey, V. (1994). Time series evidence on the sources of trends in wage inequality. *American Economic Review, 84,* 10–16.

Bound, J., & Freeman, R. B. (1992). What went wrong? The erosion of relative earnings and employment among young black men in the 1980s. *Quarterly Journal of Economics, 108,* 202–232.

Bureau of Labor Statistics. (2000). Inflation calculator. *Consumer price indexes home page.* Retrieved from http://stats.bls.gov/cpihome.htm

Cassidy, J. (1995, October 16). Who killed the middle class? *The New Yorker, 77,* 113–124.

Donohue, J. J., III, & Heckman, J. (1991). Continuous versus episodic change: The impact of civil rights policy on the economic status of blacks. *Journal of Economic Literature, 29,* 1603–1643.

Freeman, R. B. (1973). Changes in the labor market for black Americans, 1948–1972. *Brookings Papers on Economic Activity, 1,* 67–120.

Freeman, R. B. (1976). *The Overeducated American.* New York: Academic Press.

Juhn, C., Murphy, K. M., & Pierce, B. (1993). Wage inequality and the rise in returns to skill. *Journal of Political Economy, 101,* 410–442.

Katz, L. F., & Murphy, K. M. (1992). Changes in relative wages, 1963–1987: Supply and demand factors. *Quarterly Journal of Economics, 107,* 35–78.

Lee, D. S. (1999). Wage inequality in the United States during the 1980s: Rising dispersion or falling minimum wage? *Quarterly Journal of Economics, 115,* 977–1023.

Leonard, J. (1990). The impact of affirmative action regulation and equal employment law on black employment. *Journal of Economic Perspectives, 4,* 47–64.

Wood, Adrian. (1995). How trade hurt unskilled workers. *Journal of Economic Perspectives, 9,* 57–80.

4

Education and Training in an Era of Creative Destruction

Leonard I. Nakamura

OVERVIEW

This chapter provides a perspective on how the U.S. economy is changing and on the impacts that these changes are having on education.[1] Our economy is in a period of rapid and accelerating change. The kinds of work done and the corporations that employ the workers are changing at a more rapid pace than ever before. The world for which education is supposed to prepare us is changing faster than education itself and faster than educators. This is true of the most intensive education we provide—the education of medical doctors. It is even more true of the education we provide in elementary and secondary school.

The economic process we are engaged in is best described in terms of Joseph Schumpeter's theory of *creative destruction*.[2] From this perspective, the U.S. economy is increasingly devoted to *creating* new products and new work and continuously displacing—*destroying*—existing products, jobs, and firms. Under creative destruction, businesses compete to produce distinctive new products that are more valuable than existing products and to displace them from the market. When a business invents a new product, it can use patents, copyrights, trade secrets, and its advantage as the first one in the marketplace to establish a temporary monopoly over that product. If the new product is sufficiently superior, the firm reaps huge benefits from its temporary monopoly, which repay the firm for the costs and risks of the discovery process.

A rapidly growing proportion of workers is engaged in creating new products. These new products make existing products obsolete, the way computers have made typewriters and slide rules obsolete, and the way CDs have made LPs obsolete. Among these new products are many that serve to automate and expedite production, eliminating jobs directly—even when the product is not obsolete. These continuous shocks to the workplace imply that workers ought to be preparing themselves for frequent career disruption and for repeated—if not continuous—formal education. Our educational system, however, is designed more for sorting students into hierarchical categories by final degree earned than preparing them for a lifetime of learning. How then is the educational system coping with these changes? Thus far, mainly by multiplying stresses on educators.

This chapter provides an overview of economic change in the past twenty-five years in the first two parts; then it steps back to discuss occupational and educational change over the course of the twentieth century in the next two sections. It finally discusses some of the dilemmas confronting education, using the example of medicine to provide perspective.

HOW WORK IS CHANGING IN AN ERA OF CREATIVE DESTRUCTION

The economy of creative destruction divides workers and work into two parts or paths: creative workers, who change the world, and production workers, who are subjected to continuous change. As creative work is itself carried out on a leading edge that is rapidly evolving, creative workers are also subjected to rapid change.

Creative Workers

Creators are workers who first must try to imagine what has never existed before and yet is more valuable than what exists. Next, they must work with production designers, managers, and producers to discover how the new product might be efficiently mass-produced. Then, they must communicate—first to business decision makers and then to consumers—why the new product is of greater value than existing products that it would supplant, and why it is therefore worth making and purchasing.

Every act of genuine creativity provokes resistance, and should. What is familiar is usually safe; what is new possesses unknown dangers. The power of capitalism, according to the Schumpeterian theory of creative destruction, is precisely that it gives the profits of creativity to creators and the corporations that employ them, and thereby it can make creativity powerful enough to overcome the natural human resistance to change (Nakamura, 2000). That is, a corporation such as Pfizer can earn billions of dollars in profits marketing Viagra; and these prospective profits, with similar profits earned in the past, give it the power to hire workers to produce the new good, place it visibly before a wide market, and overcome the objections of those who prefer the status quo.

As we shall see in the next section, technological developments and globalization have tipped the scale decisively in favor of rapid creation, destruction, and economic change; this change has placed new demands on our educational system for more creative, better-trained workers. An important part of that system has been using success as a reward and failure as a punishment. This causes those who are labeled slow learners in our population to become averse to formal education and to terminate their education early. Fortunately, educational movements that made high school and then college education more widely accessible have, for much of the twentieth century, ensured that the supply of well-educated workers has kept pace with—and at times exceeded—the demands of new technologies. As a consequence, the wage premium for additional high-school and college education generally fell or remained low for the first three-quarters of this century, a trend that has favored income equality. Since the electronics revolution in the 1970s, that trend has reversed, and inequality has been rising.

College Education as Learning to Learn

The value of a college education has risen sharply, if we measure its comparative impact on the earnings of college graduates and high-school graduates. One important part of the value of a college education is that it better prepares the student for a lifetime of learning and change. Indeed, the ideal of the liberal college education is to prepare a broad base for continuing learning. A consequence is that college graduates, in fact, pursue more adult education than high-school graduates. Although one might guess that they need less additional formal education than high-school graduates, 58% of college graduates in 1994–95 took adult-education courses, whereas 31% to 42% of high-school graduates lacking any college education did (National Center for Education Statistics, 1995). Preparing students for relatively slow-paced careers—the traditional job of the junior high school and high school—is preparing them for a dead end.

Can we change the nature of education? The nature of education is changing already. The question is, how best can teachers and their institutions cope?

THE RISING PACE OF CHANGE SINCE 1975

Before the electronics revolution, a large sales force and clerical staff were required to place a new product in the mass market. As we shall see, from 1900 to 1980, corporations hired immense numbers of high-school graduates to staff offices and sales counters. During that period, long-run profitability and corporate leadership in a given field were rarely in doubt. As Alfred Chandler (1980, 1994), Harvard Business School's management historian, has documented, the top firms in the early 1900s remained the top firms in the 1960s and 1970s. As he discusses in the magisterial works, *The Visible Hand* and *Scale and Scope,* U.S. corporations made three investments: in mass-production facilities, in a sales force, and in a corporate office structure to coordinate production and sales.

The consequence was that a potential rival with a new invention could only very rarely challenge the corporate leader. A new invention might make the corporate leader's production facility potentially obsolete, but it could rarely take over an important market because the sales force and the corporate office took a long time to duplicate. So, the leading corporation could grind an innovative rival into submission while adopting the new technology at a leisurely and profitable pace. Thus, outside inventors had to sell their ideas to the large corporation that could use them most efficiently, and rarely were they paid full value. To summarize: Only large corporations had the wherewithal to reach consumers quickly, and as a result, the great corporations were in control of the pace of introduction of new products.

All that has now changed. Technology is no longer controlled by the corporation; instead, only those corporations that can repeatedly invent and use the next new thing are consistently profitable. Creators and creativity dominate the pace of work.

The great hurdle is to come up with a great product that is really substantially better than previous products. Being just as good is not enough. But if you have a great product, the marketplace can distribute it to millions of customers in a hurry, and distribution can be extended globally. Before the electronics revolution, setting up a distribution network for a great new product took decades. As a consequence of that revolution, new products that are worth hundreds of millions or billions of dollars in profits to their producers have become almost commonplace. And that means corporations are forced to spend, overall, hundreds of billions of dollars to try to invent and then market great new products.

What evidence do we have that the economy has changed so much? The most important evidence is that the number of workers engaged in creative occupations has risen rapidly, as we shall see in the next section. The proportion of such workers at the end of the twentieth century was very high. These workers are among our best and brightest: well-educated and experienced. They are highly paid, and their pay is justified only if they produce new products that are more valuable to consumers than existing products. That ensures continuous, rapid, and probably accelerating creative destruction.

OCCUPATIONAL CHANGE IN THE TWENTIETH CENTURY

At the beginning of the twentieth century, almost all workers were engaged in actually doing the physical work needed to produce economic output directly; they were farmers, carpenters, welders, barbers, and cooks. These are the *directly productive* occupations: They include agricultural workers; industrial workers (skilled and unskilled); and direct-service workers, such as barbers, waiters, and domestic servants. By the end of the century, fewer than half of all workers were so engaged, and the majority of workers were involved in white-collar work. These in turn are divided into two groups: *sales and clerical* workers, who, abstractly speaking, are engaged primarily in communicating information about products and data about transactions; and *managerial, professional, and technical* workers. We can usefully divide professionals into two groups: the creative professionals (those who invent, design, or create new products) and service professionals (such as doctors and teachers, who make client-based decisions).

These three groups—directly productive workers, sales and clerical workers, and managerial, professional, and technical workers—roughly correspond to three levels of educational requirements. Broadly speaking, direct production does not require a high-school education; clerical and service work requires a high-school diploma; and managerial, professional, and technical work requires a bachelor's degree. We will be using these categories to help give us a sense of how the educational requirements of work have changed over the century.

Figure 4.1 (National Center for Education Statistics, 1999, Table 384) shows the proportion of workers over age twenty-five in each occupational category with a given level of education. The overwhelming majority of both direct-production workers and clerical and sales workers have less than a bachelor's degree. What differentiates clerical and sales work from direct-production work is that, generally speaking, the minimum educational requirement for the former is a high-school diploma. Of course, there are openings for checkout clerks who lack a high-school diploma, but such opportunities, aside from being poorly paid, are surprisingly small in number.

In sharp contrast, 60% of managerial, professional, and technical workers have a bachelor's degree or higher. Only 40% range from a high-school diploma to an associate's degree (Bill Gates is in this 40%). Again, in many

Figure 4.1
Educational Background of Workers over Age Twenty-Five by Occupation, 1999 (Percentages)

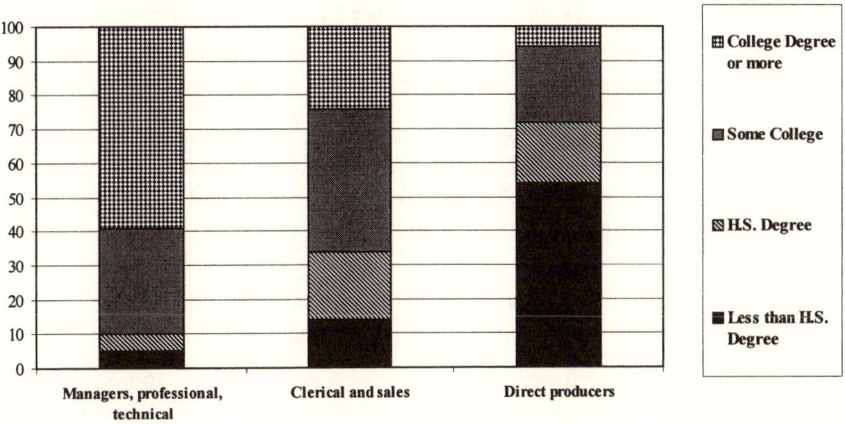

cases—doctors, lawyers, nurses, architects, engineers, scientists—college and often advanced degrees are occupational requirements.

Beginning in 1975, more workers were involved in the white-collar activities of decision making, coordination, and supervision than in actually producing the goods and services that were ultimately purchased. And as the electronics revolution tended to automate routine aspects of white-collar work, it has increasingly centered, as I have said, on discovering new, superior products.

To get a feel for recent employment dynamics, from 1990 to 1999, we can observe that the number of workers in the U.S. increased by 15 million, to 133 million.[3] More than two-thirds of the increase in new jobs was in managerial, professional, and technical occupations, whose numbers rose from thirty-four million to forty-five million. It is in this group that employment opportunity has expanded the most, and it generally requires a bachelor's degree. Direct production expanded by three million jobs, from fifty-one million to fifty-four million. And clerical and service work expanded by fewer than two million jobs, from thirty-three million to thirty-five million.[4]

Until the Electronics Revolution, the Proportion of Clerical and Sales Workers Grew Rapidly

To put these recent trends in historical perspective, we now examine how the labor-market shares of our two white-collar occupation groups have varied over the past one hundred years. Clerical and sales work rose very substantially in the first half of the twentieth century and continued rising until the electronics revolution began to rapidly automate these jobs.[5] From 1900 to 1980, these white-collar occupations rose from 7.5% of the workforce to 28%. In the first half of the century in particular, the development of mass-production techniques, in the absence of inexpensive electronic devices, rapidly multiplied the demand for workers to keep track of the multiplying array of transactions. The whole point—that is, profit—of being able to produce millions of gallons of kerosene, or millions of cars, or millions of shoes was lost if the revenue from the millions of sales did not wend its way back to the producer as efficiently as the goods were produced. During this period, as Chandler tells us, these workers were the primary line of defense of the great corporation; once they became technologically outmoded by electronics, that defense was greatly impaired. After 1980, with computers and electronics rapidly automating data processing and communication, the proportion of clerical and sales workers leveled off and then began declining, with some 26% of the workforce employed in these occupations in 1999.

The Proportion of Managers, Professionals, and Technicians Has Accelerated over the Course of the Twentieth Century

These workers, primarily engaged in creating new products and making decisions about products, now comprise 33% of the workforce. Because they are highly paid, managers, professionals, and technicians garner half of all U.S. wages and salaries, whereas direct producers earn roughly 30%, and clerical and sales workers earn about 20%.

This group includes 20 million managers, primarily employed in private businesses. These are the decision makers of the corporations, and they are increasingly engaged in deciding how to create new products and which new products to produce and market. There are about four million technical workers, including roughly a million computer programmers. And there are about twenty million professionals, of which about thirteen million are service professionals, mainly doctors, nurses, and college, secondary, and primary school teachers.

Although the number of clerical and sales workers increased faster than that of managers, professionals, and technicians in the earlier part of the century, the decision-making group has steadily accelerated. They were 10% of the workforce in 1900 and 17% in 1950. During the first two decades of the century, clerical and sales workers rose from being one-fourth less numerous than the decision makers to being 10% more numerous, and this proportion remained relatively fixed from then until 1970. From 1970 to 1999, the decision-making group grew from 23% to 33% of the workforce, while the clerical and sales group remained roughly constant. As a result, the managers, professionals, and technicians group once again outnumbers the sales and clerical workers group—just as it did in 1990.

Creative Professionals Have Grown Faster than Other Managers and Professionals

The direct work involved in the creation of new products is, by and large, in the hands of creative professionals. These professionals include the science-based creators, scientists and engineers, of which there are about five million, and the culture-based creators, designers, writers, artists, and entertainers, who constitute about two million more.[6] All told, this group now constitutes about one-sixth of managers, professionals, and technicians, and about one in sixteen of all workers.

This group's pay averages about the same as that of other managers and professionals; that is, about twice that of direct-production workers, but as any reader of *Entertainment Weekly* knows, pay within the group is wickedly dispersed. The total payroll of creativity amounts to about 10% of U.S. payrolls. It is the work of this group that is responsible for most of the huge increase in U.S. stock prices over the past two decades: Their creations temporarily exempt corporate products from the corrosive forces of direct market competition. As a consequence, products such as *Harry Potter* books, Microsoft Office, Intel Pentium microprocessors, Viagra, and Disney World can earn billions of dollars of profits.

They had better, for they represent a collective investment of between $500 billion and $1 trillion annually. U.S. prosperity is based on a high return to that annual investment, so each year corporate valuations will rise by more than $1 trillion if the investments are, on average, good ones. But that in turn requires that a large proportion of all products must change each year! And that means ongoing turmoil in the workforce.[7]

By contrast, there were only 200,000 creative professionals in the workforce in 1900, and they represented about 1% of total payrolls. Moreover, without motion photography to capture acting and without phonography to capture music, the impact of these creative professionals was much smaller. At that time, culture-based professionals represented two-thirds of the creative professions, and there were only about 60,000 engineers and scientists. So although there was a great deal of change taking place in the early twentieth century with the development of electricity, the automobile, the airplane, movies, phonographs, and radio, the pace at which these inventions affected the economy was slower, and the proportion of the economy devoted to these pursuits was smaller.

THE HIGH-SCHOOL MOVEMENT (1910 TO 1940) AND THE COLLEGE MOVEMENT (1940 TO 1970)

Claudia Goldin, an economic historian at Harvard University, has documented (1998) the striking fact that before 1900, very few Americans—roughly 10% of the population—went to high school. At that time, high-school students often went to private college-preparatory programs, and more than half of all students went on to college and became professionals: teachers, mainly, but also preachers, lawyers, and doctors.

As mass production increased, however, it became clear that corporations needed large numbers of clerical and sales workers to handle rapidly increasing volumes of sales transactions. And these workers needed to have enough understanding of science and mathematics to be able to learn how the mass-produced goods operated: How to safely handle electrical appliances, repair cars, replace vacuum tubes on radios, or operate Victrolas or nickelodeons. They also needed to be able to understand corporate forms, tally invoices and customer bills, and follow national events in the newspaper. The information flow associated with the massive quantities of production made possible by mass-production techniques required highly accurate hand recording and responsible transmission of sales data and cash receipts. Clerical and sales workers at the turn of the century were quite well-paid, typically earning twice as much as skilled factory workers, so such jobs were looked on as desirable, both in status and in pay.

A mass movement in favor of publicly supported junior high-school and high-school education swept the country, particularly the North. Goldin (1998) has pointed out that the resulting increase in the quality of the U.S. workforce helped to dramatically increase U.S. output. It represented the major investment in workforce quality America made in the twentieth century, far outweighing in quantitative importance the college movement of the postwar period, involving as it did far more of the workforce and increasing the number of years of education more rapidly.

This rapid increase in junior high- and high-school attendance rates was mainly compressed into the period from 1909 to 1939 (U.S. Department of Commerce, 1976, 1999; National Center for Education Statistics, 1999). Moreover, this movement occurred in the U.S. nearly half a century before it did elsewhere in the world. For example, the British, whose university and private-school systems were probably the most advanced in the world at the time, did not adopt universal high-school education until after World War II. The resulting increase in U.S. education not only increased real wages, but the public character of the education also dramatically increased U.S. equality.

The economic value of education is the increase in pay that a student can expect from having an additional year of successful formal training. Broadly speaking, that value is determined by supply and demand: how much the demand for educated workers is increasing and how much the supply of educated workers is increasing. If the wage premium for a given level of educational attainment falls while the proportion of such workers increases, it would appear that the supply of education is keeping ahead of the skill demands of technological progress. On the other hand, if the wage premium rises while the proportion of such workers increases, skill-biased technological progress is likely outracing the supply of education. (For theoretical discussions and more detailed analyses, see Goldin & Katz, 1999; Katz & Murphy, 1992.)

In the first half of the twentieth century, the high-school movement caused the supply of high-school educated to increase faster than demand. As a result, the relative economic value of an additional year of both high-school and college training declined (Goldin & Katz, 1999).

From the end of World War II to 1969, it was the college-going population that grew rapidly—partly because of the GI Bill and partly because of the draft deferment in the 1960s for college students. During this period, the demand for college-educated workers kept up with the increased supply, and their earnings rose slightly relative to those of noncollege-educated workers. In the 1970s, however, demand increased more slowly than supply, and the wage gap between college- and noncollege-educated workers narrowed (Katz & Murphy, 1992). Finally, over the last two decades, rapid technological change—this time in the form of the electronics revolution—again increased the demand for highly trained workers relative to supply. As a result, the wage gap between college-educated and noncollege-educated workers once more grew to significant proportions even though college attendance rates were also increasing. Data from Goldin and Katz (1999), for example, suggest that the current pay differential between high-school and college graduates is approximately the same in percentage terms as it was in 1914.

THE PROFESSIONAL SERVICES IN AN ERA OF CREATIVE DESTRUCTION

The thirteen million service professionals include some four million medical professionals and seven million teachers. Virtually all these service professionals have bachelor's degrees and additional formal training after college. Yet they are responsible—in principle—for keeping abreast of an explosion of information relevant to their duties. These occupational groups have very high rates of attending ongoing educational courses. In 1995, according to the National Household Educational Survey (National Center for Education Statistics, 1995), doctors, dentists, and veterinarians on average took two career- or job-related courses per year; registered nurses and pharmacists took 2.2 courses per year; and elementary and secondary teachers took 1.5 courses per year.

The rapid increase in creativity has meant that the amount of potentially useful information has grown extremely rapidly. This offers a challenge to the professional services: Can humans keep up with the pace of knowledge? The answer is that the pace of new products and knowledge production is outracing education. Let us view this dilemma in medicine. Medicine is now the largest industry in the United States, accounting for more than a trillion dollars in annual revenues, or more than 10% of U.S. output. The U.S. consumer buys more medicine than food. The pace of progress in medicine is unmistakable and nearly unbearable.

The Crisis in Medicine

In an editorial published in 1998 in the *Journal of the American Medical Association,* a blue-ribbon team of doctors studying the quality of medicine discussed how doctors were coping with the abundance of new scientific knowledge being produced.

One crude index of the impact of this change is illuminating. The randomized controlled trial has become the gold standard for evaluating the efficacy of health care interventions of all sorts. Yet it is a relatively recent phenomenon. The first one was published in 1952. In thirty years, from 1966 to 1995, more than 76,000 journal articles were published from randomized controlled trials (as registered in the automated database *MEDLINE*). The first five years of that period contributed less than 1% of the total, whereas the last half-decade contributed more than the previous twenty-five years combined. In the face of this avalanche of rigorous data on efficacy, our methods of training physicians and other clinicians and our systems for supporting them in the delivery of health care services have not kept pace (Chassin & Galvin, 1998, p. 1003).

That is the best-trained, best-paid, and best-informed professionals in America can no longer keep up with the amount of information generated for their patients' benefit. The dimensions of the problem can be seen in the annual averages of published randomized trials. From 1966 to 1970, the years in which the Medicare system was proposed and implemented, randomized controlled trials were published at a rate of roughly 150 articles per year, or three per week. This is a rate of publication that one can imagine a busy but conscientious professional might keep up with. From 1991 to 1995, 150 articles were published every *week*. It seems unlikely that a professional could keep up with this pace of information, even if he or she did nothing else.

The consequence is that the average doctor does not use anything resembling the full armory of medical knowledge in practice. One solution is for doctors to draw their prescription and treatment recommendations from a computerized, constantly updated database. At LDS Hospital in Salt Lake City, Utah, such a computer system has been in place for more than a decade.[8] Doctors are free to disagree with the computerized recommendation, but if they do so, they must articulate why, and these arguments may result in changes in the computerized recommendation if these treatments are successful. This permits doctors at the frontiers of specialties to improve the computer recommendations and to experiment in concert with other doctors. Several studies at LDS Hospital have shown substantially better outcomes at substantially lowered average cost.

Yet outside of a few isolated cases, doctors and hospitals have not adopted computerized systems to improve the handling of cases and the flow of information. Doctors fear, perhaps rightly, that computerization will serve to limit their freedom and may threaten their jobs because nurses and other medical personnel also can read computer output. Doctors know that the HMOs, hospital chains, and other for-profit corporate providers of medical care will seize any opportunity to cut costs, and computerization of medical diagnosis is a major way to cut costs by reducing the value of doctors. It is true that medical education in the U.S. is almost surely the best in the world, and new medicines reach our population faster than anywhere else, albeit unevenly. Yet such is the pace of economic change that our medical education and our medical system are not merely inadequate, but in crisis.

Our educational system is often sharply criticized because our students do not perform as well on standardized tests as students in many other countries. For example, as Stevenson and Lee (1998) point out, "The only countries that American eighth graders outperformed in both mathematics and science were Cyprus, Iran, Lithuania, and Portugal" (p. 9). Yet this same educational system has produced the workers who are the most creative in the world. In terms of preparing students for a world of creative destruction, the U.S. educational system is almost certainly the best. But such are the demands of creative destruction that this system is under attack from all sides. In particular, teachers are struggling to help their students integrate their knowledge and get better test results. The challenges of our economy help explain why students have expectations—whether realistic or not—of obtaining a college education and why countries around the world are moving away from apprenticeship programs.

Creativity

Creating new products is inherently risky. If creating new products that make lots of money were easy, everyone would do it. At the leading edge of innovation, no one knows exactly what the next step is. As Harvard economist Richard Caves puts it (2000), when it comes to creativity, "nobody knows" (p. 3). Creators need the ability to evaluate the existing products critically, decide which additional features or qualities new products should have, and solve the problems that lie in the path of creating the new products and publicizing them to their intended audience. Typically, they need both to communicate with others in their field as they compete with them, and to convince others outside their field of expertise to cooperate in launching the new product. Of course, no one can expect to exemplify all the complex and contradictory mix of skills needed for successful creativity.

Fortunately, not all of us are required to be creators just yet; only one worker in sixteen is employed at such work. But in the more dynamic work environments we now inhabit, we are asked far more often to change what we are doing, to help in adapting new sets of procedures, and to critique and improve them. Learning from failure is increasingly expected from all of us. Increasingly, educators are suggesting that this can be done with experimental and activist learning along the constructivist paradigm in which students actively construct their understanding in their studies.

Supporting experimental and activist learning is not impossible; it is, after all, a natural human activity, according to modern developmental psychology. Gopnik, Meltzoff, and Kuhl (1999) have emphasized that human babies naturally experiment and learn like miniature scientists. One of the coauthors of that study, Andrew Meltzoff, argues that maintaining this sort of learning requires school to provide a stress-free environment in which concrete manipulation and active, meaningful exploration is possible (as cited in D'Arcangelo, 2000). Offering opportunities for structured play and empowering students to learn effectively and to challenge authority, at the same time that we wish them to acquire large quantities of formal learning, require not only reorienting schools and teachers, but also providing substantial new resources for learning.

Perhaps the most important step in the short run is to adopt, insofar as possible, as a value and a goal that *all students leave school prepared to successfully continue their education* with recurrent, episodic job- and career-related course training. A decisive movement toward this goal is to attempt to ensure that all students, no matter how fast or slow, have successful learning experiences. Is it possible to do this and still have students learn? An intriguing example of a school reform that supports this approach is reported by Wilson,

Corbett, and Williams (2000). They describe an urban middle school that serves a poor community that is half African American and half white. The school instituted a "no excuses" attitude toward the students' learning. The basic rule adopted was a simple one: All students were required to finish assigned work at the B level. Incomplete or less-than-adequate assignments continued to be worked on until complete and satisfactory, at the same time as new work was assigned and done.

This program appears to have been reasonably successful, in that on the eighth-grade writing assessment, the school's students performed above average for the district, although it served the poorest community therein, and just below average for the state. The math assessment was not reported. As in many educational reforms, it is difficult to assess to what extent the morale of the teachers and the obvious intelligence and enthusiasm of the principal are responsible for this outcome relative to the specifics of the reform itself.

The Crisis in Education

Educators are not as well equipped, trained, or paid as doctors. And although it may be true that educational practice has not leapt forward at the pace of medical practice, educators are responsible for preparing their students for a world that in many ways is racing forward more rapidly than medicine. In any case, it is similarly true that very few educators can keep up with best practices. Consider how fast the potential for best practices is rising.

Teachers do not have time to keep up with the computer programs and games available to their students (Roschelle, Pea, Hoadley, Gordin, & Means, 2000). While the number of computers per student has risen rapidly, only 15% of teachers had nine hours of training in computer technology or more in 1998 (Chapman, 2000). English teachers do not keep up with developments in reader-response analysis and its application to the principles of writing (Williams, 1990). Math teachers are unaware of the application of projective geometry—the theoretical basis for three-dimensional perspective discovered by Renaissance painters—in the development of video games, charts in spreadsheets, and movie and cartoon production. Science labs do not take advantage of hardware to simulate virtually the physical feedback of animal dissection, although that simulation uses computer joysticks.

Perhaps most important, the prospects for automating the routines of practice and test taking in education remain bleak. Giving students computerized desks in principle could allow teachers to give and grade tests frequently and with scant effort. But we are far from being able to reach this standard. Not only is teacher training inadequate, but the hardware resources—despite a substantial investment—are outdated because most of the computers available to students are not multimedia computer and the software offerings are also lacking.

Electronic automation of data processing is now routine in most American corporate offices. Tests of arithmetic, spelling, reading, geography, and science could be both more informative and less costly in terms of teacher and student time if administered over a computer network. By downloading the results, teachers could use programs to pinpoint student weaknesses, both individually and en bloc. That would also permit teachers to perform controlled experiments testing the effectiveness of alternative lesson plans in instilling particular kinds of information. In turn, this documentation could allow teachers who produce new, more effective teaching methodologies to be identified, the methodologies shared and further tested and refined, and the originating teachers rewarded for their contributions to teaching.

Such computerization might also permit the detailed diagnosis and assessment of learning disabilities and other problems in individual students, which would then lay the basis for detailed discovery of methods for solving learning problems and catering to disabilities. Successfully applied, this could result in a system in which learning speed became less crucial to a student's ability to complete a given level of education. That would be an important step forward in a work world that increasingly demands that all workers, not merely the top ones, be sufficiently comfortable with formal education to be willing to pursue it throughout their work lives.

Yet few educational systems have embraced this level of computerization. The software tools have been slow to develop, and few schools have committed themselves to placing computers on every student's desk. Of particular concern is the fact that relatively little funding has gone into assessing the strengths and limitations of individual learning technologies (Shields & Behrman, 2000), although broad studies suggest that computer technologies are useful both in drill (as in a meta-analysis reported in Kulik, 1994) and in deepening mathematical understanding (Wenglinsky, 1998, a large-scale national study).

Moreover, it is quite possible that many teachers will resist an intensive computerization of learning, both because of the revision to their own work habits and accumulated knowledge that this would require and because of the likelihood that these evaluative tools would be used on the teachers as well as the students. These tools would permit detailed evaluation of the ability of individual teachers to improve the knowledge of their students, and could be used as a blunt instrument for forcing teachers to focus on short-term results at the cost of more intangible skills.

At the same time, many teachers are not trained to help their students develop the skills they already possess that could be the basis for their education. To give one example, at least limited curricula have been developed that help students use activities in music, art, and dance to understand concepts in math, science, language, and history. But the average nonspecialist teacher is not able to teach music, art, and dance, areas where students' abilities often outstrip their own. It may be possible one day for distance learning to fill the gap.

More generally, though, just as the bulk of a doctor's knowledge and power is in the routine part of medicine, so too is a teacher's. If computers take over the routine of education, teachers must become something more—a role that many teachers, like doctors, may be uncomfortable with.

Ultimately, it may be possible to foster learning through many channels. Our work system is pushing the entire workforce toward being either creators or those who cooperate with creativity because the machines we use to produce goods and services increasingly do not need human input. If this is the case, the role of the teacher will be more and more to foster creativity, communication, and cooperation instead of guiding the specific learning of specific pieces of knowledge, such as how to form a letter or multiply fractions.

One avenue for training for creative destruction that has already spread to many school districts is training in peer mediation and conflict resolution. Although such training is often aimed at resolving potentially violent conflicts, training in negotiation is of value in a broad spectrum of circumstances. In particular, it is useful in an economy of creative destruction. Conflict is central to creative destruction because new ideas are inherently conflictual. Most new ideas turn out to be wrong; most new products lose money. Both giving potential new ideas a fair trial and separating what is sound about a new idea or product from what is not involve conflicts that must be resolved and mediated with as little damage to egos and budgets as possible. Helping students learn techniques for rational negotiation and for helping others attain goals without harming their own is likely to prove a fundamental building block for a career in the age of creative destruction.

CONCLUSION

Over the course of the twentieth century, the United States evolved from a country in which few students went beyond the primary grades to one in which most students enter college. The century witnessed enormous change, and the pace of change appears likely only to accelerate. Already we have reached the point at which all workers must look forward to a lifetime of continuing education.

Just as the education of doctors has not prepared them for the pace of change the medical profession is experiencing, so too the education of teachers has not prepared them for the pace of change the educational process is experiencing. It is hard to prepare students for a lifetime of continuing education, and it is even harder to prepare them for a lifetime of creativity.

It is possible that electronic advances may eventually make it more possible for educators to meet these challenges. In the meantime, dissatisfaction with education and educators is likely to deepen. Learning techniques of conflict resolution may be helpful for teachers and students alike.

NOTES

1. The views expressed are those of the author, and do not necessarily reflect those of the Federal Reserve Bank of Philadelphia or of the Federal Reserve System.

2. Schumpeter's theory is set forth in *Capitalism, Socialism, and Democracy* (1942). This theory poses direct challenges to the mainstream theory of the invisible hand first enunciated by Adam Smith (Nakamura, 2000).

3. Data are from the Current Population Survey of the Bureau of Labor Statistics (1991, 1999), which measures unemployment every month.

4. Because managers, professionals, and technicians tend to retire later than other workers, these figures on new employment exaggerate the difference in job availability because there tends to be more attrition in the other occupations.

5. U.S. Census Bureau (1980), Bureau of Labor Statistics (1991, 1999), and U.S. Department of Commerce (1999). Sales and clerical workers include sales workers and administrative support, including clerical workers. Managers, professionals, and technical workers include executive, administrative, and managerial workers; professional specialty workers; and technical and related support workers.

6. Professional creative workers consist of architects, engineers, mathematical and computer scientists, natural scientists, social scientists, urban planners, writers, artists, entertainers, and athletes. I have made minor multiplicative adjustments to exclude teachers of dance, music, and art from the artists and entertainers category in earlier years.

7. Rising productivity has both positive and negative impacts on the workforce. Rising productivity in the U.S. has supported strong and sustained expansion of the economy and falling overall rates of unemployment while keeping inflation modest. This cyclical impact has reduced layoffs and stabilized overall employment. On the negative side, individual corporations and jobs have become riskier, so the job tenure of workers overall has become more uncertain for any given level of national unemployment. This uncertainty has particularly affected experienced male workers.

8. See Garibaldi (1998) and references therein.

REFERENCES

Bureau of Labor Statistics. (1991). *Employment and earnings, 1991.* Washington, DC: U.S. Department of Labor.

Bureau of Labor Statistics. (1999). *Employment and earnings, 1999.* Washington, DC: U.S. Department of Labor.

Caves, R. (2000). *Creative industries: Contracts between art and commerce.* Cambridge, MA: Harvard University Press.

Chandler, A. (1980). *The Visible hand: The managerial revolution in American business.* Cambridge, MA: Harvard University Press.

Chandler, A. (1994). *Scale and scope: The dynamics of American capitalism.* Cambridge, MA: Harvard University Press.

Chapman, G. (2000). Federal support for technology in K–12 education. *Brookings Papers on Education Policy, 3,* 307–342.

Chassin, M. R., & Galvin, R. W. (1998). The urgent need to improve health care quality: Institute of Medicine national roundtable on health care quality. *Journal of the American Medical Association, 280,* 1000–1005.

D'Arcangelo, M. (2000). The scientist in the crib: A conversation with Andrew Meltzoff. *Educational Leadership, 58,* 8–13.

Garibaldi, R. A. (1998, January 22). Computers and the quality of care—a clinician's perspective. *New England Journal of Medicine, 338,* 259–260.

Goldin, C. (1998). America's graduation from high school: The evolution and spread of secondary schooling in the twentieth century. *Journal of Economic History, 58,* 345–374.

Goldin, C., & Katz, L. F. (1999). *The returns to skill across the twentieth century United States* (NBER Working Paper No. 7126). Cambridge, MA: National Bureau of Economic Research.

Gopnik, A.M., Meltzoff, A. N., & Kuhl, P. K. (1999). *The scientist in the crib: Minds, brains, and how children learn.* New York: Morrow.

Katz, L. F., & Murphy, K. M. (1992). Changes in relative wages, 1963–1987: Supply and demand factors. *Quarterly Journal of Economics, 107,* 35–78.

Kulik, J. A. (1994). Meta-analytic studies of findings on computer-based instruction. In E. L. Baker & H. F. O'Neil, Jr., *Technology Assessment in Education and Training* (pp. 9–33). Hillsdale, NJ: Erlbaum.

Nakamura, L. I. (2000, July–August). Economics and the new economy: The invisible hand meets creative destruction. *Federal Reserve Bank of Philadelphia Business Review,* pp. 15–30.

National Center for Education Statistics. (1995). *National household education survey, 1995.* Washington, DC: U.S. Department of Education.

National Center for Education Statistics. (1999). *Digest of education statistics, 1999.* Washington, DC: U.S. Department of Education.

Roschelle, J. M., Pea, R. D., Hoadley, C. M., Gordin, D. N., & Means, B. M. (2000). Changing how and what children learn in school with computer-based technologies. *The Future of Children, 10,* 76–101.

Schumpeter, J. (1942). *Capitalism, socialism, and democracy.* New York: Harper.

Shields, M. K., & Behrman, R. E. (2000). Children and computer technology: Analysis and recommendations. *The Future of Children 10,* 4–30.

Stevenson, H. W., & Lee, S. (1998). An examination of American student achievement from an international perspective. *Brookings Papers on Education Policy, 1998, 1,* 7–38.

U.S. Census Bureau. (1980). *U.S. census of population, 1900–1980.* Washington, DC: U.S. Department of Commerce.

U.S. Department of Commerce. (1976). *Historical statistics of the United States, colonial times to 1970.* Washington, DC: Author.

U.S. Department of Commerce. (1999). *Statistical abstracts of the United States, 1999.* Washington, DC: Author.

Wenglinsky, H. (1998). *Does it compute? The relationship between educational technology and student achievement in mathematics.* Princeton, NJ: Educational Testing Service.

Williams, J. M. (1990). *Style: Toward clarity and grace.* Chicago: University of Chicago Press.

Wilson, B., Corbett, D., & Williams, B. (2000). A discussion on school reform—case 1: All students learning at Granite Junior High. *Teachers College Record Online.* Retrieved from http://www.tcrecord.org/PrintContent.asp?ContentID=10619

5

Old Economy or New Economy? The Educational Implications

William C. Dunkelberg

INTRODUCTION

As the year 2000 started, a quote from the *Wall Street Journal* caught my attention. "So Long, Supply and Demand. There's a New Economy Out There—and It Looks Nothing Like the Old One" (Petzinger, 2000). This January 1 pronouncement characterized the views of many in the U.S. as the Internet Age became headline news. But we woke up in the same bed and watched the same, if much-improved, television to get the early news. We drove to work in cars that worked and looked pretty much as cars have for 20 years (a car may have 15 to 20 computer chips in it, but it also has improved mechanical brakes, valves, much better paint, and other "old-economy" improvements). For the past five years, we have been looking for that "new economy" that "is nothing like the old one," but we have not found it, a fact that has been confirmed by the evaporation of many "dot-com" companies and the retreat of the NASDQ from over 5,000 to under 1,500 points.

Every year, there are inventions, improvements, new information and knowledge, new gadgets and gizmos—events that have occurred throughout our entire history. Change is a fact of life, sometimes rapid, sometimes slow, but inevitable. The economy is newer every day, as some industries shrink and other industries grow, old jobs disappear, and new jobs are created. The hype was wrong; there is not a host of new products and services all made possible by the Internet and the chip. But the economy has been changed significantly, much as the introduction of electricity changed our lives. And the educational demands of the market have changed with it.

NOT SO MUCH A NEW ECONOMY AS A MORE EFFICIENT ONE

Although it seems as if there is a computer chip in everything these days, this has not created a new economy, just a more efficient one. Much of what the chip has contributed to our economy is invisible. The Internet existed in 1995 when the stock market "discovered" the new economy. People were learning how to use it, and businesses were looking at ways to get into new markets or reach more customers or suppliers, but there was nothing new about these activities. Firms were performing the same basic functions, but in more efficient ways. Moreover, science and medicine have been profoundly impacted, as the chip has helped make the impossible possible and has ramped up the speed of discovery and progress. The rate of change is stunning, but not "new"—such progress has been happening for centuries. The major impact of the new technologies has been the improvement of the old economy, not the creation of entirely new firms and new products.

For example, UPS uses scanners to track and direct parcels, cell phones are making phone lines obsolete, and full-length cartoons can be made in no time at all—but they are still cartoons, nothing new. Inventory management has been streamlined by bar-code scanners that feed transactions to computers that track sales and automatically order more product. *Business Week* reported business-to-business (B2B) transactions on the Internet well in excess of $100 billion, up from "almost zero a few years ago" (Cohn, 2000, p. 37). But these are not "new" sales of "new-economy product." It's the same old stuff. Goldman Sachs estimated that B2B could "slash processing costs by more than 20% in industries such as electronics and freight transport," and a Boston Consulting Group study estimated that over five years, B2B alone "will boost productivity [output per working hour] by 9%" (Cohn, 2000, p. 37). Firms are performing the same basic functions, but they now have more efficient ways to do them. And because of the low cost of computers, software, and the Internet, this technology has become available to businesses of all sizes, not just the big guys (in the old days, you could not fit a computer into a small business, much less afford the cost of programmers and software). As a consequence, the benefits of the Internet and chip innovations are very pervasive and the impact of this technology on costs, quality, and service is more substantial.

Examining the notion of a "new economy," Professor Robert Gordon defined it as "the post-1995 acceleration in the rate of technical change in information technology together with the development of the Internet" (2000, p. 72). Indeed, Oliner and Sichel concluded that "information technology accounted for about two-thirds" of the step-up in labor productivity growth between the first and second halves of the decade" (2000, p. 21). Brynjolfsson and Hitt examined the business use of the new technology and concluded that the evidence points "to organizational complements like new business processes, new skills, and new organization and industry structures as a major driver of the contribution of information technology" (2000, p. 45). What this means is that you cannot see most of what the new technology is doing because it is making old-economy companies more efficient. Products and service may improve in quality, prices may not rise or rise by less than might otherwise have been the case, and labor productivity may rise, all because of computers and the Internet, but all "invisible" to the consumer.

So, we do not have a *new* economy, but a *newer* economy that has changed in response to the development of new technologies and information. We can be sure of two things: (a) technology has changed how we do business, has improved the quality of many products, and lowered many prices, but it has had less of an impact on what we do, including what we buy (are there brand-new products, or just better ones?); (b) the chip, the computer, and the Internet are at the core of the change that has occurred. Within the next five years, we can expect the percentage of U.S. households with computers, Internet access, and cell phones to rise to at least 65% (Joint Economic Committee, 2000). The growth of this "high-tech" sector has accounted for about a third of our gross domestic product (GDP) growth in recent years (including heavy high-tech exports to the rest of the world, which have doubled since 1990) and these industries now account for about 8% of our GDP (Joint Economic Committee, 2000, p. 1). Employment in these industries has grown at twice the rate of job growth in the overall economy (32% versus 15% over the past six years; Joint Economic Committee, 2000, p. 1).

THE NEW ECONOMY, THE STOCK MARKET, AND THE INVESTMENT BOOM

The so-called new economy was discovered by financial investors in 1995. At that point in time, the S&P 500 index had reached five times its 1968 level. From 1995 to 2000, however, the S&P 500 soared to sixteen times its 1968 level, an unprecedented run-up in the valuation of firms that produce our real GDP. Somehow, a handful of firms were thought to have so much value (on the basis of expected future earnings from new-economy products and services) that investors were willing to pay $1,000 for $1 of expected future earnings (meaning it would take 1,000 years to get your money back unless earnings grew dramatically) and to value companies with no earnings (such as Amazon.com) at hundreds of billions of dollars in the hope that someday these companies would make a fortune doing business in the new economy. The financial pages in the late 1990s focused on the new-economy concept and touted the use of the Internet as a communication device with the consumer. The new-economy technology was supposed to open up all sorts of new untapped markets that would be supplied with a plethora of unspecified new-economy goods and services. But it is not clear that these companies produced any new good or service beyond the convenience of communication over the Internet. After all, Amazon.com just sold books, and there's nothing new about those. Yet this company was valued at more than twice the market capitalization of Borders and Barnes & Noble combined.

Huge amounts of capital were invested in what were thought to be the new-economy companies. In 2000, investment spending on capital goods (buildings, equipment, power distribution, telecommunications, and so on) accounted for a record 20% of our GDP, the culmination of a big-time capital-spending boom that took off in the mid-1990s. Spending on IT (information technologies) as a percentage of total investment almost doubled, rising from 19% to 35% (we should note that the economists' concept of "investment" embodied in the measurement of GDP is the creation of new capital goods, not the purchase of an existing share of stock or building). But as we entered the twenty-first century, it became clear that there was a lot that was better but very little that was new. Most of this investment went toward improving old-economy businesses, as we should have expected.

The pace of change is certainly faster, and that may have confused people. But change has been under way for a long time. Banking provides a typical example. Once the telephone was invented, banking started changing. Then came the push-button phone (allowing bill-paying and account management by phone), then the fax (allowing transmission of complex instructions, signed documents, and so on), and then the personal computer (which can support more sophisticated communication systems in the home) and ATMs (which give access to your bank anywhere). But the nature of the changes in banking was predictable; it was just a question of "how fast" they would happen, which depended on the technology as well as consumer acceptance. Credit cards were also changing the way things were done, and it was easy to see where it was all going; it was just a question of how fast it would happen (e.g., how fast chips improved). Financial analysts observed AOL (and others) giving away "product" to grow their market as something new, but what's new about using "samples" (as drug companies, cigarette producers, and food processors do) to develop a market?

It is hard to find new products made by the Internet, and few products can be delivered by the Internet (only audio, video, and information). Huge numbers of dot-coms have gone out of business (such as K-Tel, Value America, and Pets.com), and most have lost all the market value that they once commanded. Why? Because they produce little of value and consequently cannot make money and have little prospect of doing so in the future. The Internet reduces the cost of what business always did, and the chip makes it possible to do it better, more efficiently, and with higher quality. But so did electricity, the telephone, and the internal combustion engine. You can now have your garage sale worldwide by advertising your items on e-Bay rather than with a sign at the corner of your block. This is more efficient in getting the products into the hands of those that value them the most, but it is basically the same event—a garage sale.

THE IMPACT ON EMPLOYMENT

Rapid change historically alters the nature of jobs available in the economy as businesses look for new skills and training in their workers. This investment boom of the 1990s was no exception. Not surprisingly, employment in new-economy manufacturing industries (such as electronice equipment) grew more rapidly than total manufacturing employment over this period. New-economy services—particularly those in the writing, installation, customization, and maintenance of software—grew even faster.

Historically, our educational system has responded well to the changing needs of our commercial structure, although recent work by the National Bureau of Economic Research suggests that this responsiveness has diminished over time. In spite of the current level of criticism, there is little reason to believe that the system will not continue to respond. Economic incentives have always redirected the allocation of educational effort, and this decade and century will be no exception. However, responding to today's more complex set of educational demands may be more difficult than simply providing more high-school graduates, the task facing the educational system 100 years ago.

Few investment booms have been as pervasive as the chip boom, and the pace of change is now faster because discovery and learning occur at a faster pace, but it's the old economy using the new technology that makes it all work. The car, the jet plane, electric lights—those were at the core of major investment booms, and you could "see" and "touch" the results. The impact of the chip is more subtle. The personal computer is tangible and pervasive, but it is not the major output of the chip and the Internet. Although the composition of output in the economy has changed—including computers, cell phones, and other chip-based products—it is not a new economy, just a changing one. The economy is experiencing yet another major boom driven by technological innovation. After electricity was successfully "invented," it still took decades for its use to widely penetrate the economy. The same is true for the chip and the Internet, although we will experience time compression—it all will happen more quickly.

IMPLICATIONS FOR THE EDUCATIONAL SYSTEM

At the risk of overgeneralization, one can assert that there is no new economy and that the *Wall Street Journal* was wrong—it's not "so long, supply and demand," there is *not* a "new economy out there," and what is out there looks like the old one, not "nothing like" the old one. It is the old economy, doing what it always does, just faster and better. Chips have been around for quite a while now, but the immense increase in their power and the huge reduction in their cost has made it possible for firms to do what they always do much better—find ways to make products and services less expensive and better and distribute them to consumers more cheaply. There is nothing new about that in our economy. It is the force of competition and the innovation that is driven by the promise of financial returns to the endeavors of entrepreneurial activity. And like all such change, it creates demands for new skills and training. For example, with the invention of the car came the need for driver skills, new regulations, mechanics, and new skills to create and distribute the fuel. As a consequence of today's changes, the percentage of the population with degrees of all types has continued to grow in response to this demand. Perhaps the major issue we face today is whether or not people can keep up with the progress. This is at the core of the major challenge to our educational system.

The technology that is associated with the new economy has changed the face of the labor market in many ways. The widespread impact of the computer has altered job content more pervasively and for more workers than has any other investment boom in history. Workers need computer skills at all levels of business. In addition, the boom has created a large demand for some new skills and talents (as is always the case with change) that our educational system is addressing only slowly, as has historically been the case (integrating computers into a curriculum is difficult if faculty members do not know how to use them). There is a shortage of the skills needed by the faster growing IT sector of the economy. There is clearly a higher return to education in this boom—but again, that has always been the case. Few workers lack a high-school education today, but 100 years ago, that lack would have been pervasive in the workforce. When the economy is changing rapidly, the skills of the teachers become obsolete at a faster pace as well. The rapid growth in in-house training at major corporations has, in part, been a result of the sluggish response of our educational institutions at all levels to the changing educational-content needs of businesses.

There has also been a reduction in the skill requirements for many blue-collar jobs in manufacturing and other sectors of the economy as computerized processes have increased reliability and performance and replaced workers or reduced the skill levels required. At the far extreme, "hamburger flippers" no longer need to be able to read or do math or communicate well with co-workers because picture-driven computer systems that compose and communicate orders and make change do the job. This is actually a positive result of the IT revolution, making it easier for low-skilled workers to enter the labor force and get on-the-job training and socialization. Welfare reform was instituted at a fortuitous time with the demand for labor at an all-time high. Even if unfortunate economic events return many of these workers to the welfare rolls, their period of employment will have improved their human capital and work skills, upgraded the average quality of the workforce, and made it easier for these workers to reenter the labor force.

THE NEED FOR FINANCIAL SKILLS AND KNOWLEDGE OF THE ECONOMY

A major factor in the rapid growth experienced in the 1980s and 1990s has been the changing role of capital markets. Stock ownership has soared, exceeding 50% of all families. A real investment boom must be supported by strong saving. At the peak of the most recent expansion (the end of 1999 and early 2000), total saving in the economy (business saving and government surpluses plus personal saving) was strong. In addition, huge amounts of foreign savings flowed into the U.S. A well-functioning economy and investment expansion also require an increasing sophistication among consumers about financial management and an understanding of how the economy works. Here, the educational system faces some major challenges. A recent series of studies undertaken by the American Financial Services Association Education Foundation (Mandell, 2000) indicates that the financial literacy of our young people is not high. Only 40% of the high-school students taking a financial literacy exam administered by the foundation received a passing grade. Whites and Asians did somewhat better than blacks and Hispanics, but overall scores were low for all students—including those from well-to-do families. Even "rich kids" lack good financial skills. These children are destined to inherit trillions of dollars earned by their parents, but they are not gaining the skills needed to wisely manage this capital.

Over the past twenty years, the private sector has probably provided more computer-based skills training to consumers (students) and workers than has the educational system. Worker skills and consumer or life skills are not as different as they were historically. In a manufacturing- or production-dominated economic process, there was little overlap between job skills (running a screw machine) and life skills (e.g., teamwork, communication, reading and learning, financial management, and investing). Today, the overlap is much larger, and growing.

The role of entrepreneurship in the creation of what has been called the best economy in history has been widely acknowledged. In Los Angeles, aerospace and defense employment has declined to 200,000, while employment in business related to international trade (including banking and warehousing) now exceeds 400,000. Ninety-five percent of the firms in Los Angeles now employ fewer than fifty employees ("Mayoral Election," 2001, p. 29). These small firms are the research-and-development sector of the U.S. economy. Many different ideas are tried (new firms started); some fail, and some succeed. Those that succeed are those supported by consumer votes (dollars) that provide the capital to expand. "Failures" are not losses for society—the resources are simply repriced, and a new experiment is started until a profit is made (a signal that the resources are being used to do something that has value to consumers). The successes provide guidance for how to do it right. But change of this magnitude creates many strains on the social fabric and particularly on the educational systems.

To better meet the changing demands on our educational system, a logical next step might be to employ the concepts of entrepreneurship in the restructuring of the educational system. This is happening through the development of such approaches as voucher systems and charter schools in their various forms. The driving principle behind these changes is the private-sector principle that as consumers of education, parents will direct resources toward those schools that deliver, whether public or private. Might some of these experiments fail? Certainly. However, better the failure of a few educational experiments than the failure of the entire system (in the U.S., we have firms that fail but a strong economic system, whereas the USSR had no firms "fail," just the whole system). In this type of system, successful enterprises (public or private schools) attract students who want to succeed and develop their human capital (or their parents want them to). Critics say that some students will be left behind. This is certainly happening today and at alarmingly high rates. And averaging all of these students together is handicapping those who wish to excel and on whom the future more heavily depends. What we must do is find ways to make our educational system more responsive to the needs of the firms and organizations that hire them—that is, prepare our students to take advantage of the opportunities in life that await them.

CONCLUSIONS

There is no new economy, but certainly a changed and rapidly changing one. It's all about the impact of the computer chip and the Internet. It appears that, at least now, the direct impact on consumers has been far less than anticipated—there is not a plethora of new consumer products on the market as many investors betting on the future of the new economy had hoped. The failure of the many dot-com companies that came into existence to sell directly to consumers confirms that this is not what the new economy is about. Far more pervasive is the impact that the Internet and the high-powered computer chip are having on business. And, most of this is not B2B, but internal to each company. Business process is being transformed as information flows and related decision making is enhanced. Workers have more power at their fingertips and more programs to assist in using that information to lower costs, and the power of the tools available to support research and development is phenomenal and still improving. But in many ways, the impact of the new economy is little different from the development of electricity, the internal combustion engine, and the telephone. The challenge to our educational system is (a) to provide an educated labor force that is prepared to take advantage of this change and the job opportunities it presents, and simultaneously (b) to learn how to use this new technology to transform the educational process in ways similar to the deployment of the technology in the private sector to enhance the productivity and performance of our educational enterprises.

REFERENCES

Brynjolfsson, E., & Hitt, L. (2000). Beyond computation: Information technology, organizational transformation, and business performance. *Journal of Economic Perspectives, 14*(4), 23–48.

Cohn, L. (with Brady, D., & Welch, D.). (2000, January 17). B2B, the hottest net bet yet? *Business Week*, p. 37.

Gordon, R. J. (2000). Does the "new economy" measure up to the great inventions of the past? *Journal of Economic Perspectives, 14*(4), 49–74.

Joint Economic Committee. (2000, June). *High technology and the U.S. economy* (Document No. 224–0367). Washington, DC: Author, Office of the Chairman, U.S. Senator Connie Mack.

Mandell, L. (2000). *Improving financial literacy.* Washington, DC: American Financial Services Association Education Foundation.

The mayoral election in Los Angeles: Is he up to it? (2001, June 9). *The Economist, 359,* 29–30.

Oliner, S. D., & Sichel, D. E. (2000). The resurgence of growth in the late 1990s: Is information technology the story? *Journal of Economic Perspectives, 14*(4), 3–22.

Petzinger, T., Jr. (2000, January 1). So long, supply and demand: There's a new economy out there—and it looks nothing like the old one. *Wall Street Journal*, p. R31.

Part III

The School-to-Work Movement

6

Has School-to-Work Worked?

Alan M. Hershey

The School-to-Work Opportunities Act of 1994 (STWOA) set an ambitious agenda for changing American schools. It was a response to concerns about how American schools prepare youth for careers, the role of American industry in a competitive global economy, falling real wages of young adults without college degrees, poor performance of American students on international skill measures, and employers' disappointment with young labor-force entrants. Observers such as Stern (1991) noted that unless the U.S. prepared youth better for work, there would be a shortage of the "skills required in the kinds of jobs *that will have to be created* if the nation's economy is to regain its competitive edge" (p. 27).

The 1994 STWOA drew on theories of how students learn best, models of technical education practiced in Europe, and elements of American vocational education. It envisioned four changes in American education:

- *Local Partnerships of Educators and Employers Would Play a Central Role.* Collaboration among schools, postsecondary education and training institutions, employers, labor, and others would help schools produce graduates with the skills for the new economy. Employers would help guide curricular changes and give students opportunities to develop and practice skills in the workplace.
- *Students' Experiences Would Change.* Students would get opportunities to learn about careers and formulate goals, and engage more in "career majors"—programs that integrate academic and vocational instruction, with links to work-based learning.
- *Student Outcomes Would Improve.* With greater focus on career goals and more opportunities to learn in a work context, students would achieve better outcomes, be more motivated, do better academically, and make smoother transitions to employment or further education.
- *STW Ideas and Practices Would Become Embedded in American Education.* Federal STW funds would trigger development of durable systems of policies, programs,

curriculum, and opportunities for students as well as collaborative relationships that would outlive the period of federal funding.

Evidence on the extent of such changes comes from broad national studies as well as studies of particular local programs. Much of what is reported here comes from the National Evaluation of School-to-Work Implementation (National STW Evaluation), conducted by Mathematica Policy Research, Inc. (see Hershey, Hudis, Silverberg, & Haimson, 1997; Hershey, Silverberg, Haimson, Hudis, & Jackson, 1999; Silverberg, Haimson, & Hershey, 1998). This National STW Evaluation has included surveys of all federally funded local STW partnerships; longitudinal surveys of cross-sectional samples of the high-school classes of 1996, 1998, and 2000 in thirty-nine local partnerships in eight states; and case studies of thirty-three of those local partnerships.[1] Over the same period, national "progress measure" surveys of partnerships have been conducted by the National STW Office through MPR Associates (see Medrich, Giambattista, & Moskovitz, 1997; Medrich, Merola, Ramer, & White, 2000; Medrich, Ramer, Merola, Moskovitz, & White, 1998). Studies done at the Institute on Education and the Economy at Teachers College, Columbia University, have contributed to our understanding of employer roles, curriculum change, and the uses of work-based learning (see, for example, Bailey, 1995; Bailey, Hughes, & Barr, 1998; Hughes, 1998; Hughes, Moore, & Bailey, 1999). A few studies have attempted to estimate impacts on student outcomes of STW program interventions. Experimental estimates of impacts on students in career academies in nine sites are being developed by the Manpower Demonstration Research Corporation, and others have attempted to estimate impacts of particular academy programs (see Hollenbeck, 1996; Kemple & Snipes, 2000; Maxwell & Rubin, 1997).[2] This range of studies provides a basis for some broad conclusions about how well the four goals of the STWOA have been realized.

THE ROLE OF PARTNERSHIPS IN STW REFORMS

A central premise of the STWOA was that accomplishing necessary changes in American education required partnerships at the state and local level to bridge the divide between schools and their communities. Partnerships would link schools to employers and businesses, focus school curricula more on skills that employers value, and create workplace-learning opportunities. They would include school districts and postsecondary institutions, and foster articulated programs so that students could follow progressively more advanced programs toward a career goal. Organized labor would facilitate skill instruction in workplaces and ensure that such opportunities are consistent with labor agreements. Federal funding was to "seed" these partnerships, not provide ongoing support.

The four surveys of STW partnerships undertaken for the National STW Evaluation provide a basis for gauging the role of these local entities and the growth of activities for students that the STWOA aimed to promote. The surveys included all federally funded local partnerships: substate grantees in states that had received STW implementation grants and grantees funded directly by the U.S. Department of Labor. This universe of partnerships surveyed grew from 908 in 1996 to 1,152 in 1997, 1,291 in 1998, and 1,611 in 1999.[3] Response rates to the survey were high: 91% in 1996, 89% in 1997, 88% in 1998, and 82% in 1999.

Widespread Local Partnerships Have Been Forged Throughout the Nation

The creation of partnerships was a precondition for the STWOA funding at the local level, and all states created a local infrastructure and distributed substate grants, as foreseen in the Act. Federal implementation grants to states, totaling $798 million, were issued in stages: to eight states in 1994, nineteen states in 1995, ten states in 1996, and finally to the last thirteen states and Puerto Rico and the District of Columbia in 1998. By fall 1999, states had distributed substate grants to 1,894 partnerships that included more than 48% of all U.S. public school districts.[4]

Educators Usually Take a Lead Role, but Employers Participate in Large and Growing Numbers

Local STW partnerships have brought schools and employers together in vast numbers, with educators usually in a coordinating role. Educators and private-sector employers or groups share about equally in the formal governance of local partnerships, but both survey data and field observation suggest that educators and employers play different roles. Responsibility for defining an agenda and making initiatives happen typically lies with educators; STW coordinators most often call the school district or key participating schools the "lead organization" (and the fiscal manager for the partnership).[5] Indeed, Hughes (1998) concluded from case studies of 12 apprenticeship programs in the mid-1990s that "although the word partnership implies accommodation . . . we have more commonly found educators adhering to employers' needs" (p. 18) in an effort to elicit and sustain their support and cooperation.

Local STW partnerships have the support of large numbers of employers. Employers have participated on governing boards and provided workplace learning for students, ranging from brief worksite visits and job shadowing to more intensive internships and apprenticeships. In school year 1997–1998, Medrich et al. (2000) found that nearly 178,000 private, public, and nonprofit employers participated in some aspect of STW programs in the 770 local partnerships that provided data. The number of participating employers has grown in large part because STW grants continued to be awarded to more states, which in turn funded more local partnerships. In addition, partnership schools have continued to expand their networks of employers, focusing primarily on increasing employer involvement in providing low-intensity student activities like job shadowing (see Figure 6.1; all figures and the table are based on data from the Mathematica National STW Evaluation; see Hershey et al., 1997, 1999).[6] The National STW Evaluation found that, per school, the average number of employers providing job shadowing increased from fifteen in school year 1995–1996 to more than twenty in school year 1998–1999. However, employer provision of more intensive STW activities, such as paid jobs or unpaid internships related to career-major programs, has shown no consistent growth.

The lack of consistent growth in employer involvement in more intensive STW programs reflects the balancing of student interest, employer motivations, and school–employer agreement on program design that is needed for such programs. Taking on students for an afternoon of job shadowing requires little commitment of resources. Taking on students for extended worksite activities, however, forces employers to consider costs and benefits more carefully. They may participate, according to Bailey (1995), from a spirit of philanthropy; a sense that their firm will benefit in a business sense, a belief that their overall industry will benefit, or some combination of these motives. In a study of twelve STW programs, Hughes (1998) found that program staff have to determine whether employers are interested in public relations, short-term inexpensive labor, or long-term labor recruitment, and then tailor appeals to potential employer partners accordingly. At the same time, program designs have to meet the concerns of educators, students, and parents, who are typically concerned that the experience be a foundation for broad career and educational options, not just for a particular occupation. Hughes notes that employer motivations can sometimes conflict with the aim of providing high-quality ex-

Figure 6.1
Employer Involvement in Providing STW Activities for High-School Students: School Years 1996–1997 through 1999–2000

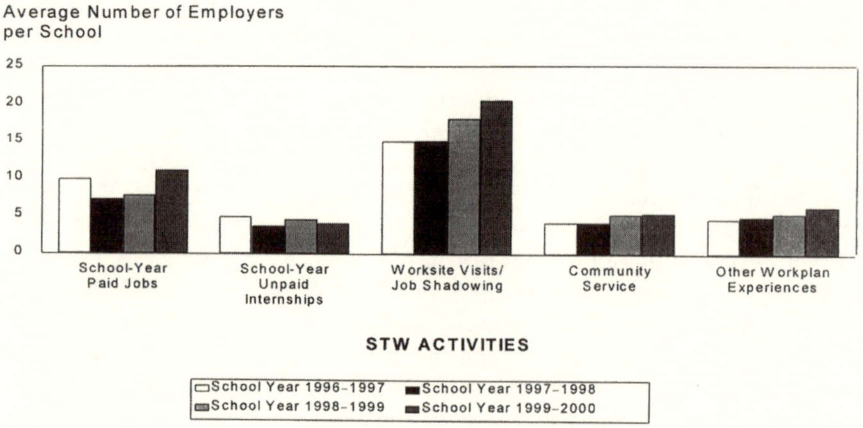

periences for students. Reconciling educators' and employers' goals in ways that attract enough students to sustain a program is complicated and is not always achieved.

Partnerships Have Contributed to Expansion of Career-Development Activities

STW partnerships have been conduits for ideas and funding and promoted program initiatives in individual schools and across their entire membership. Most partnerships that span multiple school districts have made small grants to their member schools or special task forces to support specific programs, events, or materials that address goals agreed to by partnership members.[7] This minigrant approach often supports an agenda ratified by a STW governing board and its constituent school, employer, and labor members; and it yields products useful throughout the partnership, such as curricula, procedural guides, or public-relations materials.[8] Aside from providing funding for specified purposes, STW partnerships have been a channel for conveying policy priorities adopted by state and national STW offices. The ways in which STW partnerships have presided over expansion of STW activities for students have reflected these policies, the processes used for distributing funding, and the constraints of preference and practicality inevitably encountered in schools and at employer workplaces.

The priorities of STW partnerships and the incentives and constraints they face are visible in the relative expansion of various STW components. The National STW Evaluation charted the rates at which partnership schools offered and expanded three components emphasized in the STWOA: career-development activities, career majors, and integrated programs combining career-focused academic and technical instruction and workplace learning linked to the school curriculum.

Comprehensive career-development programs have become more widely available in schools, along with specific activities that schools offer as part of these programs. Career-development programs aim to give students from elementary through secondary years a sense of the world of work and how they might fit into it. Some states, even before the STWOA, had already made career development part of education policy. They were encouraging the coordinated, sequenced use of activities such as workplace visits, self-awareness and interest inventories, career-information courses or units in other courses, job shadowing, and students' development of career plans to guide their educational choices.

From school year 1996–1997 through 1999–2000, virtually all parts of a career-development program typically conducted in high schools have become available in an increasing percentage of STW partnership high schools (Figure 6.2). In many schools, it remains a challenge to weave these activities together

Figure 6.2
Growing Availability of Career-Development Activities: School Years 1996–1997 through 1999–2000

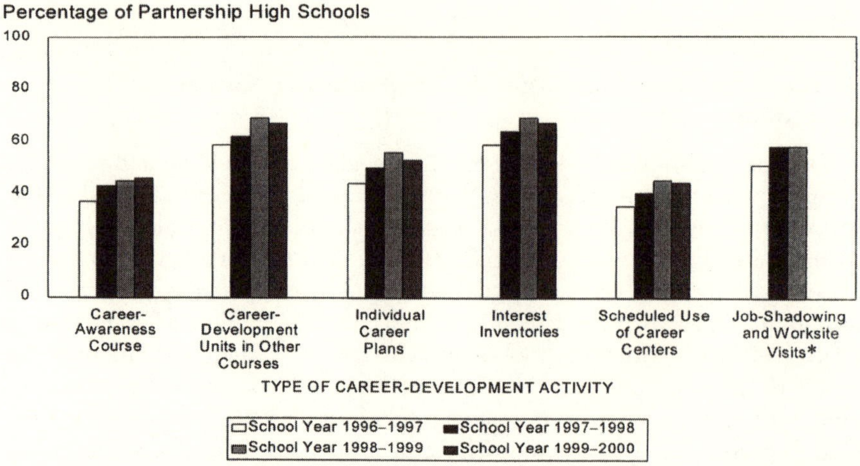

*The latest data from local partnerships on worksite activities are for school year 1997–1998.

for the individual student, but it is hard to dispute the gradual progress in expanding use of specific career-development activities.

Schools have expanded not only career-development activities within their walls, but also the opportunities students have to learn about careers and occupations at the workplace. Most notable is the increasing percentage of schools that offer worksite visits or job shadowing—brief experiences, occurring in one day or a few part-day sessions, in which students observe the work process or tag along with employees in careers that interest them. The percentage of partnership high schools offering such experiences rose from 49% in 1996 to 58% in 1999, in large part because of the proliferation of job shadowing programs. This growth in job shadowing was fueled by the National STW Office's promotion of Groundhog Day job shadowing and the efforts of state STW offices to set participation targets for local partnerships. Schools have expanded these programs, involving increasing numbers of employers.

Changes in Curriculum Have Been Modest

Several curricular changes were anticipated in the STWOA. Students would be given the opportunity to organize their studies around a "career major." In the legislation, this term suggested the integration of academic and technical or vocational content, with links between secondary and postsecondary programs with the same career focus. In reality, however, the idea of a career major has been interpreted and implemented in quite diverse ways.

Schools are gradually making more use of what they call career majors or career pathways, but there is great variety in the roles these programs play in students' school experience and the range of students they affect. In the most basic career pathway, students are exposed to information about careers and then asked to indicate a preference for either a particular career goal or a broad career area. Although some schools refer to this process as "selecting a career major," it falls far short of the career-major concept envisioned in the STWOA. Visits to the eight in-depth study states for the National STW Evaluation suggest that many schools go beyond that simplest interpretation of career majors, but to varying degrees. Three models can be distinguished:

- *Written Course Sequences.* Many partnerships, often in concert with state STW offices, have developed "career cluster" charts of careers and occupations and the academic and vocational courses students are advised to consider as preparation for each cluster. Guidance counselors use these maps to help students choose their classes. In some cases, all students must choose a career pathway and select courses accordingly, but more often these materials serve a more flexible advisory purpose.
- *Defined Programs of Study with Some Student Clustering.* Some schools have developed structured programs that cluster students with like career interests together for at least some of their classes. These programs may be called "career-magnet" or "academy" programs. They often offer intensive workplace activities such as internships and typically serve a fraction of a high school's students.
- *Intensive Programs with Integrated Curriculum and a Required Workplace Component.* Programs that most closely match the model emphasized in the STWOA incorporate both academic and technical classes, cluster students together by their career selection so the program can be tailored to their needs, and make a paid or unpaid internship a required part of the program. These programs are often called "career academies."

The prevalence of all three of these interpretations of career majors has expanded, but the most modest interpretation is most common. The four school years beginning in 1996–1997 saw gradual increases in the percentage of schools using the three types of career majors. The most common way that schools implement career majors is simply to include careers as a factor in the guidance process by using written course sequences; between 1996 and 1999, the percentage of partnership schools following this practice increased from 41% to 48%. The percentage of schools using the "defined program of study" and "intensive-program" forms of career major for at least some students increased, respectively, from 33% to 40% and from 25% to 27%.

There are only marginal increases in use of strategies for integrating academic and vocational instruction. The percentage of high schools using commercially available or home-grown curricula that incorporate applied instruction in academic subjects such as mathematics or science have just inched up over the years of the National STW Evaluation surveys, and the use of collaborative teaching involving academic and vocational teachers has remained roughly constant. The strategy of involving employers with faculty to develop new curricula has not become markedly more common. The percentage of schools using block scheduling—often described as a precondition for applied instruction and team teaching—has continued to climb slowly, from 26% in 1996 to 31% in 1999.

The enhancement of linkages between secondary and postsecondary institutions has similarly advanced slightly. From 1996 to 1999, the percentage of partnership high schools that have signed articulation agreements with colleges granting credit or advanced standing for relevant courses completed in high school climbed from 54% to 58%. There has been a slight increase in the percentage of schools that share employer contact networks with a local college. Other possible forms of secondary–postsecondary collaboration have remained fairly constant.

Workplace Learning Availability Has Increased, but Usually without Strong Career-Major Links

Schools now are more likely to offer workplace learning, but growth is most apparent for workplace activities unrelated to career majors (Table 6.1). As the number of partnerships and member schools has grown, the absolute number of schools reporting that they make workplace learning available has increased. However, the percentage of partnership schools offering intensive workplace activities related to a student's chosen career major has grown only marginally.

Table 6.1
Availability of Workplace Learning Activities in Partnership High Schools: 1995–1999

	Percentage of Partnership High Schools Offering Activity by School Year			
Type of Workplace Activity	1995–1996	1996–1997	1997–1998	1998–1999
Related to Chosen Career Major				
Paid Jobs in School Year	28.4	27.3	28.7	30.6
Unpaid Internships in School Year	24.5	23.9	26.0	28.0
Paid Summer Jobs	18.5	17.4	20.6	20.7
Unpaid Summer Internships	6.9	9.2	10.3	11.0
Not Necessarily Related to Chosen Career Major				
Worksite Visits/Job Shadowing	48.8	51.1	58.1	58.0
Community Service/Volunteer Work	29.2	30.6	35.8	37.9
Workplace Experience	23.7	27.0	30.3	31.5
Assigned to a Workplace Mentor	18.1	20.0	20.4	22.8

In contrast, schools were considerably more likely in 1999 than in 1995 to be offering brief job shadowing, community-service opportunities, or other experiences not related to a career major.

Most STW proponents have viewed linkages between workplace learning and school-based curriculum as an important feature of STW programs, but the effect of such linkages on students have been more asserted than empirically demonstrated. Hughes et al. (1999) distinguish two ways in which workplace learning could strengthen student's academic performance: by motivating students to work harder in school and by providing opportunities in the workplace to learn, apply, and master academic skills taught in the classroom. They note that the STW legislation set rather limited goals for workplace learning. It would be useful by "engaging student interest" and giving them a chance to "learn in context " (p. 2), but the concept of contextual learning has typically been used to refer not to classroom teaching but to workplace skills. In response to criticisms from opponents that STW programs would substitute watered-down applied curriculum and workplace experience for rigorous academics, proponents have asserted that workplace activity reinforces academic learning. Hughes et al. found in their field research, however, that even in workplace activities of high quality, students do not frequently learn academic concepts or apply academic skills. Stasz and Kaganoff (1997) similarly found a weak connection between workplace learning and students' academic program in three programs they examined.

Whether and how workplace activities help students succeed in school thus remains uncertain. There is abundant anecdotal evidence of increases in students' motivation to succeed and work harder in school, but there is no strong evidence of greater mastery of academic skills. Given the increasing emphasis on school accountability for student performance—typically measured by standardized tests of academic skills—this uncertainty will probably continue to weaken arguments for expanding workplace experience as part of the school curriculum. High-quality workplace learning may still be advocated as part of preparation for careers, but clear evidence that such experiences are commonly implemented in ways that reinforce academic skills is still missing.

TRENDS IN STUDENT EXPERIENCES

Progress in implementing a STW system can be measured not only by the programs that schools and their partners put in place but also by changes in students' experiences. The previous section focused on the extent to which schools make various STW activities available to students, without regard to the scale of the STW programs or how many students they really affect. To be sure, the STWOA did not envision that STW activities would be universal or mandatory. Instead, STW activities would be widely available to all students. In the end, however, it would be hard to assert that implementation efforts had succeeded in creating a new system unless growing fractions of the American student population participated in some way.

Participation in three STW components can be used as a gauge of implementation progress: (a) career-development activities designed to expose students to career options and encourage planning, (b) career-focused school curricula that integrate academic and vocational instruction, and (c) work-based learning linked to school curricula. The National STW Evaluation has tracked the prevalence of these experiences among high-school students through cross-sectional surveys of representative samples of the classes of 1996, 1998, and 2000 in the eight in-depth study states.[9] With data on only two cohorts of students available for analysis for this chapter, it is difficult to put forward conclusions about trends, but some observations from the 1996 and 1998 surveys are consistent enough with partnership survey findings on program development trends and with field observation to merit reporting.[10]

Students Report Increasing Participation in Career-Development Activities

The increasing emphasis schools are placing on promoting career-development activities is reflected in students' recollections of their high-school experiences. Even before the STWOA, of course, schools offered these opportunities, and many students participated. Over the first few years of STW implementation, however, there was a slight upward shift. For example, more students recalled having taken a work-readiness class about careers or having gone on a worksite tour or job shadowing experience (Figure 6.3).

Figure 6.3
Participation in Career Development: Activities Students Ever Did in High School, Classes of 1996 and 1998

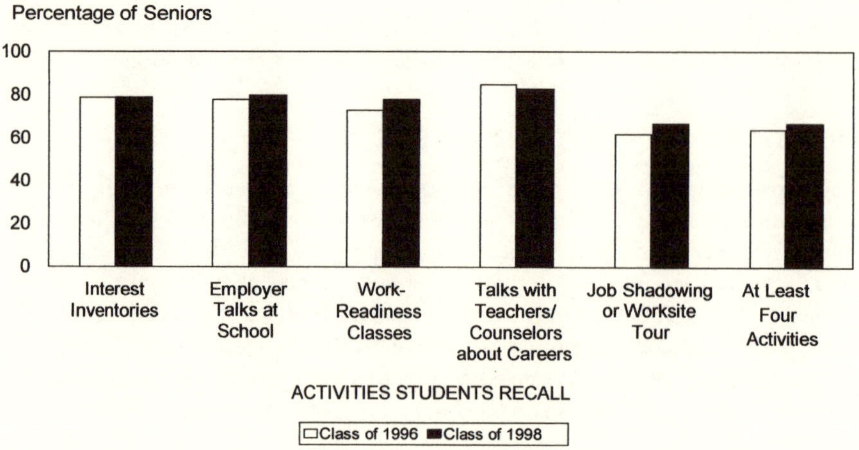

Students' Sense That Curriculum Relates to Career Direction May Be Growing

It is one thing for schools to offer career majors or even require them, but another question whether students perceive that they are organizing their studies around a career focus. If career majors are implemented simply as career-related guidance brochures, students' course choices may be guided by career goals, but the curriculum that they experience may not be any different than it would have been in the absence of career majors. Deeper interpretations of career majors might imply tailoring class content and assignments to students' career focus. The National STW Evaluation surveys attempted to discern student participation in something like a career major indirectly, by examining whether students (a) recalled having been asked to select a career area focus for their education, (b) had ever taken an academic class they thought was for students with their career interests (called here "career-related academic" classes), and (c) recalled assignments related to their career interest in any academic classes.

Students' perceptions suggest that some modest progress is being made in focusing their attention on the connection between the courses they choose in high school and their future career aims. In the eight in-depth study states, more students in the class of 1998 recalled being asked to select a career area to plan for than was true in the class of 1996, and there was also growth in the percentage who perceived at least one of their academic classes as being tailored to their career interests. No increase was noted, however, in the percentage of students who recalled getting career-related assignments in class.

There was a substantial increase, from 12% to 18%, in the percentage of students who reported all three of these experiences and were thus described as having taken a "career-related academic class." Hershey et al. (1999) found this pattern consistent with the finding that guidance in course selection is the most common school approach to promoting a career focus, rather than more structured programs that cluster students in classes with a career focus.

Intensive Forms of Workplace Learning Are Not Markedly Expanding, but Quality Is High

STW partnerships and member schools are but one of several sources through which students might find workplace activities. Even before the STWOA, students were working in summer and after-school jobs, doing community service and volunteer work, and finding internships. They have traditionally found such activities on their own, with the help of relatives and family friends, and through some school-based programs of long standing, such as cooperative education. Important issues for the National STW Evaluation have been whether students are engaging in increasing numbers in the activities STW partnerships and schools are helping to arrange and are getting more of a learning experience in the workplace.

Partnerships' emphasis on recruiting employer partners has so far increased students' participation in career-development activities, but not in more-intensive forms of workplace activity linked to the school curriculum. Participation in brief job shadowing is rising, but not in paid or unpaid positions obtained through their schools, such as apprenticeships, internships, or paid employment (Hershey et al., 1999). In both 1996 and 1998, about 28% of high-school seniors reported that they had ever obtained a paid or unpaid position through their school. Of course, particular schools have been creating new career-focused programs, many of which have offered workplace opportunities. However, the students who participate may be those who would have otherwise participated in cooperative education or other preexisting programs offering internships or work-study opportunities, so there is no noticeable net participation increase.

There are indications, however, that students get more of a learning experience in STW programs than if they find a job on their own. Student surveys in the National STW Evaluation identified five qualitative differences when students gain workplace positions through STW programs. First, paid STW program positions offer more training; participants are more than twice as likely to report spending at least half of their worksite time in training than students in paid jobs they got on their own. Second, they get more career information through discussions of careers with their employers. Third, they are more likely to get an evaluation of their performance. Fourth, for unpaid as well as paid positions, students perceive more links between their program activity at the workplace and their classroom activity than is true for workplace activities they find on their own. Finally, they get involved in more diverse workplaces; STW program positions are far less likely to be in restaurants and retail trade, and more likely to be in fields such as manufacturing, finance, education, and public service.

Expanding the Scale of Intensive STW Program Participation Is Difficult

Whatever the apparent advantages, expanding participation in programs that fit the model emphasized in the STWOA has been slow. By available measures, the percentage of students who experience a curriculum that integrates technical and academic instruction does not appear to be increasing. Links between workplace activity and school classes showed no increase from the class of 1996 to the class of 1998. For example, the National STW Evaluation survey showed no consistent increases from 1996 to 1998 in the percentage of seniors who reported links between workplace and school (Figure 6.4). These surveys suggest that the percentage of students who could be regarded as participating in all three STW components—comprehensive career-development activities,

Figure 6.4
Selected Quality Indicators in Positions Obtained through School: Changes from 1996 to 1998

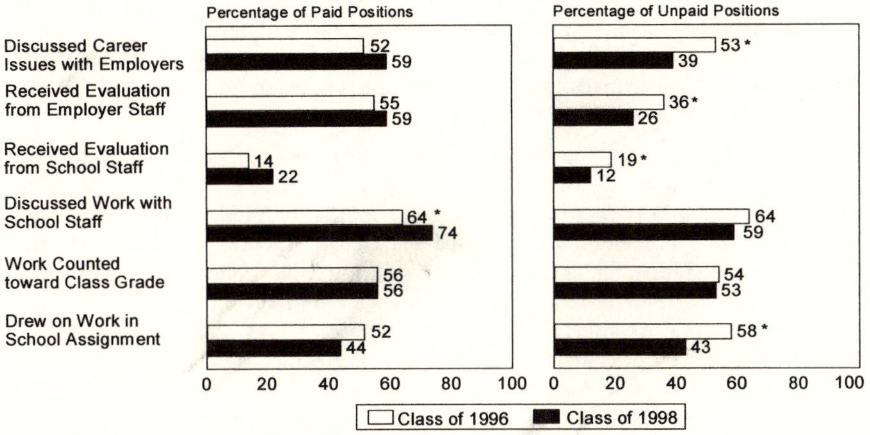

*Difference between the class of 1996 and class of 1998 is significant at .05 level, two-tailed test.

career-related academics, and workplace experience linked to school—was just 2% in 1996 and still less than 3% in 1998.

Expanding integrated, intensive STW programs is complicated. Difficulties arise from factors affecting employers, school staff, and other educators as they attempt to balance their respective concerns about program design with the ways in which these design decisions affect students' interest and ability to engage in such programs. Four major factors are at work:

- *Costs to Employers.* Surveys suggest that employers most often get involved in STW programs for philanthropic or public-relations reasons, rather than primarily to recruit employees (Bailey et al., 1998). Estimates of employer costs for training and supervising students in STW programs can reach $10,000 per student (Bassi, Feeley, Hillmeyer, & Ludwig, 1997), yet few students stay as permanent employees.
- *Burden on School Staff.* Schools must recruit employers, negotiate program design with employers, balance competing views of school staff and faculty, match students with employers, help employers develop activities, and monitor students' progress. This burden is substantial, in part because most employers provide positions for only one or two students; school staff must work with many employers to place large numbers of students. Shifts in employers' circumstances and ability to take on students make it necessary for school staff to engage in ongoing employer negotiations and recruiting. Even with STWOA funding, many schools visited for the National STW Evaluation found that staffing constraints limited prospects for growth.

- *Tensions Between Workplace Activities and Academic Success.* Past research suggests that student employment beyond a reasonable number of hours can contribute to lower performance. Pressures for accountability created by states' high-stakes testing reforms add to concerns among teachers and parents that work-based learning may eat into the time students have for classes and homework. Although vocational teachers often support work-based learning, academic teachers are generally slower to recognize its value or invest the time required to make strong connections between workplace and academic learning.
- *Difficulty of Integrating Vocational and Academic Instruction.* Many states and local partnerships have invested heavily in curricular integration. Some states have developed curriculum frameworks emphasizing application of academic skills, a form of integration, and many have sponsored teacher workshops on blended instruction or project-based learning, as well as teacher institutes on applied academic curricula and instructional methods. Site visits and partnership surveys suggest, however, that academic teachers are still less interested than vocational teachers in changing instructional strategy or course content, out of concern that moving toward more applied learning may detract from teaching traditionally defined academic content, and jeopardize students' chances for admission to competitive colleges and the school's overall performance on state academic tests. This concern is reflected in the fact that "resistance of academic teachers" is among the three obstacles to further development of STW reforms most commonly cited by partnership coordinators (analysis of data from 1999 Local Partnership Survey, National STW Evaluation).

EFFECTS ON STUDENT OUTCOMES

Advocates argue that STW reforms would improve student performance in several ways. The integration of technical and academic instruction and the emphasis on work-based learning would create opportunities for learning in context, which theorists and advocates have maintained is a more effective way for students to acquire skills than instruction that is purely theoretical. Students who have not been inspired to great academic efforts would be energized by the hands-on style of work-based learning and motivated to apply themselves. All students, helped by STW career-development activities to formulate, test, and refine their goals for the future, would have a clearer idea of why they are in school, be more highly motivated, and make smoother transitions to further education or the labor market.

Testing the effects of the broad sweep of STW reforms on student outcomes, however, has proven difficult. The very nature of the STW agenda makes it difficult to know which students should be considered STW students and which ones should not. The National STW Evaluation and other studies have made it clear that STW partnerships and member schools engage in a wide variety of initiatives. Some engage virtually all students to some degree, and others engage subgroups, some large and some small, with varying degrees of intensity.

Even when researchers focus on determining the impact of specific STW *programs* rather than overall STW reforms, evaluation-design constraints have limited the confidence that can be placed in their results. Most often, efforts to estimate impacts have been undermined by the difficulty of identifying a suitable comparison group or controlling adequately for differences between the two groups. Hanser and Stasz (1999), for example, estimated the relative impacts of the Los Angeles Unified School District's Transportation Career Academy Program (TCAP) in three comprehensive high schools and the impacts of the same schools' magnet programs relative to the schools' general-education programs. Because students were not randomly assigned to the three programs, the authors adopted as a comparison sample the overall student body in demographically similar schools that had general and magnet programs but no career academy; and they controlled for ethnicity, gender, school, age, and prior-year test scores. Their analysis found that TCAP students performed significantly better than general-track students, but they concluded that these results were undermined by their inability to deal with selection issues: the possibility that TCAP students were systematically different from general-track students in ways they could not measure, such as motivation, and in ways that might be measured but for which they had weak data, such as prior performance.[11]

Maxwell and Rubin (1997) interpret more optimistically the impact results they derived from career academies in a large West-Coast school district with six comprehensive high schools, despite evaluation-design constraints. They found that attending a career academy increased students' rates of graduating on time from high school by about 10% over the graduation rate for general-track students. They also found significant increases in self-reported measures of ability to focus on work and development of critical thinking and study skills, at least for students who went on to two- or four-year colleges. However, this study was based on data from a survey with only a 12% response rate, and data constraints limited the researchers to controlling in the analysis for just a few demographic characteristics. Furthermore, the researchers acknowledge that the effects of career-academy participation in comparison to the general track were not significantly different from those observed for academic or vocational tracks, and that it may thus be that "providing structure, per se," rather than the career focus of the academy, "provides the motivation to enhance work and education knowledge and skills" (p. 15).

Sometimes, what appear to be encouraging indicators of impacts turn out to be less convincing when researchers carefully control for the diverging characteristics of program participants and the group. For example, Hollenbeck's study (1996) of the Manufacturing Technology Partnership (MTP) program in Genesee County, Michigan, found promising differences between outcomes for participants and comparison-group students. The MTP, operating out of an area vocational school, predated the STWOA, but embodied the essential features of integrating technical and academic instruction. Simple comparisons of MTP students with comparison groups drawn from unsuccessful applicants to the MTP and similar students from another county were encouraging. However, multivariate analysis controlling for students' characteristics showed that there were no significant effects on postsecondary enrollment, employment, or career aspirations.

Against this backdrop of inconclusive efforts to assess the impact of intensive STW programs, the ongoing Career Academies Evaluation offers more rigorous evidence that at least modest positive impacts on certain groups of students can be achieved (Kemple & Snipes, 2000). Comparing entrants to career academies in nine high schools to academy applicants randomly assigned to a control group, this study found that for at-risk students, the academies reduced dropout rates, improved attendance, increased academic course taking, and enhanced the rate of on-time graduation. Across all students, however, the academies had modest effects, slightly increasing credit accumulation and causing a shift from academic to vocational classes, largely because academy participation appears to have reduced emphasis on academic courses among low- and moderate-risk students. Kemple and Snipes note that in those sites where academies were tightly organized as personalized and nurturing learning environments and stood in greatest contrast to the regular school program, there was a more consistent pattern of positive effects for a broader range of students. One possible interpretation is that it is not so much the programs' career focus as this smaller, more intimate learning setting that benefits students. Clearly, however, the adoption of a career focus may be a useful strategy to win support for the creation of small learning environments, and thus indirectly be a path for improving student outcomes.[12]

THE SUSTAINABILITY OF STW REFORMS

Whether the STWOA has succeeded in the long run depends on whether it has planted seeds for enduring change in American education. It is thus worth asking what prospects there are for continued development as federal STW funding ends. The efforts of local STW partnerships, state STW teams, and the National STW Office could have resulted in several changes that could continue to affect American education. The STW movement may have added momentum to trends already evident before the STWOA, such as the creation and refinement of comprehensive career-development programs. STW concepts may have been embedded in school organization and curriculum in at least some places. Implementation of the STWOA may have established patterns of collaboration that go beyond what was practiced in earlier years—between schools and employers, between academic and vocational faculty, and between schools and postsecondary institutions. The value of local partnership structures created as the result of STW funding may have been proven clearly enough that states and local communities will make maintaining them a priority and provide resources to sustain their work. It is impossible to predict whether such enduring results will emerge, but it is possible at least to report on several indicators of what aspects of STW reforms and institutions are surviving beyond the end of federal STW funding.

State-Level STW Efforts Are Continuing in Some States

States' federal STW funding has begun to expire, but there are some indications that certain policies and institutional commitments to STW reforms will survive in at least some states. Since five-year federal grants were first awarded in 1995, many states exhausted their federal funding before the legislation's sunset in 2001. Despite the end of federal funding, many states report plans to provide continuing support for STW programs. In a forum held toward the end of the STW funding period in which thirty-six states participated, more than half reported that their state-level STW offices would continue operating even after federal funding ends, although in more than two-thirds of these cases, staffing would probably be reduced (Public Forum Institute, 2000).

Many states have passed legislation that supports some aspect of STW reforms and programs, although the laws do not always provide a broad basis for pursuing a comprehensive STW agenda. Almost half of the states have passed legislation supporting STW initiatives (American Youth Policy Forum, 2000). In some instances, such as Kentucky's Education Reform Act of 1990, legislatures have adopted comprehensive policies making STW concepts part of ongoing educational reform. In other instances, however, legislation has focused on particular elements of the original STW agenda: creating a youth apprenticeship program, providing tax credits to employers who take on student apprentices, or clarifying liability for student workers, for example. In many instances, these more narrowly defined acts have had limited consequences and are unlikely to be decisive factors in the growth or survival of the more-intensive STW models they were intended to support. In a few states, however, comprehensive state initiatives mirroring much of the STWOA have been created. Michigan, most notably, has created a Career Preparation System that funnels state funds in excess of the previous federal STW resources to the local level for very similar purposes.

Most Local Partnerships Cease to Operate When STW Funds Expire, but Some Survive

Partnerships at the local level can be viewed simply as habits of collaboration, but the resources and institutions created under the STWOA have played a role in fostering those relationships. The work that partnerships have accomplished has usually depended on having staff and other resources to convene partners, often across school district boundaries, for professional development;

agenda-setting; and sharing of problems, progress, and useful products. In some instances, of course, local or substate regional professional bodies, such as associations of guidance counselors or area career technical-education consortia, can accomplish similar goals. In many instances, however, federal STW resources have been vital in creating a center of gravity and local momentum for discussion; goal setting; and development of curriculum, procedures, and systems. Some of the collaborative relationships observed in STW partnerships are likely to endure, but others may dissolve or weaken without institutional support.

Without federal STW funding, it appears that most local STW partnerships will cease to function as distinct operating entities or substantially reduce their roles in promoting STW reforms and program development. Almost half of the thirty-six states participating in the 2000 State STW Directors' Dialogue Session (Public Forum Institute, 2000) said their states would offer no funding to local partnerships after federal funding ends, and approximately another one-third would offer support, but at lower levels than was possible with federal funds. This finding is consistent with the results of the local partnership surveys in the National STW Evaluation (Hulsey & VanNoy, 2000). The sequence of partnership surveys shows that after partnerships have been without federal funding for more than a year, about one-half or more stop functioning.

The negative effects of loss of federal funding will certainly not be universal, however. Some partnerships will continue to operate even without federal funding, and at the school level, many STW initiatives are continuing without federal funding. Among partnerships that exhausted their federal funding in 1997, more than one-third were still functioning in fall 1999, and a quarter of those whose funding ended in 1996 were still operating. Partnership survey results suggest that some partnerships may shrink as less-committed schools or districts disengage. However, the remaining schools in unfunded STW partnerships—perhaps those that were more active during the period of federal funding—continue to offer STW activities for students at rates at least comparable to the rates found in partnerships still receiving federal STW funds. Loss of federal funding may be pruning partnerships of less-interested schools, but many schools find ways to sustain STW activities. The question remains whether local and in some cases state funding will be adequate to sustain for the long term the accomplishments of the STW partnerships: maintaining and cultivating employer partnerships; finding workplace activities for students; operating job shadowing programs; and in some instances, refining and supporting intensive, integrated academy programs focused on particular careers.

The question whether the "STW movement has worked" must be answered "to some extent." An overall judgment must take into account the systematic survey data about partnerships and student experiences, the beginnings of rigorous impact estimates for the relatively rare intensive STW programs, and qualitative impressions of how schools are incorporating STW concepts and of the forces that create resistance to them. Survey data suggest that the infusion of the STWOA resources stimulated widespread attention to career-development concepts and the expansion of opportunities for students to learn about careers and educational paths to them and to formulate career goals. Field observation by many researchers identified shining examples of intensive STW programs combining academic and workplace learning that was fostered with the STWOA and other resources, but the survey data do not reveal any systematic widespread trend in the development of such programs or in students' participation in them. Emerging research suggests, however, that when such programs are well implemented, they can improve student outcomes.

Development of such intensive, integrated STW programs is slow, in part because of the pressures to improve that schools face from multiple directions. In many states, emphasis is being placed on standards-based reforms and high-stakes testing. Increasing time and energy are being devoted to preparing students for standardized tests whose results are used to gauge school performance and determine student promotion. This emphasis can crowd out the efforts required to develop such STW programs, discourage teachers from straying in their instruction from the expected focus of state tests, and make it more difficult for students' schedules to accommodate the activities that distinguish STW programs. STW reforms are thus in competition with standards-based reforms for resources and attention, even though STW proponents see their program activities as another valid strategy for improving student performance in the long run.

Despite uncertainty about whether STW concepts will play a lead role in redirecting schools, field observation suggests that the STWOA has achieved some noticeable purposes. It has helped to nudge a notch higher the level of awareness among educators, students, and parents of the contribution that career exposure, workplace experience, and goal-oriented educational decisions can make to a successful future. Although the STWOA has not achieved the ambitious goals it set forth, it has probably contributed a constructive thread to the evolving fabric of American education.

NOTES

1. The National STW Evaluation has focused at the state and local levels on Florida, Kentucky, Maryland, Massachusetts, Michigan, Ohio, Oregon, and Wisconsin.

2. Numerous local evaluations have also been performed, and some states have conducted or are still conducting ongoing evaluations of their STW initiatives.

3. Most of the sample in each year consisted of substate grants in states that had received federal implementation grants. States were included only if they had received their implementation grant by July of the survey year, and several states refused to participate in the survey, so the number of states included in the survey did not always match the number of implementation-grant states. In 1996, the first year, twenty-seven

states were included; there were thirty-four states in 1997, forty-three states (including Puerto Rico) in 1998, and fifty-two states (including Puerto Rico and the District of Columbia) in 1999.

4. These 1,894 partnerships include 434 that were funded for the first time in fall 1999. Many partnerships were funded for the first time in fall 1999, even though their states received their implementation grants earlier, because of the time required to form partnerships and apply for funding at the local level and to process applications and make awards at the state level. The total number of partnerships also includes 340 that are no longer funded or functioning by late 1999; many partnerships funded in the early implementation years had already exhausted their funding (Hulsey & VanNoy, 2000). An additional 100 local partnerships have received direct funding from the federal government under the Urban/Rural Opportunity Grant category or the Direct Local Partnership Grant category.

5. Among the roughly 70% to 75% of partnership coordinators who recognize one of their partner entities as having a lead role, K–12 educational districts or schools are about ten times more likely than private-sector firms or associations to be named as the lead organization (Hershey et al., 1999; Hulsey & VanNoy, 2000).

6. The earliest local partnership survey (LPS) collected data on program characteristics in school year 1996–1997. Results for that year constitute a quasi-baseline, reflecting to a large extent pre-STWOA programs, given the time it took for most states to award local partnership grants and for the partnerships to set and act on agendas. To some extent, however, local partnerships may already have been influencing the scale and direction of programs. In later years, the LPS has included the earliest-funded partnerships as well as those funded later, so the LPS has captured a mix of the growth and emerging direction of partnerships created earlier with an early snapshot of later partnerships as their STWOA funding began. The results reported here thus understate the growth of some STW activities engendered by the STWOA funding, but the main conclusions reached are borne out by separate analyses that focus on just those partnerships that were included in all the surveys.

7. About 58% of local partnerships in 1999 encompassed more than one school district (analysis of 1999 Local Partnership Survey data, National STW Evaluation).

8. In other instances, however, partnerships simply share out much of their STW funding to individual school districts on a proportional basis, without first forging a common agenda and using minigrants to address the agenda and foster ongoing collaboration and mutual benefit.

9. At this writing, data are available only for the classes of 1996 and 1998.

10. The student survey sample consisted of 2,739 students across sixty-nine schools in thirty-one partnerships in the eight states in 1996, and 2,846 students in those jurisdictions in 1998. Response rates were 80% in 1996 and 83% in 1998.

11. Hanser and Stasz (1999) note that controlling for prior performance of student samples in programs that begin in the early high-school years is especially difficult, not only because of weaknesses in schools' record systems but particularly because of disparities between record-keeping systems in middle and high schools and between the different school systems among which students move.

12. In a study of selected schools in which a career-focused curriculum was adopted as a strategy for reshaping entire school programs for all students, Hudis (2001) found that in several cases adopting a career focus was motivated by the more basic goal of creating smaller learning environments.

REFERENCES

American Youth Policy Forum and the Center for Workforce Development, Institute for Educational Leadership. (2000). *Looking forward: School-to-work principles and strategies for sustainability.* Washington, DC: American Youth Policy Forum.

Bailey, T. (Ed.). (1995). *Learning to work: Employer involvement in school-to-work transition programs.* Washington, DC: The Brookings Institution.

Bailey, T., Hughes, K., & Barr, T. (1998). *Achieving scale and quality in school-to-work internships: Findings from an employer survey.* Berkeley, CA: National Center for Research in Vocational Education.

Bassi, L., Feeley, T., Hillmeyer, J., & Ludwig, J. (1997). *Learning an employer's look at school-to-work investments.* Alexandria, VA: American Society for Training and Development.

Hanser, L., & Stasz, C. (1999, April). *The effects of enrollment in the Transportation Career Academy Program on student outcomes.* Paper presented at the annual meeting of the American Educational Research Association, Montreal, Canada.

Hershey, A. M., Hudis, P., Silverberg, M. K., & Haimson, J. (1997). *Partners in progress: Early steps in creating school-to-work systems.* Princeton, NJ: Mathematica Policy Research, Inc.

Hershey, A. M., Silverberg, M. K., Haimson, J., Hudis, P., & Jackson, R. (1999). *Expanding options for students: Report to Congress on the National Evaluation of School-to-Work Implementation.* Princeton, NJ: Mathematica Policy Research, Inc.

Hollenbeck, K. (1996). *An evaluation of the Manufacturing Technology Partnership Program.* Kalamazoo, MI: The W. E. Upjohn Institute for Employment Research.

Hudis, P. (2001). *Making schools career-focused: Final report.* Princeton, NJ: Mathematica Policy Research, Inc.

Hughes, K. (1998). *Employer recruitment is not the problem: A study of school-to-work transition programs.* New York: Columbia University, Teachers College, Institute on Education and the Economy.

Hughes, K. L., Moore, D. T., & Bailey, T. R. (1999). *Work-based learning and academic skills.* New York: Columbia University, Teachers College, Institute on Education and the Economy.

Hulsey, L., & VanNoy, M. (2000). *The 1999 national survey of local school-to-work partnerships: Data summary.* Princeton, NJ: Mathematica Policy Research, Inc.

Kemple, J. J., & Snipes, J. C. (2000). *Career academies: Impacts on students' engagement and performance in high school.* New York: Manpower Demonstration Research Corporation.

Maxwell, N. L., & Rubin, V. (1997). *The relative impact of a career academy on post-secondary work and education skills in urban, public high schools.* Hayward, CA: California State University, School of Business and Economics, Human Investment Research and Education Center.

Medrich, E., Giambattista, J., & Moskovitz, R. (1997). *School-to-work progress measures: A report to the National School-to-Work Office for the period January 1, 1996–June 30, 1996.* Berkeley, CA: MPR Associates, Inc.

Medrich, E., Merola, L., Ramer, C., & White, R. (2000). *School-to-work progress measures: A report to the National School-to-Work Office for the period July 1, 1997–June 30, 1998.* Washington, DC: U.S. Department of Education.

Medrich, E., Ramer, C., Merola, L., Moskovitz, R., & White, R. (1998). *School-to-work progress measures: A report to the National School-to-Work Office for the period July 1, 1996–June 30, 1997.* Berkeley, CA: MPR Associates, Inc.

Public Forum Institute. (2000). *Perspectives on progress: The school-to-work national dialogues. Interim dialogue report #2: Session held for state school-to-work directors in Washington, DC, on June 1, 2000.* Washington, DC: Author.

Silverberg, M. K., Haimson, J., & Hershey, A. M. (1998). *Building blocks for a future school-to-work system: Early national implementation results.* Princeton, NJ: Mathematica Policy Research, Inc.

Stasz, C., & Kaganoff, T. (1997). *Learning how to learn at work: Lessons from three high school programs.* Berkeley, CA: National Center for Research in Vocational Education.

Stern, D. (1991). *Combining school and work: Options in high schools and two-year colleges.* Washington, DC: U.S. Department of Education, Office of Vocational and Adult Education.

7

School-to-Work Governance

Bari Anhalt Erlichson

INTRODUCTION

In 1994, Congress passed the School-to-Work Opportunities Act (STWOA). The act provided a framework and seed money for states to improve the transition from secondary education to either postsecondary institutions or the workforce. The act specified three types of activities that states and localities should pursue: work-based learning, school-based learning, and connecting activities. Beyond these initial specifications, the STWOA left it to the states to determine how to structure, implement, and govern such a system.

In comparison with other federal initiatives, the STWOA was unique in several respects. The act allowed states to define goals and processes for obtaining those goals. Thus, the STWOA structured funding much like a block grant, flowing through the governor's office. Governors initially formed school-to-work (STW) planning committees that included representatives from state agencies as well as from the private sector to determine what the goals and governance structure would be. Most states began by detailing desired outcomes. Some chose to focus on broad or *comprehensive goals,* such as making their STW programs levers for systemic school reform. Others focused on *intermediate goals,* such as improving vocational education or workforce training programs. Still others focused on limited or *programmatic goals,* such as instituting the use of skills assessment. States chose and formulated goals for their STW programs within unique state policy contexts. For example, Iowa is the only state in the nation that has not formulated state-level curricular standards. Instead, local school boards fiercely guard their responsibility for these decisions. Therefore, Iowa's STW structure reflects and respects this policy environment of local control by focusing efforts at the local level. As I outline the experiences of other states in this chapter, I will emphasize the extent to which policy environments shape the goals as well as the implementation and sustainability of the STW initiative.

On the comprehensive end of the spectrum are states that undertook systemic school reform or systems-level change. Activities of states pursuing comprehensive goals included embedding STW programs within curricular reform or standards-based reform efforts and developing a state-level assessment strategy that included STW programs. In the middle, states are pursuing intermediate goals. These states intended STW programs to impact on particular pieces of the state's education agenda or workforce-development activities. Activities included improving the delivery of workforce-training programs, linking STW endeavors to other workforce-development programs, or broadening the scope of vocational education. Finally, some states chose programmatic goals for STW programs. In these states, STW activities enhanced the connections between business and education or instituted an assessment tool without linking it to curricular reform or school-improvement efforts.

The STWOA was structured to taper and sunset funding. Therefore, developing a plan for sustaining the STW initiative was an immediate issue. As described in this chapter, some states chose an embedded strategy, locating STW programs within existing agencies, such as an education department. Others chose to link STW efforts to larger workforce-development reforms, anticipating the 1998 passage of the federal Workforce Investment Act (WIA).

SCHOOL-TO-WORK GOVERNANCE STUDY

This chapter summarizes a larger study that was originally conducted as the School-to-Work Governance Project by the Consortium for Policy Research in Education with support from the National Institute on Educational Governance, Finance, Policymaking and Management, Office of Educational Research and Improvement, U.S. Department of Education. (The opinions expressed in this chapter are the author's and do not necessarily reflect the views of the National Institute.) The research team conducted the study from October 1997 to July 1998. The central purpose was to examine governance structures for STW programs to assess the impact of these structures on STW implementation. The primary methodology for the study was interviewing, either by telephone or in person. The conclusions in this chapter rely on 342 interviews.

This research proceeded in three phases. During Phase 1, we conducted telephone interviews in all thirty-seven states that had received STW implementation funds. We interviewed the STW-program state coordinators, major state agency partners, and a representative from the state Workforce Development Board or Human Resources Investment Council. In all, we conducted 113 interviews from October 1997 through January 1998.

At the conclusion of Phase 1, ten states were chosen to focus on in Phase 2: Colorado, Indiana, Iowa, Maryland, Nebraska, North Carolina, Ohio, Oklahoma, Oregon, and Pennsylvania. Because Pennsylvania was undergoing a major transition in STW goals and structure at this time, it is not included in this report. In this phase, we broadened the scope of interviewees to include respondents from the regional- and local-level partnerships; other state partners; and other state, regional, or local sources of knowledge. Phase 2, which was conducted between February and May 1998, included 162 interviews.

We chose three states to include in Phase 3: Colorado, Ohio, and Oregon. Phase 3 included a site visit during either June or July 1998. We spent a day at the state level interviewing the STW state coordinator, state-level agency partners, important private-sector partners, and representatives from other workforce-development programs. We spent a day in three separate regions of the state as well. During our regional visits, we interviewed regional coordinators, regional partners, local STW coordinators, and their partners. In all, we conducted sixty-seven interviews during our three site visits.

For this study, we utilized a networking or relational approach, in which we allowed the people interviewed to direct us to other people to interview. At times, we interviewed someone who, although not a formal partner, had programmatic interests related to STW activities. During our site visits, we allowed regional and local partnership coordinators to direct us to major players in their organizations. In this way, we attempted to steep ourselves in the available knowledge about governance structures and relationships between them.

POLICY AND IMPLEMENTATION CONTEXT

States implementing STW programs faced significant policy challenges. Among the most significant was the fragmented nature of the policy context. In constructing a "policy map" of federal legislation related to STW programs, Moore and Waldman identified twenty federal programs or statutory mandates that functioned to provide "services or other supporting elements needed in a system of career preparation for youth between the ages of 14 and 21" (1994, p. 133). Among the most prominent existing policies and programs were the JTPA Youth Training Programs, the National Apprenticeship Act, the Wagner-Peyser Act, the Fair Labor Standards Act, the Perkins Basic and Perkins Tech-Prep Acts, the College Work-Study Program, Goals 2000 legislation, the Pell Grants, and the Elementary and Secondary Education Act. The STWOA was to provide a vehicle for integrating these policies and programs into a coherent system of career preparation. Moore and Waldman articulated the challenge in the following way:

> The creation of School-to-Work Opportunities systems based on collaborative service delivery will require considerable staff time and energy if they are to establish effective links between different educational levels, between the school and work sectors, and across programs. They will have to initiate contacts, develop partnerships, follow up on plans and agreements, resolve barriers, coordinate schedules and paperwork, and cajole a diverse group of individuals who serve different organization masters to work together. (p. 134)

Moore and Waldman (1994) also predicted difficulty establishing collaboration across federal programs because "other claims on these federal program funds are likely to dampen their impact on the envisioned system of career preparation significantly," such as the "requirements that target federal funds to disadvantaged youth and youth with disabilities" (p. 137). They also noted that the "divergent missions and cultures that have become attached to federal programs are likely to hinder state and local efforts to leverage other federal resources on the School-to-Work Opportunities initiative" (p. 138).

A second significant challenge was the structure and history of vocational education. Vocational education began in earnest in the early 1900s with the passage of the Smith-Hughes Act. Vocational education was then a separate educational endeavor. As noted by researchers at the National Center for Research in Vocational Education, "The 1917 Smith-Hughes Act created federal support for a separate kind of vocational education that became well-established in subsequent decades" (Urquiola et al., 1997, p. 68). The separation continued to endure in policy until the reauthorization of the Perkins Act.

As Hayward and Benson (1993) pointed out, the 1990 reauthorization of the Carl D. Perkins Applied Technology and Vocational Education Act (Perkins Act) "represented the most significant policy shift in the history of federal involvement in vocational-technical funding. For the first time, emphasis was placed on academic as well as occupational skills" (p. 3).

The Perkins Act was intended to revolutionize vocational education, turning the system "90 degrees, requiring that the basic federal grant to the states . . . be spent only on programs that [in the act's words] 'integrate academic and vocational education'" (Urquiola et al., 1997, p. 69). Tech-prep, a "major programmatic vehicle" of the act, "represented an attempt to institutionalize the role of high school vocational education as a step in the preparation for continued learning and instruction" (p. 23).

The Perkins Act also enabled states to build educational systems that included postsecondary institutions. As Urquiola et al. (1997) indicated, "In addition to the required integration of academic and technical skills, the 1990 Perkins reauthorization called for articulation and coordination between secondary and postsecondary educational institutions" (p. 23).

These two foci of the Perkins Act—integration and the inclusion of postsecondary institutions—helped lay a foundation for implementing STW programs. However, the Perkins Act, in opposition to the "all students" goal of the STWOA, focused "largely on special targeted populations, especially what had traditional been considered under-served populations such as minorities, women, individuals with handicaps and of limited English proficiency, and the economically disadvantaged" (Urquiola et al., 1997, p. 23).

In its attempt to capitalize on these revisions and to coordinate with other policy and program arenas, the STWOA represented a unique type of education policy. Three distinct characteristics separated it from other programs. First, its focus on all students, without eligibility requirements, set it apart from previous educational funding legislation. Second, it was a program to be jointly administered by two federal agencies: the U.S. Departments of Education and Labor. Finally, the funding stream was deliberately intended to sunset. Consequently, states were immediately challenged with finding ways to leverage other educational and workforce training programs to continue implementation.

The passage of the WIA in 1998 may provide such an opportunity. The act called for substantial alteration of the structure of workforce training and development. The following six principles form the basis of the WIA: (a) streamlined services through one-stop service centers, (b) empowering individuals to make informed choices about jobs and training programs, (c) universal access for employed and unemployed individuals, (d) increased accountability, (e) new roles for local workforce-investment boards, and (f) enhanced youth programs. Moreover, the WIA consolidated sixty separate existing programs into three block grants and three funding streams for adult job seekers, dislocated workers, and in-school or out-of-school youth. Within the promise of improved youth programs, the WIA significantly revised the JTPA program by creating a Youth Services block grant that combines youth and summer youth programs, incorporates the philosophy of the STW program, reforms the Job Corps system, and authorizes the youth opportunities initiative. Some of the elements include tutoring, study-skills training, and instruction leading to the completion of secondary school; paid and unpaid work experiences; and occupational-skills training. Given the incorporation of the STW philosophy and many of the core STW activities such as internships and job shadowing, many respondents viewed the WIA as a way to continue STW initiatives, at least for youth at risk of dropping out of school.

GOVERNANCE DECISIONS

One distinguishing characteristic of the federal STW program is the discretion left to states and localities to define their goals and strategies. Although all of our respondents applauded this level of discretion, it led to some difficulties in practical terms. Most important is the lack of a standard definition across the United States, or sometimes even within a particular state, of what the goals of the initiative should be. The choices states made in terms of governance structure reflect this variety of goals and priorities.

In each participating state, structuring the initiative began by developing an understanding of what the desired outcomes or goals would be. From that understanding, states devised different approaches to governing the initiative. Thus, those states that wanted to pursue education reform chose a different governance structure from those that wanted to reform workforce development. The structure in turn shaped the actual outcomes. A representation of this process appears as follows:

Desired Outcomes → Decisions about Governance Structure → Actual Outcomes

In designing the STW initiative, states faced important decisions about structure. The first concerned the location of the state STW office within the executive branch of government. Additionally, states needed to define the process for interaction between the state STW office and other state agencies, stakeholder groups, and policy areas. Finally, states needed to decide how to structure the substate system of STW implementation.

State Structures

Perhaps the most important strategic decision a state made was where to locate the STW office. The location of the office could stimulate instant allies or instant opposition to the STW program. Locating the STW office in an agency could spur the agency to change, whereas not locating it there could guarantee that the agency would do nothing to embrace the STW program and could possibly hasten resistance to the implementation effort.

Of the states, twenty-two chose to locate the office within departments of education. Of the other states, two chose departments of labor or commerce, eight chose to grant workforce-development boards direct oversight, and five located state STW offices in a governor's or lieutenant governor's office.

Another point of variation is the activity of other agencies in the STW initiative. Nearly every state created an interagency implementation team that attempted to integrate STW efforts in their home agencies. However, the actual activities of the interagency teams varied. The majority of the states reporting the presence of interagency teams typically employ these teams in a networking role to establish communication among state-agency partners.

Each state formed a stakeholder council comprised of business and private-industry people and agency heads and staff. The governors appointed these councils to play an advisory role concerning STW policy and oversight. As the roles of the governor and legislature vary across states, so too does the role of the stakeholder council and its location within the executive branch.

The most common form of a stakeholder council is the Workforce Development Council or Human Resource Investment Council. These councils were typically already in existence in these states and played a role in overseeing the traditional JTPA programs. Seventeen states reported such a structure. In these instances, the council oversaw all workforce-development efforts, of which they considered the STW piece to be the youth component. In many instances, these councils have subcommittees dedicated specifically to the STW initiative. The stakeholder councils typically engage in the role of a policy advisor to the governor. Indeed, twenty-two states mentioned the advisory role as the stakeholder council's most important activity, whereas two states commented that the stakeholder council actively worked to promote coordination across agencies, and four states reported that the stakeholder council played an evaluative role. Despite the fact that states reported a pleasant working relationship with their stakeholder council, it appears that the stakeholder council played primarily a symbolic role in most instances.

Substate Structures

States also constructed "rollout plans" or implementation strategies for the substate partnerships. These plans resulted in a tremendous diversity in the types of relationships existing between the substate partnerships and the state-level governance structure.

Eighteen states chose to have only one level of partners beneath the state-level partnerships, forming either regional boards/consortia or many local partnerships. Another eleven states chose to create two levels of partnerships, usually a regional board and then local partnerships. However, the states varied in relationships between regional and local partnerships. Some states funded the regional board, which then reviewed funding proposals from local partnerships. Others funded the local partnerships, and the regional body served a coordination function. Some funded both the regional and local partnerships directly.

The determination of the delivery-service boundaries of these substate partnerships also is an area of extreme diversity. Some states chose to define the local partnerships along the same lines as the school districts. Other states collapsed all delivery of social programs into the same boundaries under comprehensive regional workforce-development boards. Some states used economic-development-zone boundaries, whereas others simply used the draw areas for the community-college systems. At least two states reported that they have not instituted boundaries below the state level.

The state STW structure also determined the degree and frequency of communication between the state and substate partnerships. Most respondents indicated that these relationships were open, informal, and frequent. States and active agency partners provided technical assistance to the substate partnerships. In addition to this type of communication, coordinators reported that they held monthly meetings, in person or through conference calls, with the partnership level beneath them. Additionally, the state office typically required monthly or quarterly narrative reports and other specific data collection.

Variation also existed among states regarding how much control the state STW office exerts over the substate partnerships. In the most common relationship, the substate partnerships have a great deal of independence from the state and are free to pursue whatever STW activities fill their defined needs. Usually, the state STW office articulated requirements for substate partnerships during the funding process. Most states reported that the structure of the funding relationship required an ongoing reporting relationship. Often, states encouraged substate partnerships to engage in specific STW activities by issuing targeted funding opportunities to support these activities.

COMPREHENSIVE-GOAL STATES

Comprehensive-goal states typically defined the STW program as part of the state's ongoing education-reform or systems-change efforts. Thus, these states pursued explicit linkages between STW endeavors and other education-reform efforts, often as a result of strong and consistent leadership at the state level. Participation in the STW program was widespread at every level of STW governance and within school buildings themselves. Often, comprehensive states capitalized on a hospitable policy environment. Most states or regional partnerships redirected funding for STW activities. Some states had even adopted state-level education policy that reinforced the STW program. The likelihood that STW endeavors will continue is highest in these comprehensive-reform states.

State context is important for understanding how goals and governance structure are related. Oregon instituted career-related learning standards through state legislation. Iowa, on the other hand, pursued education reform by building buy-in from school-level curriculum coordinators. Maryland is also attempting to integrate STW concepts by using statewide assessment plans as an incentive. However, the link between the STW program and curriculum reform is not yet formal in Maryland, leading some to feel that the STW program is an additional reform effort, separate from higher academic standards. Each of these states is discussed separately as follows.

Oregon's initiative began in 1991 with the passage of the Oregon Educational Act for the 21st Century. Two certificate programs—the Certificate of Initial Mastery (CIM) and the Certificate of Advanced Mastery (CAM)—formed the major elements of the act. After earning the CIM in the tenth grade, students devote the remaining years of high school to achieving the CAM. To earn the CAM, students participate in an "endorsement area" or career pathway, achieve twelfth-grade mastery of all academic content areas, achieve career-related learning standards, and participate in career-related learning experiences.

Oregon illustrates the pros and cons of attaching a STW program to legislative education reform. Although the legislature was able to act decisively in establishing a direction for education reform in 1991, lawmakers left the implementation to the state's department of education, an agency that had not developed the capacity to implement the reform. Furthermore, the state sought to effect change in the classroom without simultaneously building teacher buy-in or overcoming teachers' resistance to change. In choosing to pursue comprehensive goals through legislation, the state engaged in a high-stakes strategy that could potentially lead to great successes or high losses. At risk in Oregon are the larger education-reform effort, the dismantling of the STW program, and continued pessimistic public opinion that efforts to improve education are doomed to failure.

Iowa has a long history of local control over education. Embedded within the choice of the STW structure is the strategy of using that local-control tradition to involve the community through building the linkages between schools, businesses, and communities. Local curriculum coordinators led the local initiatives, and the state STW office chose to take on the roles of facilitator and technical-assistance provider. Overall, the structure encourages active participation without duplication of effort in every school district.

Implicit in this strategy is linking the STW program to school improvement initiated at the school. This linkage enabled the STW program to broaden its scope and become a mechanism by which schools alter their teaching and curricular practices to improve their instruction. Respondents in Iowa typically did not view the STW endeavor as a program that would expire after the federal funding sunsets. The link between the STW program and school improvement also led local districts to buy into the overall initiative.

The connection between the STW program and Maryland's education reform will occur with the state's new High School Assessment. The linkage between the STW program and workforce and economic development is established through the state's use of the Private Industry Councils, the Employer Incentive Fund, and the requirement that a proportion of funds be used as incentives for business partnerships at the substate level.

In sum, Oregon, Iowa, and Maryland present examples of states pursuing comprehensive goals. Underlying the STW initiative in these states is the goal of obtaining systemic school improvement. Oregon and Maryland are pursuing this goal through their legislatures and other education-reform efforts such as Goals 2000. The state departments of education are active partners in, if not drivers of, the STW initiative. Sustainability in these two states depends on support from the state legislature and the alignment of goals among those at the substate level. Iowa's STW initiative is deceptively simple in its appearance. Iowa has not engaged in a state-mandated, standards-based reform effort. Thus, the STW program is a lever for such reform, not merely a means through which to accomplish an already-stated goal.

INTERMEDIATE-GOAL STATES

Half of the Phase 2 states pursued intermediate-level goals: Ohio, North Carolina, Colorado, Oklahoma, and Pennsylvania. Respondents articulated their goals as improving workforce-development activities, raising the skill level of the emerging workforce, or strengthening vocational education. Some states were concurrently pursuing systemic education reform. In contrast to the comprehensive states, the education reform has had a less-formal connection to the STW program. The major difference between comprehensive and intermediate states has been the degree to which STW activity is a collaborative activity among stakeholders that focuses broadly on school reform and improvement. In intermediate states, characteristically a subset of stakeholders was leading the initiative. States in this category have had particularly strong leadership and involvement from business and other private sectors, but have had limited participation from education. It is too early to conclude what impact this lopsided involvement has on the long-term sustainability of the STW program. In practice, it meant that the STW initiative was more likely to be linked to workforce-development reform, and in some instances the structure of the initiative itself anticipated the WIA.

The lieutenant governor of Ohio oversees an independent STW office. Five state agencies worked to align their internal policies and contribute to the implementation of the STW program. The decision to create an independent STW office gave the initiative higher visibility and allowed the formation of linkages with other workforce-development programs. Although the initiative enjoys support from businesses, the STW program is not institutionalized in supportive policy within the Department of Education. Prospects for sustainability depend on whether local partnerships generate interest, support, and buy-in from school districts.

North Carolina also has strong business support. The initiative began in the governor's office and subsequently moved to the Department of Commerce. JobReady Partnership Councils, led in most areas by school districts, community colleges, or chambers of commerce, run the STW initiative at the substate level. Each local partnership includes a coordinator, a business chair, and a JobReady Council.

Colorado's STW office is located in the lieutenant governor's office, but the state used an interagency approach that intended to root the STW activities in state-agency policy. Colorado, although engaged in standards-based education reform, has not formally linked the STW program to this. Colorado saw its STW initiative emerge from an office completely separate from other education-reform efforts. Because a variety of resources to assist local curricular-reform efforts is provided—including identification of career pathways, model lesson plans, and a publication linking workplace competencies to state standards—Colorado hopes that its STW program is a means of implementing the larger standards-based reform.

Oklahoma's STW office is located in the Oklahoma Department of Vocational and Technical Education. Viewed as primarily an effort to provide students with a range of postsecondary options and necessary skills and knowledge to succeed in the workplace, The STW program is a strategy toward meeting both local and state needs for a skilled workforce. Most respondents viewed the location of the STW office as a strength. This agency possesses the capacity and commitment necessary to implement the effort statewide. However, because Oklahoma has separate state agencies for vocational and common education, a few respondents claimed that the STW initiative is viewed as a limited vocational initiative.

In sum, these four states have had goals that are more narrowly defined than the goals of the comprehensive states. The largest difference is the degree of implementation of the STW program in schools. Comprehensive states attempt to change what occurs in each classroom. Intermediate states have not pursued

STW activities to that point, partially because their efforts and success at establishing the necessary collaborative partnerships is more limited.

A PROGRAMMATIC-GOAL STATE

One of the states in Phase 2 pursued a programmatic goal. Nebraska sought to fund a testing program enabling a business to determine the extent and appropriateness of a student's skills. In choosing a governance structure, Nebraska faced three major challenges. First, the state has a strong principle of local control. A second challenge was the state's geography. In many instances, the substate partnerships cover an enormous amount of territory. This led to approximately 86% of the students being involved in STW programs, whereas only 31% of the school districts are. However, a third issue presents the greatest challenge to sustainability: the overall structure of school funding. Thus, poor, rural school districts find themselves struggling to first marshal resources for the improvement of regular education programs.

CONCLUSIONS

States pursuing comprehensive goals are most likely to reap large benefits from their STW programs. However, they also have the most at risk. Among the risks are (a) contributing to a perception that efforts to improve public education are doomed to failure, (b) raising the expectations of important state-level stakeholders, and (c) derailing other education-reform efforts or workforce-development activities. The three comprehensive states used a variety of governance structures and strategies. In each of these states, the initiative united its activities with change in the classroom. Chances of sustainability are particularly high where the full integration of STW ideals and academic standards and assessment takes place.

The future of intermediate states is more difficult to predict. Activities included improving the delivery of workforce-training programs, linking the STW program to other workforce-development programs, or broadening the scope of vocational education. Most of our intermediate-goal states anticipated the passage of the WIA, choosing to mimic the WIA's governance structure. Therefore, this subset of states continues funding for a smaller set of activities through the WIA. Having chosen goals that are less comprehensive and less risky, the intermediate states are somewhat more likely to achieve their goals. However, achieving these limited goals may not be enough to guarantee the continuation of the broader initiative. In intermediate states, the education sector is not playing an active role. As a result, these states have been unable to institutionalize their STW initiatives in the schools, posing a significant challenge to statewide sustainability.

States with programmatic goals differ in that their activities are less integrated with existing state agencies or policies. Often, this was not the original intent, but has resulted from exogenous forces such as a vocal opposition group or statewide economic conditions. However, programmatic states have lower chances of sustainability absent additional resources.

REFERENCES

Hayward, G., & Benson, C. (1993). The changing role of vocational-technical education in the United States. *CenterWork, 4*(2), 1, 3.

Moore, M., & Waldman, Z. (1994). Opportunities or obstacles? A map of federal legislation related to the school-to-work initiative. In *School-to-work: What does research say about it?* (pp. 131–146). Washington, DC: U.S. Department of Education, OERI.

Urquiola, M., Stern, D., Horn, I., Dornsife, C., Chi, B., Williams, L., et al. (1997). *School-to-work, college, and career: A review of policy, practice, and results 1993–1997.* Berkeley, CA: National Center for Research in Vocational Education.

8

School-to-Work: The Wisconsin Experience

Mark C. Schug
Richard D. Western

Throughout the industrial era, Wisconsin educators and parents had concerned themselves with questions about how the schools ought to serve broad social goals, and school districts developed vocational-education programs to serve the needs of prospective workers and employers. By the late 1980s, however, this tradition of school policy and practice seemed in need of a major overhaul, given two overlapping problem areas that loomed large in the state. One problem had to do with Wisconsin's workforce; the other had to do with the K–12 schools. Performance in each area looked unsatisfactory. A large-scale policy initiative seemed to be in order. The reexamination and developmental activity that followed produced the STW program in Wisconsin. This chapter, revised and adapted from Schug and Western (1999), reviews the background, development, and implementation of the STW program in the state.

BACKGROUND

The Workforce Development Problem

Twenty years ago, Wisconsin's economy looked bleak. Fearing a steep slide, leaders in business and education examined the state's education system. The vocational and agricultural programs associated with an earlier era now seemed obsolete; it would not do merely to update them. Nor would it suffice to encourage more high-school graduates to continue their studies in college programs. College and university enrollment appeared to be a poor choice for many young people, as evidenced by the fact that many who enrolled in baccalaureate programs failed to complete them, while many who did earn degrees found themselves lacking skills demanded in the labor markets.

Reflecting this mood, the state legislature in 1987 approved an Education for Employment standard requiring that all students in grades K–12 have access to an education-for-employment program. Although it represented an effort to move beyond traditional vocational programs, this initiative emphasized in-school activity to be designed and carried out largely by K–12 educators. In a subsequent assessment of the state's needs, Wisconsin's Commission on Schools for the 21st Century (1990) envisioned a more far-reaching set of initiatives, including new partnerships between businesses and schools, youth-apprenticeship programs, and a tech-prep program to align K–12 curricular requirements with those of the state's technical colleges.

These developments in Wisconsin paralleled the STW agenda evolving concurrently at the national level. The Clinton administration had identified job training as a national priority, assigning Secretary of Labor Robert Reich to develop publicly supported programs for skill enhancement. In addressing this task, Reich sought to draw upon a consensus in policy circles about the need to upgrade the skills of American workers. The consensus view held that new programs were needed to cope with a set of urgent problems, including a growing inequality in wages and incomes, especially among the young; a decline in the quality of the workforce, with productivity problems linked to weak skills and motivational shortcomings; and an upper limit on our capacity to improve productivity through investment in physical capital. In response to recommendations associated with this view, President Clinton proposed the establishment of a nationwide system of youth-apprenticeship programs to provide school- and work-based training for young people not bound for college.

The argument for apprenticeship programs derived support from a premise that the transition from school to work in the United States is at best inefficient. Observers asserting this view pointed to large numbers of poorly educated young people who could be seen wasting time in what seemed to be aimless activity: working at dead-end jobs and dabbling at college or university studies for which many were ill-prepared. This premise ties the discussion of the workforce-development problem to the second problem associated with the rise of STW programs in Wisconsin: the problem of low effort and achievement among pupils in K–12 schools.

The K–12 Schools Problem

Throughout the 1980s, observers of schooling in the United States generally reported low levels of effort and achievement on the part of K–12 students. Goodlad (1983), for example, described a general picture of passivity and slack effort among students. Sizer (1984) similarly described students as characteristically docile, compliant, and without initiative. Powell, Farrar, and Cohen (1985), introducing a metaphor that became well-known, described high-school students as shoppers passing casually through a shopping-mall high school, deciding on their own terms what they would consent to learn or whether they would consent to learn anything at all. Boyer (1983), commenting on a high school he took to be typical, described classroom work as mostly routine, with relations between students and teachers marked by a tacit agreement: Don't expect much from me, and I won't expect much from you.

Additional evidence of low effort and expectations appeared in studies of how students spent their time. Studies of time use in school showed that, on average, students engaged actively in efforts to learn during about half the time they spent in school, with about half lost to absences, lateness, and inattention (Bishop, 1989). Data from the High School and Beyond survey (again during the 1980s) showed that students spent an average of 3.5 hours per week on homework. "When homework is added to engaged time at school, the total time devoted to study, instruction, and practice is . . . 18–22 hours per week. . . . By way of comparison, the typical senior spent 10 hours per week in a . . . job and about 24 hours per week watching television" (Bishop, 1989, p. 6).

Similar concerns prevailed in Wisconsin. The Commission on Schools for the 21st Century spent seven months examining Wisconsin schools in light of the priorities it saw arising from developments in the global economy. Its report identified a host of problems. In Wisconsin, it said, the schools' academic mission had drifted out of focus. Uncoordinated efforts at improvement had left school programs cluttered and diffuse. High-school students faced inadequate opportunities to learn, especially in relation to technology, work, and citizenship. And teachers and administrators faced increasing difficulty in trying to engage students in serious effort and in keeping order among them.

Of the various explanations offered for these observations, one had special relevance for the STW idea. It was an explanation emphasizing the irrelevance of the schools' academic programs. According to this view, a constellation of changes—in technology and in the nature of work, leadership, and citizenship—had rendered traditional school practices, focused on the study of single subjects, obsolete (Commission on Schools, 1990). Especially in high schools, teachers were said to focus too narrowly on formal, disciplinary learning (see Gray & Herr, 1995; Milwaukee Public Schools, 1997). This narrowly focused academic activity, moreover, was carried out in school settings that seemed designed more for custodial purposes than for learning. Isolated from adults, confined in classrooms, restricted to work on textbook problems, and rewarded more for compliance than for accomplishments, students did not exactly fail to achieve, according to this view. Instead, they declined to take up the learning tasks posed for them. Inappropriate goals and practices thus were said to produce the disaffection and slack work habits about which educators and others complained.

It was not a new criticism. In previous formulations, it had been the stock-in-trade of critics in the Progressive movement in education. They argued after World War I for a transformation of the schools, to be ushered in by an expansion of school programs addressed to social goals (Krug, 1969). It was an old idea—to accommodate disaffected students, expand the curriculum and infuse it with opportunities for practical learning—redescribed for presentation as a bold departure. The need for redescription arose in part from acknowledgment of the failures of vocational education. In addition, a new line of scholarship about situated learning—learning as it occurs in actual workplace settings—suggested what seemed to be a solid basis for new directions in thinking. This scholarship elaborated and provided confirmation for the view that working in school on academic tasks bears little resemblance to the dynamic reality of working and learning on farms or in offices, laboratories, hospitals, design studios, and so on.

In her presidential address to the American Educational Research Association, Lauren Resnick (1987) summarized research findings that contrasted learning in school and out. Learning inside school emphasizes "pure mentation," for example (no use of the dictionary during an impromptu essay), whereas situated learning emphasizes the use of tools (task-specific tables, for example, used by street vendors in currency transactions). Observations of this sort were taken by many educators to imply that general applications might be made of the situated-learning idea in school programs. Brown, Collins, and Duguid (1989), for example, argued that in order to produce robust academic learning, educators should turn to activities of *cognitive* apprenticeship, embedding teaching and learning in activities simulating work as it might be carried out by practitioners in workplace settings.

This formulation of the situated-learning idea does reinterpret the earlier line of Progressive criticism. In practice and not occasionally by outright declaration, Progressive educators had extolled practical, experiential learning *in opposition* to academic learning, which many of them disparaged as bookish, medieval, and aristocratic (see Hofstadter, 1963; Krug, 1969). In contrast, the situated-learning theorists contended that academic learning *and* learning for civic and work-related purposes would be better served if schools could find ways to reintroduce key elements of apprenticeship experience throughout their programs. To teach science, mathematics, history, or English *and* to prepare young people for life outside school, educators should engage their students as workers in the respective domains. How to do this had by no means been settled, and the power of the idea to transform schools was therefore only a matter of speculation. Nonetheless, even in barest outline, the situated-learning idea captured the attention of reformists who sought to reorient school programs toward work-related goals without creating new versions of the old vocational-track dumping grounds (see Olson, 1997).

Even given the cachet bestowed on it by research, the situated-learning idea remained little known outside academic circles. It most likely could not have carried the STW initiative forward as a promising new program except for the timely fact that additional evidence about situated learning seemed also to be at hand from a real-world source. That source was the German school system, with its program of apprenticeships designed to help young people move smoothly from school to work while continuing their education on the job. The German system looked compelling. By providing for work-based learning, it apparently addressed motivational problems, imposed order on the transition from school to work, and reduced wasteful drifting and job shopping. Moreover, it placed young people in contact with adults outside school, where their interaction would be based on reciprocal responsibilities, not the ministration of the helping professions. And it seemed to improve on old-fashioned vocational education by placing responsibility for skills development in the hands of employers, thus ensuring that training priorities would reflect market requirements.

Attracted by the German system, many Americans educators embarked on study tours of German schools, returning to recommend aspects of the German model for adoption in U.S. schools. Among the visitors were Wisconsin's Governor Tommy Thompson and Superintendent of Public Instruction Herbert Grover. Thompson and Grover subsequently cited the German example in their endorsements of STW programs. By 1996, when apprenticeship programs in the state had enrolled 730 students, the governor credited Wisconsin's adaptation of the German model (see Olson, 1997, p. 87).

THE STW PROGRAM EVOLVES AS A COMPREHENSIVE REFORM PROGRAM IN WISCONSIN

In its visionary tone on the one hand and in the discretion it granted for variations in local implementation on the other, the School-to-Work Opportunities Act (STWOA) has proved to be compatible with two different conceptions of its purpose (Hershey, Silverberg, Haimson, Hudis, & Jackson, 1999). It may be understood as calling for programs focused on career-related preparation for students not planning to enroll in college. Implementation guided by this interpretation would emphasize, for example, youth-apprenticeship activity closely linked to in-school instruction. In provisions related to the large goal of *transforming* K–12 education, however, the STWOA also stressed the importance of STW activity for *all* students (the word *all* occurs with marked frequency in STW documents), only some of whom would participate in a complete package of career-related STW activity. Implementation guided by this interpretation would emphasize school-based learning activities, including career exploration units and academic courses enhanced by career-related applications.

As a "leading-edge" implementer of the STWOA, Wisconsin embraced the comprehensive STW vision, encompassing academic and work-related goals. The vision is prefigured in reform proposals recommended by the Commission on Schools for the 21st Century. Its proposed curricular framework for Wisconsin's schools listed career and occupational development among the overarching categories to be used in conceptualizing K–12 programs (Commission on Schools, 1990). Subsequent documents have echoed this view, hailing the STW program as a means for "transforming Wisconsin's educational system" (Skills for the Future, 2001a). The transformation would provide both "a strong academic foundation and technical know-how" (Skills for the Future, 2001b), and its benefits would extend to all students: By the year 2000, all high-school graduates "will have had at least some exposure to the workplace" (National School-to-Work Learning & Information Center, 2000). In addition, one of three graduating seniors would have a career major linked to an associate degree, and one of five seniors would earn or be in the process of earning a state skill certificate.

On the surface, at least, no Wisconsin school district bought into STW programs more enthusiastically than the Milwaukee Public Schools (MPS). In 1993, in light of the district's chronic problems with truancy, dropout rates, and low achievement, MPS Superintendent Howard Fuller established a task force to examine STW as a reform program. The 1993 task-force report, *School to Work: Learning for Life*, embraced an expansive vision of what might be achieved through STW activities, asserting that decisions taken within MPS should in future be guided by a concern for students' success in the workplace. The entire MPS curriculum, accordingly, stood in need of reconfiguration as a STW program. Resources and effort within the district and the larger community would be used in a new fashion to alter students' experiences radically (Wilson et al., 1995). STW activity would begin in kindergarten; STW programs would usher in rigorous academic and experiential goals; they would address citizenship, problem solving, and personal growth for students of all strengths and skill levels (Milwaukee Public Schools, 1997). It would in fact approach the sublime, engaging students "in the practice of freedom to transform the world" (Wilson et al., 1997, p. I-1).

To govern and administer STW programs, Wisconsin developed a complex infrastructure. It consisted initially of the Office of the Governor (advised by a Council on Workforce Excellence), the Department of Workforce Development (DWD), the Department of Public Instruction (DPI), and the Wisconsin Technical College System (WTCS). The Department of Workforce Development would be responsible for work-based learning, including youth-apprenticeship programs. The Department of Public Instruction would be responsible for tech-prep. These state agencies would interact variously with local school districts. The districts in turn would be organized within STW consortia established by the Department for Public Instruction to foster coordinated planning.

Apparently acknowledging opacity and bureaucratic excess in this governance structure, Wisconsin moved in 1999 to consolidate STW authority in a single body: the Governor's Work-Based Learning Board. Oversight of work-based learning programs administered by the DWD, DPI, and WTCS has been transferred to this board in an effort to enhance the accountability, sharpen the focus, and improve the effectiveness of STW programs.

STW PROGRAMS IN WISCONSIN'S SCHOOLS

STW programs in Wisconsin encompass a broad range of practices, with variation from district to district. District programs, moreover, are in flux, expanding or contracting as district priorities change. To indicate the range of activities and identify patterns among them, we have reviewed data from STW implementation reports and follow-up surveys. We have also interviewed curriculum directors from 45 Wisconsin school districts in an effort to learn about situation-specific developments.

Implementation Studies

Wisconsin reports STW implementation data by reference to nine benchmark categories, providing in each case a participation-count statistic. Using these reports, the Center on Education and Work compiles implementation profiles. The profiles for 1995–1997 have been published (Mason & Thorn, 1997); additional information updated to 1999 is available online at an STW website (National School-to-Work Learning & Information Center, 2000).

Data from these sources show steady growth in STW-program participation overall; they also show that this growth has occurred preponderantly in school-based learning activities. Many Wisconsin students now participate in career-awareness activities and develop career majors, but few (in percentage terms) participate in STW activities that connect them to a workplace. Moreover, participation rates in work-based categories have been flat. In the youth-apprenticeship category, in which state projections had called for a 20% participation rate by 2000, the rate (as of 1999) is 1%, up only 0.7% from 1995. And the 1% figure reflects Wisconsin students *enrolled* in apprenticeship programs, not the number from the cohort group in question having *completed* an apprenticeship program.

The disparity in participation rates between school- and work-based activities can most likely be explained by the relative ease with which school-based activities can be assimilated to ordinary patterns of classroom activity. Alternative explanations may also be relevant to rates of participation in paid and unpaid work experience (the two categories are conflated in the updated 1999 report). Wisconsin employers faced a tight labor market late in the 1990s, and many of them sought new ways to solve staffing problems. In this context, it would be surprising if paid and unpaid work experiences had not increased for Wisconsin students at the time.

STW Programs as Curriculum Directors See Them

In 1998, we conducted telephone interviews with curriculum directors in Wisconsin school districts, selecting 45 districts at random from the total set of 426. We interviewed curriculum directors rather than STW coordinators in order to learn about district-wide perspectives on STW programs. As would be expected in this random sampling, most participating districts represented small towns or rural areas of the state. Several districts representing larger population areas also participated, however, as did several Milwaukee-area suburban districts. Because the MPS district is unique in size and in the nature of its early commitment to STW programs, we conducted separate interviews with MPS personnel.

STW Activities

Nearly all curriculum directors (forty-two of forty-five) reported that schools in their districts had implemented aspects of STW programs. Most identified STW programs with work-based learning activities, mentioning cooperative work placements, apprenticeships, job shadowing, and instruction provided in workplace settings. The school-based activities mentioned most frequently included career awareness and the provision of integrated academic and applied coursework. Connecting activities included business-partners programs and programs for dual-credit articulation with technical colleges.

STW Effects on the Curriculum

Here, several curriculum directors initially mentioned attitudinal effects, stating that STW implementation had made teachers more aware of their responsibility to use real-world examples and to encourage good work habits in their instruction. For the most part, however, curriculum directors reported that STW programs had their main effects in business and technical fields. "Technical education has boomed," one curriculum director stated, elaborating the point by reference to course offerings in medical technology, foods, and agriculture. Courses of this sort were said to be required of students in only a few districts, however; typically, they appear as electives in school programs.

The general curriculum has been little affected by STW programs, most curriculum directors (thirty-two of forty-five) said. Some spoke bluntly of "no impact on the curriculum." Others struggled to describe curricular effects, as in the case of one who said she believed that language-arts teachers were now doing more with the writing of business letters, only to add that business letters had always been a part of the curriculum. Several curriculum directors echoed this point: What the schools now count as STW activity is often indistinguishable from activity (in agriculture, consumer economics, and work-study programs, for instance) that predated STW programs and is now repackaged under new names. A long-standing tradition of elementary-school visits to a fire station or a zoo, for example, might now be said to yield instances of worksite observation.

The failure of STW programs to penetrate the general curriculum caused some directors to speak ashamedly, deploring what they saw as a lack of interest in STW programs among mainstream teachers. Others had a more matter-of-fact analysis. "In my district, the priority now is development of [Wisconsin's state academic] standards," one said; "STW is not going to get much attention because it is not in the standards."

Which Students Participate in STW Programs?

Here, curriculum directors provided mixed responses. Many (nineteen of forty-five) said initially that STW programs affected students across the board. Follow-up discussion usually disclosed that the claim of across-the-board effects referred to across-the-board *access* on the one hand ("Our STW opportunities are open to all"), and to elementary- or middle-school career-awareness activities on the other. When curriculum directors turned to the high-school grades, they spoke more typically of work-based STW activity; and in respect to these activities, participation tended to be concentrated among those students not bound for college. "College-prep kids do college-prep stuff," one director stated.

The number of students said to be involved in work-based learning activity was typically small (especially in the case of apprenticeships) as a percentage of school populations. Some districts had no students doing apprenticeships; most reported numbers ranging from two to six. "Apprenticeships? We have only . . . " was a typical opening remark.

By way of explanation for low rates of apprenticeship participation, curriculum directors emphasized three points: Apprenticeship programs make time demands that many students are not willing to accept, small-town and rural districts have limited access to placement opportunities, and districts can afford apprenticeship placements only on a small scale. Some rural and small-town curriculum directors expressed resentment about what they saw as an inequitable emphasis on apprenticeships in STW policy; they believed that cooperative work-placement programs, which they found more feasible, merited stronger state support.

About the split between college-bound students and others in STW participation, two qualifications emerged. First, some curriculum directors reported strong interest among college-bound students in technology and applied academics courses. "We've got a great technology course," one explained, "and a lot of juniors and seniors take it. It's a good course, and they need some electives anyway." Second, apprenticeship programs also appealed strongly to some college-bound students. "At first we pushed these [apprenticeships] just for the kids we thought would not be going on [to college]," one curriculum director said, "but now everybody wants in." He and others emphasized that apprenticeship programs should not be thought of as a catchall for at-risk students.

Which Faculty Members Participate in STW Programs?

Faculty involvement in STW programs is generally low, most curriculum directors (thirty-five of forty-five) said. It tends to be concentrated among teachers in technology, business, and vocational courses and programs. Other teachers are said to be less involved or not involved at all. Despite the fact that money for STW staff development and externship activity was available in her district, one curriculum director said, few teachers had shown an interest in either. Another said of STW staff development that those teachers who have experienced it were the ones now most apt to seem "saturated" with and tired of STW programs.

Some curriculum directors attributed the lack of interest they described to the subject-matter orientation of high-school teachers. Middle-school teachers, according to these curriculum directors, were more receptive to integrated, thematic teaching. "But in the high school," one said, "they are into content." Or again, "The wall goes up when you hit high school." As to why such resistance might be widespread among high-school teachers, we heard mostly circular explanations ("because they are into content"). The only substantive explanation came from one curriculum director who stated that within her district, high-school teachers had no clear sense of what the "applied academics" concept meant or how they might make use of it in their work.

One might expect to find higher levels of STW involvement among elementary-school teachers, given the nondepartmentalized classroom settings in which most of them work. But except with respect to career-awareness activities, the curriculum directors did not report significant STW-program involvement among the elementary-school teachers. "No elementary-school involvement," one curriculum director said. "Our elementary-school teachers don't know much about STW so far."

How Do Students Benefit from STW Programs?

In response to questions about how students benefit from participation in STW programs (in improved achievement, attendance, or school-completion rates, for example), curriculum directors agreed (forty-five of forty-five) that school districts had no reliable information about such effects. Several believed, on the basis of informal observation, that STW participation (especially work-based activities) helped students learn to think more clearly about vocational decisions and to make better course selections. For students who moved from apprenticeship programs directly into jobs after high-school graduation, curriculum directors agreed that there seemed to be a benefit in improved access to good jobs.

But all who spoke to the main question emphasized that as STW programs are designed and carried out in Wisconsin, there is no way to assess effects on learning. The STW activities tend to be integrated with other school programs, some said, so it is not possible to isolate the STW component for analysis. Some students make gains according to various measures during their STW participation, others said, but these tend to be good students in the first place, so it is hard to know what STW programs might have to do with the changes.

"There is no system in place for tracking GPAs, graduation rates, or other measures in respect to STW," one curriculum director said; "nothing targeted specifically to STW. The state does not ask for that."

STW Programs in Milwaukee

As noted previously, STW proponents in Milwaukee thought of STW programs as a driving force for broad education reform. Early goals included developing new, integrated curricula for all students, aligning STW activity with curricular requirements, developing assessment programs to evaluate STW initiatives for achievement effects, developing partnerships and working relationships with the business community and postsecondary schools, and providing requisite staff-development programs.

Among these possibilities, staff development became an early priority, reflecting a view among administrators that the broad goals of the project should be approached initially by efforts to improve school-based learning. A series of summer STW institutes ensued; the institutes emphasized uses of integrated teaching focused on themes and projects. Other early efforts also emphasized school-based activities. An evaluation of these first-round implementation initiatives found all participating MPS schools to have shown progress in the school-based components of STW programs, but implementation of work-based components was very limited (Wilson et al., 1995).

Two subsequent phases or waves of implementation followed. An evaluation of the cumulative effort yielded a summary that looks telling in retrospect. Under a rubric entitled "What's Working," the summary focused on STW inputs or capacity building, not results. It listed committee work related to STW activities; STW job shadowing experiences provided for school principals, partners, and teachers; a new initiative for improving the teaching of mathematics and science; increased involvement in STW programs on the part of the Guidance Department, especially in respect to supplying data bearing on MPS's progress in STW implementation; administrative restructuring; and helpful participation by STW teacher-facilitators (Wilson et al., 1997). Nothing in the summary suggested that outcome goals—for example, improved academic learning, growth in opportunities for apprenticeship experiences, improved job-placement rates for graduating seniors, or improved articulation of MPS academic requirements with those of the technical colleges—had been addressed in the time period 1993–1997.

The "What's Working" account was followed by one titled "What's Not Working" (Wilson et al., 1997). It was more extensive, and the problems it spelled out say a great deal about the difficulties MPS experienced in trying to impose STW efforts onto its complex system of programs. Heading the list was a finding that MPS educators never came to an agreement about what STW meant: "After three years, the definition and goals of STW are still not settled" (Wilson et al., 1997, p. III-27). Other problems followed. High-school teachers had often balked, contending that STW emphases would dilute the academic curriculum. Some principals, called upon by STW policy to serve as instructional leaders, found that their other obligations within a decentralized administrative system required them to focus on resource management instead. STW activity had not been coordinated with the vocational-education programs that predated STW programs in MPS. Nor had graduation requirements been aligned with STW goals. As a result and because procedures for data collection had not been aligned with STW programming, there was little evidence about the effects of STW programs on student learning. Student participation in work-based learning activities had remained low. And people charged with responsibility for doing so had found it difficult to "scale up": to obtain cooperation and participation on a broad scale, so that the goal of making MPS over in a new mold, shaped by STW programs, might be realized.

As of fall 1998, the future of STW programs in MPS looked doubtful. Its early promise had not been borne out, and events had apparently passed it by. Business and political leaders in Milwaukee had increasingly voiced support for revitalizing the city's vocational-technical education programs (a new, fifty-million-dollar trades and technical high school is now under development). The MPS Board of School Directors had reallocated STW money within the MPS budget, and MPS's STW director had resigned, stating that there was no longer a need for her position.

STW AS A POLICY RESPONSE TO WORKFORCE AND K–12 EDUCATION PROBLEMS

Here, we revisit the two main problems that gave rise to STW initiatives. As a statewide policy initiative, how well has Wisconsin's STW program served the main purposes for which it was established?

Good things clearly have been done in its name, benefiting individual students and employers. Follow-up studies (Heidenreich, 1999; Phelps & Fulton, 1997; Phelps & Jin, 1997; Phelps, Scribner, Wakelyn, & Weis, 1996) of youth-apprenticeship graduates describe high levels of satisfaction reported by the graduates regarding their program participation. They believe generally that their program experiences have enhanced their earnings and employment potential, their sense of self-responsibility, and their ability to work well with others. Evidence from a survey of recent youth-apprenticeship graduates (Heidenreich, 1999) suggests that they are correct in their beliefs: A majority of the 1997 youth-apprenticeship graduates received and accepted offers of full- or part-time employment from their apprenticeship employers. Parents responding to recent surveys also report overall satisfaction with apprenticeship programs, as do participating employers.

Questions remain to be asked, however, about the statewide impact of STW programs. We turn next to these questions.

Workforce Development Revisited

STW programs in Wisconsin emerged as a policy response to a human-capital problem that seemed dire in a time of economic decline. The problems had prompted consideration in some circles of a national Japanese-style industrial policy, so that the government could influence decisions that otherwise would be determined, perhaps inefficiently, by market forces. In this climate, it seemed plausible to contemplate an analogous effort in K–12 education. Many young people and their parents were not approaching education-related decisions prudently. Why should the state not take steps, then, to influence these decisions? Education was the legal responsibility of the state, and the schools always had been deemed responsible, among other things, for preparing young people for work. From this perspective, the STW movement came into view as a forward-looking exercise in rational planning.

But circumstances at the end of the STW funding period were much changed in Wisconsin and elsewhere. While Japan struggled with a long period of economic contraction and Germany struggled with meager growth and high rates of unemployment, Wisconsin's economy rebounded (see White, 2000). Between 1991 and 1999, employment in the state grew by 21%, surpassing the nation's 13% growth rate. Manufacturing employment grew by 14%, services by 35%, and retail by 17%. The state added nearly 25,000 high-tech jobs between 1991 and 1999. Average earnings—up in all areas of the state by 1999—varied from a high of $31,908 in Milwaukee to a low of $23,936 in the rest of the state. Unemployment—lower than the nation's average rate throughout 1991–1999—was (early in 2001) below 4%.

As a result, the challenges facing Wisconsin at the beginning of 2001 differed greatly from those emphasized at STW launch time. The new challenges arose largely from strength in the economy, not weaknesses. As the adult population approached the limits of its capacity for workforce participation, Wisconsin faced a labor shortage.

What impact might STW programs have had on the turnaround in Wisconsin's economy, and what is their potential to alleviate the problems employers face in an unusually tight labor market? The starting point from which to consider these questions is one of scale. The overriding fact is that in percentage terms, very few Wisconsin students have participated in "cornerstone" work-based STW experiences. Since 1994, for example, 1,491 students have completed youth-apprenticeship programs (Governor's Work-Based Learning Board, 2000). The number for 1996–97 was 347 students. By comparison, 258,965 students were enrolled (Grades 9–12) in Wisconsin's public schools in 1994–95, and 2,892,400 workers were employed in Wisconsin's 1996 workforce. The 347 apprenticeship graduates in 1996–97 represented, in other words, about .001 of Wisconsin's 1994–95 high-school-student population and about .0001 of the state's 1996 workforce.

On the face of it, these participation counts and ratios look very small, as Heidenreich (1999) indicates: "The Youth Apprenticeship Program continues to serve only a small percentage of the state's high-school population" (p. 31). What might they imply about the economic impact of apprenticeship programs statewide? One way to estimate that impact is by reference to the effects of additional income flowing into Wisconsin's economy by virtue of wage increments that might be attributed to STW apprenticeship training.

Suppose that all 347 of the 1996–97 apprenticeship graduates had gone directly to work after graduation and had jumped immediately to earning the 1996 average annual wage for Wisconsin workers: $26,018. (In fact, many apprenticeship graduates do not begin full-time work immediately upon graduation; of those who do, not all would jump immediately to an average wage. See Heidenreich, 1999, pp. 5–6.) The annual wage total for those 347 workers would come to $9,028,246. Especially given Wisconsin's tight labor market, however, the same 347 individuals almost certainly could have found full-time employment, earning at least the minimum wage, if they had merely completed high school without any STW-apprenticeship training. At the 1996 minimum wage of $4.75 per hour, and assuming an average 2,080-hour work year, the annual wage total for such a group of non-STW workers would be $3,428,360. The difference between the two wage totals ($9,028,246–$3,428,360) is $5,599,886. This amount is the additional income attributable, according to the assumptions stated previously, to STW-apprenticeship training at the time in question.

Directly and indirectly, the $5,599,886 generated in this manner would provide a dividend from STW-apprenticeship training paid into Wisconsin's economy, because portions of the sum would flow to the support of public services (through taxes) and to purchases of goods and services in private markets, producing, in a multiplier effect, additional rounds of spending. But in fact, that dividend turns out to be very small. The reason becomes apparent if we compare the hypothetical dividend to wage totals for the larger workforce. Wages paid (again assuming Wisconsin's 1996 average earnings from wages) to the other 2,892,400 Wisconsin workers would total $75,254,463,200 (2,892,400 × $26,018). This means that STW-apprenticeship training statewide would account for about .00007% ($5,599,886/$75,254,463,200) of the money flow generated in 1996 by wages earned in the state.

Apprenticeship-participation rates may continue to climb slowly, of course; and a complete analysis of STW impact would also entail attention to effects of other STW program components. Unless the numbers in question were to change dramatically, however, the case for STW impact on workforce development looks weak. Despite the resources it has absorbed to date, STW programs in Wisconsin have reached too few young people *at crucial points of impact* to have the large, statewide effects envisioned by its proponents.

The K–12 Schools Revisited

It is not only the economic environment that changed in Wisconsin after 1990. A new education initiative based on state-level curricular standards and statewide curricular examinations came into play during the last half of the 1990s. As a result, Wisconsin's education-reform agenda is informed now by two different lines of thought. One is reflected in continuing efforts to sustain the STW initiative and to represent it in its original guise as a double-barreled program aimed both at improved academic learning and at workforce development. The other is reflected in the standards and assessment movement, developed by the Governor's Council on Model Academic Standards.

The standards are now regarded as a first-order priority by many K–12 educators in Wisconsin (Schug & Western, 2000). Whatever is excluded from their scope will seem of little importance to school administrators eager to show satisfactory achievement profiles. STW programs are not aligned with the standards, nor do STW programs provide any independent evaluation system to assess their effects on learning. In this regard, STW programs in Wisconsin have become an anomaly, unable to generate evidence related to their own academic goals and disconnected from the state's principal academic initiative. It is perhaps for this reason that the Milwaukee Public Schools, recently facing pressure to improve achievement or face state-imposed restructuring, has backed away (Williams, 1998) from its early commitment to STW programs. Had STW programs in fact been able to galvanize MPS after 1993, a prudent superintendent would have showcased his STW program, not abandoned it, in the crisis over achievement effects.

If the standards initiative continues to drive reform activity in Wisconsin's schools, it will marginalize the STW efforts. Apprenticeships and other work-related activities will retain their importance in some school districts; they may be expanded, in fact, as new initiatives come into play. But the early vision of the STW initiative as a comprehensive academic reform—one that would not merely improve teaching and learning but "transform" it—will fade and be forgotten.

IN RETROSPECT: STW PROGRAMS AND THE REFORMIST TRADITION IN AMERICAN EDUCATION

If STW programs fade away in Wisconsin, what might educators learn from their demise? Maybe nothing: The history of education in the United States is replete with examples of failed projects that are simply passed over and forgotten. The causes of failure are then not available for consideration when new versions of old programs are wheeled out for use in redemptive campaigns; and instead of learning from the record of experience in their own profession, educators flush with enthusiasm march off toward dead ends, retracing the false steps of their predecessors. In light of this possibility for the present case, we offer the following remarks about the STW initiatives in Wisconsin as a cautionary tale.

It Is a Mistake to Launch an Initiative Aimed at *Academic Reform* without Providing an *Academic Program* to Sustain It

Proponents touted the STW initiative as a workforce-development program and a program that would transform learning for all K–12 students. But Wisconsin's STW program came with no curricular or instructional component to give substance to the large claims made on behalf of its academic side.

Some STW proponents did envision new forms of integrated teaching derived from research (e.g., Resnick, 1987) on situated learning. This research, they supposed, would guide K–12 educators in their development of new forms of apprenticeship learning, including *cognitive* apprenticeship learning, thus strengthening academic and work-related programs. But this was a naive assumption. Consider the situated-learning idea first as it might be understood in a general, nonprescriptive sense. (That is how reform initiatives are typically understood in the schools.) Teachers understanding it in that sense would take STW activities as a reminder that they should bear workplace needs in mind, with respect to explicit lessons but also with respect to the school and classroom setting—the day-to-day routines common in schools and the norms implicit in them. The reminder would be unlikely to cause large changes. Teachers would point out that their norms and practices—emphasizing the importance of good work habits, basic skills, and the soft skills of cooperation and communication—are already compatible with workplace priorities, and they probably would be right about that. But such norms and the practices associated with them have been the stock-in-trade of the K–12 schools for a long time; and, worthy as most people believe they are, they have not ushered in anything like a transformation in learning.

But suppose that the situated-learning idea is understood to mean something more precise and far-reaching, such that teachers would need to reconceptualize their work fundamentally by reference to specific workplace circumstances and problems. This obviously would imply real change, but it is not a change we are likely to see any time soon. The reasons become clear as soon as we try to imagine in concrete detail what such recasting would entail. Could K–12 teachers in fact simulate—not once or twice, on special occasions, but as a matter of course and across the entire curriculum—the situation-specific work involved, say, in writing and producing a technical manual on the uses of electronic controls in fluid-power manufacturing, or in carrying out market research for a new mutual fund, or in doing an environmental-impact analysis related to the proposed construction of a new football stadium or hospital? Could they create analogues in the classroom for the market forces that induce people outside of school to undertake such projects and to complete them on time and under budget? Or could they—shifting over to the notion of *cognitive* apprenticeship activity in academic domains—effectively simulate in classrooms the work done elsewhere by editors, economists, translators, microbiologists, cartographers, and geologists? Jerome Bruner (1960) and others associated with the structure-of-the-disciplines movement in the 1960s advocated exactly that conception of academic work for K–12 students. Their work gave rise to several large-scale, federally funded curriculum-development projects, many of them directed by distinguished scholars and carried forward by talented K–12 educators. But these ambitious efforts did not come close to transforming school programs, and the movement now has generally been forgotten.

What would be different this time around? What new steps would educators take to ensure that instruction guided by the situated-learning idea would differ qualitatively from the instructional practices emphasizing themes or problems and group projects that many teachers have used routinely, to little effect, since the dawn of the Progressive era? Why might teachers succeed now, where others have failed, in using authenticity and relevance as touchstones for new programs that would foster high levels of achievement in history and chemistry, in mathematics and literature?

Perhaps the situated-learning idea could have provided answers to these questions, serving as the wellspring for a distinctly new STW approach to teaching and learning. It could have done so, however, only if it had been developed in ample, concrete detail and had then been introduced systematically to teachers: first, in carefully controlled pilot programs and then, as warranted by early results, more broadly. A research-and-development project of this sort might have produced a rich supply of sample problems (such as the fluid-power controls manual or the environmental-impact analysis) and supporting materials, suitable for use at various grade levels and in various curricular areas. Then teachers could have studied these sample problems and experimented with them in order to gauge the potential value of the underlying idea.

In addition, teachers also would have needed an analysis and demonstration showing how their academic objectives might be addressed in work related to STW problems. Advocacy for integrated, problem-oriented teaching often ignores this point. But teachers who have explored problem-oriented teaching have often found it poorly suited for use with any but the most basic of their objectives. As a result, actual instances of integrated teaching are often long on low-level skills of computation and transcription, and short on attention to advanced skills and ideas. How, exactly, do prealgebra concepts get built into a unit of instruction involving operation of a simulated travel agency? A middle-school math teacher would need to examine many examples of problem-oriented teaching as an approach to advanced concepts in order to make an informed judgment about the advantages and disadvantages of that approach.

Even given plenty of sample problems and an analysis showing how such problems might embody a full range of curricular objectives, teachers still might have wondered whether the effort required to develop and sustain integrated, applied teaching were worthwhile, given the alternative of focused, disciplinary teaching. Disciplinary teaching linked to systems of external examinations has been shown to have powerful effects on student achievement (e.g., Bishop, 1998). Could stronger effects be obtained by means of integrated teaching oriented to workplace conditions and problems? What does the evidence show?

As STW endeavors unfolded in Wisconsin, these questions were not addressed. The STW program was not preceded or accompanied by a research-and-development project of the sort suggested previously. Thus, its effects on learning could not have been assessed even if educators had wanted to do so, and the STW program could not be broached to teachers or parents as a tested program, worthy of support on its merits. Instead, it was put forward by sloganeering and admonition; the implication being that enlightened teachers and parents would get on board, and only hidebound traditionalists would drag their feet. The aggressive hard sell and the rhetoric provoked antagonism in some districts, so that people responsible for scaling up STW efforts met with resistance that could have been avoided had parental and student *demand* for STW programs been the primary consideration in decisions about program expansion.

It Is a Mistake to Conceive of Educational Programs as Vast, Totalizing Projects

Some school districts in Wisconsin went farther than others in making STW programs central to their missions, but STW programs never did come into play as a dominant, comprehensive scheme for shaping district-level policy and practice. Earnest, emphatic declarations about the power of the STW initiative to attack *all* problems for *all* students turned out, invariably, to be hyperbolic and divisive.

The hyperbole created more than a problem of tone or sensibility. It provided cover for an overall tendency to do little with core STW components: articulated technical studies, apprenticeship programs, and co-op work experiences. If *everything*—parental involvement, block scheduling, cooperative group learning, small children's field trips to the zoo—can be viewed as an STW problem or an STW practice, then the task of STW implementation has no focus and no end; it is compatible with anything and distinctive of nothing. You can be heavily involved in STW programs, according to this view, even if you do mostly what you were doing before, while doing little to connect your students with norms and practices that might add value to schooling precisely because they lie outside the K–12 world.

Why could STW programs in Wisconsin not play the lead role its proponents had envisioned? One might observe simply that no single reform campaign ever has succeeded in transforming the American schools, not even when the issue at stake has been more sharply focused than it was in the case of STW programs. In the case of STW endeavors, however, there is more to be said. STW programs in Wisconsin did encounter some resistance from parents and teachers, and, more importantly, they failed to excite many others. But resistance and weak demand were symptoms of a deeper problem of policy incoherence.

This problem arises in part from a political climate of strong support for higher education. Incentives associated with this climate of support, from the GI Bill to the present, bolster college and university enrollments by reducing students' direct costs. The state of Wisconsin, particularly, spends large sums to support the University of Wisconsin system and expands student access to it. Within the system, it is taken as a given that high enrollments are a good thing, and parents and young adults in Wisconsin seem to agree. Higher-education enrollments are strong in the state, and interest in getting a head start on college work and credits has recently surged. Wisconsin high-school students took ten times more Advanced Placement exams in 2000 than they did in 1987. The increase between 1999 and 2000 alone was 13% (Borsuk, 2000).

Accordingly, even if parents and teachers push too many young people toward college enrollment (e.g., Gray & Herr, 1995), current enrollment trends are driven by something stronger than an irrational "mania." People unhappy about those trends only poke at the fire from the top when they respond by trying to coax skeptics to get on board with STW programs. If they really were serious about changing college and university enrollment trends, they would bend their efforts to attacking the subsidies, tuition tax credits, Pell grants, discounted loans, and easy access to remedial college coursework that make college and university enrollment relatively easy and inexpensive.

As for academic teachers balking at STW programs, their response also raises an issue of policy incoherence. K–12 teachers are frequently subject to criticism for the low levels of academic learning attained by many American students. Teachers are admonished by community members to do better, and state policies—for example, Wisconsin's state standards and assessment policy—are developed to hold them accountable for improvement. But teachers also work in an environment shaped by previous traditions of reform, including the one that unfolded after World War I, when schools influenced by Progressive doctrines turned increasingly toward expanded programs emphasizing practical and vocational courses. The assumption was that by expanding offerings in this way, educators could secure commitment from an increasingly large, diverse student population and, at the same time, serve workforce needs in the industrial economy. It was a vision that combined pessimism about most students' academic abilities with high optimism about the schools' capacity to engineer reform on a large scale (Powell et al., 1985). In its emphasis on themes and topics rather than disciplinary learning, and on activities and projects rather than verbal and quantitative analysis, it channeled efforts to improve teaching into a path marked by relaxed academic standards, thus creating a climate that discouraged serious academic work (Powell et al.).

Academic teachers now live with this legacy, and it gives them reason to be skeptical about new incarnations of it. Many Wisconsin teachers saw a new incarnation of it in STW programs (see Mason & Thorn, 1997), especially because the STW initiative was not linked to Wisconsin's standards program. Given the standards program and other policies focused on their responsibility to foster academic achievement in the disciplines, it is hardly surprising that these teachers found the STW campaign to be ill-advised and intrusive.

These outcomes were not inevitable. Few parents or teachers would have balked had Wisconsin initiated a more-focused, less-grandiose STW initiative. Most would have viewed it as a good thing if the state had affirmed, as one goal among others, the public's interest in helping young people get ready to earn a living. For some, this would have meant qualifying for admission to college and university programs. For some, it would have meant moving directly from high school to postsecondary technical training. For some, it would have meant spending time during their high-school years doing worthwhile work and getting paid for it. All three courses of action could have been affirmed and targeted for ongoing improvement without the pretense of a "transformation" in which institutional authority would be brought to bear in a new manner aimed at shaping parents' and students' choices by reference to bureaucratic goals.

REFERENCES

Bishop, J. H. (1989). Why the apathy in American high schools? *Educational Researcher, 18,* 6–10.

Bishop, J. H. (1998). The effect of curriculum-based external exam systems on student achievement. *Journal of Economic Education, 29,* 171–182.

Borsuk, A. J. (2000, Aug. 30). AP exams, classes gain momentum across state. *Milwaukee Journal Sentinel,* pp. A1, A7.

Boyer, E. L. (1983). *High school: A report on secondary education in America.* New York: Harper & Row.

Brown, J. S., Collins, A., & Duguid, P. (1989). Situated cognition and the culture of learning. *Educational Researcher, 18,* 32–41.

Bruner, J. S. (1960). *The process of education.* New York: Vintage.

Commission on Schools for the 21st Century. (1990). *A new design for education in Wisconsin.* Madison, WI: Department of Administration.

Goodlad, J. (1983). *A place called school.* New York: McGraw-Hill.

Governor's Work-Based Learning Board. (2000). *Youth apprenticeship June 2000 program profile.* Madison, WI: Author.

Gray, K. C., & Herr, E. L. (1995). *Other ways to win: Creating alternatives for high school graduates.* Thousand Oaks, CA: Corwin.

Heidenreich, W. (1999). *Follow-up survey of 1997 Youth Apprenticeship graduates.* Madison, WI: Department of Workforce Development.

Hershey, A. M., Silverberg, M. K., Haimson, J., Hudis, P., & Jackson, R. (1999). *Expanding options for students: Report to Congress on the National Evaluation of School-to-Work Implementation.* Princeton, NJ: Mathematica Policy Research, Inc.

Hofstadter, R. (1963). *Anti-intellectualism in American life.* New York: Knopf.

Krug, E. A. (1969). *The shaping of the American high school, 1880–1920.* Madison, WI: University of Wisconsin Press.

Mason, S. A., & Thorn, C. A. (1997). *Wisconsin school-to-work implementation: A study of enacted practices, 1996–1997.* Madison, WI: Center on Education and Work.

Milwaukee Public Schools. (1997). *School to work and your child.* Milwaukee, WI: Author.

National School-to-Work Learning & Information Center. (2000). *Wisconsin school-to-work opportunities—1999 profile.* Retrieved from http://www.stw.ed.gov/states/profiles/WI.htm

Olson, L. (1997). *The school-to-work revolution.* Reading, MA: Addison-Wesley.

Phelps, L. A., & Fulton, D. V. (1997). *Follow-up survey of 1996 youth apprenticeship graduates.* Madison, WI: Department of Workforce Development.

Phelps, L. A., & Jin, M. (1997). *1997 Wisconsin youth apprenticeship employer survey.* Madison, WI: Department of Workforce Development.

Phelps, L. A., Scribner, J., Wakelyn, D., & Weis, C. (1996). *Youth apprenticeships in Wisconsin: A stakeholder assessment.* Madison, WI: Department of Workforce Development.

Powell, A.G., Farrar, E., & Cohen, D. K. (1985). *The shopping mall high school: Winners and losers in the educational marketplace.* Boston: Houghton Mifflin.

Resnick, L. B. (1987, December). Learning in school and out. *Educational Researcher, 16,* 13–20.

Schug, M. C., & Western, R. D. (1999). *School to work in Wisconsin: Inflated claims, meager results.* Thiensville, WI: Wisconsin Policy Research Institute.

Schug, M. C., & Western, R. D. (2000). *Standards-based education reform in Wisconsin: What it will take to make it work.* Thiensville, WI: Wisconsin Policy Research Institute.

Sizer, T. (1984). *Horace's compromise: The dilemma of the American high school.* Boston: Houghton Mifflin.

Skills for the Future. (2001a). *School to work overview: Transforming Wisconsin's educational system.* Retrieved from http://www.dwd.state.wi.us/gwblb/stw/about1

Skills for the Future. (2001b). *School to work overview: Why is this fundamental change in education needed?* Retrieved from http://www.dwd.state.wi.us/gwblb/stw/about2

White, S. B. (2000, August). *The roaring nineties: Wisconsin's regional employment growth.* Thiensville, WI: Wisconsin Policy Research Institute.

Williams, J. (1998, June 16). School-to-work reforms committee disbands. *Milwaukee Journal Sentinel,* p. 7B.

Wilson, C. L., Padilla, C., Powell, J., Faltz, C., Robertson, S. R., Hawkins, E., et al. (1997). *Evaluation of school to work in Milwaukee: Phase 3 final report.* Menlo Park, CA: SRI International.

Wilson, C. L., Powell, J., Kelly, F., Faltz, C., Shield, P.M., Marder, C., et al. (1995). *Evaluation of Milwaukee's school to work implementation plan: Phase 1 final report.* Menlo Park, CA: SRI International.

9

A Melding of International Perspectives

Robert Zemsky

Portraits of education in the United States are inevitably cast in the hues of local control and national pride. Every once in awhile, however, the conviction that America knows best becomes shaken. Usually, there is some sort of crisis, some gnawing suspicion that the American way is not working, that somewhere someone else has a solution to what ails our education system. On at least two fronts, the 1980s and 1990s were such a time of questioning.

First, research throughout the period showed that American schools were failing to teach the basics of science and math. In the Third International Mathematics and Science Study (TIMSS) of 1995, U.S. students in eighth grade performed just above the international average in science and actually below the average in mathematics. It was, however, the results for twelfth graders that stunned the education community. Here, American students finished substantially behind the students in those countries the United States sees as principal economic competitors (National Center for Education Statistics, 2001).

The second crisis that spurred American education to search beyond its own borders involved many of those same countries that outperformed America in TIMSS. From the mid-1980s through the early 1990s, there was growing concern that the U.S. economy, as well as its educational system, was not keeping pace. Just as the nation was falling further behind in the competition to produce students competent in math and science, so too was it lagging in its quest for economic security. At that time, the most popular explanation for the U.S. economy's proving to be less competitive was simply that the skills and attitudes of American workers no longer matched the changing nature of work in a global marketplace. That mismatch suggested there was something inherently wrong in general with the way Americans acquired job skills and in particular with the link between schooling and the workplace.

This perspective found voice in a national report with a title that said it all: *America's Choice: High Skills or Low Wages!* (Commission on the Skills of the American Workforce, 1990). *America's Choice* suggested that the United

States had much to learn from its economic rivals about how best to teach skills and build effective school-to-work (STW) transitions. Specifically, *America's Choice* argued that the United States could learn a great deal about the link between skills and work that had served as the foundation of Japan's system of on-the-job training and of the business–government partnerships that made apprenticeship systems, such as those of Germany and Switzerland, so successful.

A decade later, when the American economy was once again an engine of economic growth and when much of the rest of the world began to emulate American strategies for restructuring firms, it was hard to find many outside the STW movement who recalled just how loud a chord *America's Choice* had sounded in 1990. By 1992, its recommendations for recasting the STW transition were deeply embedded in Bill Clinton's first presidential campaign. School officials rushed to learn about German apprenticeships and Japanese on-the-job training schemes. The term *school-to-work* titled a new federal office and became an effective slogan. Money was appropriated. Model programs were launched. Study teams were dispatched abroad—all in pursuit of foreign remedies for what until then had been considered to be uniquely local or national problems (Zemsky, Shapiro, Iannozzi, Cappelli, & Bailey, 1998).

Had some of those early study teams been more observant, they might have noticed that many of the programs they admired were themselves coming under increased pressure and scrutiny in their own countries. A few scholars did begin to question the extent to which these models and ideas could be successfully imported from abroad. Peter Cappelli, for example, described the difficulties the British had gotten themselves into when trying to import Continental ideas about the training of first-time workers into their own education system. Cappelli's work made it clear that importation itself was a risky proposition and that the phenomena being reported across Europe were probably less successful than advertised (1993; see also Zemsky & Cappelli, 1998).

In the end, it probably did not matter. The economic boom that began in earnest after 1992 either settled or papered over most of the perceived problems. Few people—the young included—had trouble finding jobs. Whatever was amiss with American schools seemed to matter less in a stronger economy. Most STW programs completed their assigned tasks and prepared to close shop. Vocational education, particularly secondary vo-tech programs, continued a downward spiral. In the mid-1980s, roughly one-quarter of all high-school students were enrolled in formal programs of vocational education; by 1992, just 12% of high-school students were so enrolled. These dwindling numbers simply reinforced the long-standing stigma attached to vocational education in American schools. In 1997, among students in the lowest-ability quartile (as measured by standardized test scores), one in four was enrolled in a vocational program; among high-ability students, less than one in twenty was enrolled. Students in vo-tech were more likely to be from rural communities, from poorer families, and from African-American or Hispanic backgrounds than from white or Asian American households (National Center for Education Statistics, 1997, Table 135).

At the close of the century, almost all young people were learning about work on the job, principally through a progression of after-school, summer, and holiday positions. Although most of these jobs require few specific skills and offer almost no training, they do introduce young people to the basic discipline of the workplace—what it means to first look for and then hold a job. In general, young people in the United States remain on their own in deciding when and how to acquire job skills. And somehow most succeed. By the time most young people reach their thirties, they have engaged in a wide set of work experiences, which they successfully turn into productive careers (Zemsky & Cappelli, 1998).

While the STW crisis was largely passing in the United States—yet another example of the power of benign neglect—elsewhere, the issue was becoming increasingly salient. Less inclined to let time, the market, and inertia design their educational systems, school and governmental officials in countries that American STW experts had once thought worthy of emulation began to ask new questions of their own programs while looking abroad for proven models of success. One result of those inquiries was a multinational project on vocational-technical education (VTE) involving senior research teams from Japan, Singapore, Switzerland, and the United States. (For a full account of the study and its qualitative methodology as well as general descriptions of each country's education system, see Metzger et al., 2001).

The study was conducted under the auspices of the Six-Nation Educational Research Project sponsored by the University of Pennsylvania, and it was headed by Christoph Metzger of the University of Saint Gallen in Switzerland. Metzger's procedure was simple but effective. The full research team, which included one senior scholar from each of the four participating nations and a senior official from the Swiss federal government, conducted site visits in all four countries. In each nation, a single community was chosen as the research site: In the United States, the site was the Lehigh Valley in Pennsylvania; in Japan, the site was Hamamatsu, located just outside of Tokyo; in Switzerland, the site was the eastern university city of Saint Gallen; and in Singapore, the site was the city-state itself. By design, the study focused in general on highly developed economies and in particular on localities within those economies with substantial investments in manufacturing. The selection of the four countries was a happenstance that, in the end, proved to be remarkably fortunate. The balance of this chapter represents a distillation of the American team's notes and conclusions on all four countries, presented in a simplified but not (as the reader is about to discover) standard format. What follows, then, are impressions and observations—testimonies, really—that reflect an American perspective reshaped by the questions and observations of the rest of the research team.

THE LEHIGH VALLEY

The Lehigh Valley, an older industrial community north of Philadelphia in the state of Pennsylvania, has undergone substantial economic restructuring over the last decade. Emblematic of this trend has been the demise of Bethlehem Steel, whose massive capital investments have been either abandoned or demolished, and whose slick company headquarters has been converted into an extension of the local university and an incubator site for new business start-ups. Since 1970, each decennial census has marked a decline in both population and manufacturing jobs in the region as well as an increase in the ratio of older to younger people (Hendrick, 2001).

Underlying these numbers is a steady exodus of young people from the Lehigh Valley and a steady increase in the number of residents who pursue education beyond high school. Young people—and their parents to a surprising extent—have sought educational and economic opportunities elsewhere. As in most parts of the nation, the educational attainment of young people has been rising in the Lehigh Valley. High-school dropout rates have been reduced, and many school districts now report that approximately 70% of their high-school graduates proceed to postsecondary education rather than to full-time work.

Though this is an undoubtedly oversimplified characterization, VTE and the STW transition in the Lehigh Valley can be summarized as follows:

- As in most of the United States, VTE in the Lehigh Valley is being reshaped by the escalating social ambitions of its students and their families, leading to what one member of the research team called "rampant college mania."
- Vocational training itself is becoming less formal, more attuned to the needs of an economy increasingly dominated by service firms. Formal vocational training is seen less and less as a viable educational alternative. However, in response to dwindling demand for their programs, the Valley's network of vo-tech schools has exhibited remarkable flexibility in designing new offerings and rethinking how they teach their students.
- Vocational-technical education in the Lehigh Valley is confronting a growing stigma that is associated with skilled handwork, with the manufacturing enterprises that require such work, and with the schools and students whose curricula stress manufacturing and related vocational skills.
- Local manufacturing employers are becoming increasingly angry at the failure of local schools to produce a sufficient number of graduates who want to work in the jobs they have to offer and at the wages they want to pay in order to remain economically competitive.
- Vocational-technical education is not seen as having a substantial social role—as a means of either providing expanded educational access or knitting together companies and communities. At the same time, although local businesses have a need for young workers, they do not exhibit a strong sense of institutional responsibility for the success of the educational system. This finding was particularly apparent to the mem-

bers of the visiting team who were most knowledgeable about traditions of employer responsibility in Europe.

- The VTE system in the Lehigh Valley is characterized by both free choice and postponed training, particularly when compared with Switzerland and Singapore. Young people in the United States are given wide latitude regarding when and how they acquire job skills. Their first introduction to work probably occurs through a part-time job, where there is little—if any—training and even less of an occupational or career track. Frequently, specific job training does not occur until after graduation from high school. On the other hand, by the time most young people reach their thirties, they are able to emerge from a wide set of work experiences into a productive career.

The story of the Lehigh Valley exemplifies how technological advancements and global competition translate into a restructured local economy that seems increasingly at odds with an area's ambitions. It is a tale about the way young people, amidst this restructuring, make career decisions by determining what is socially valued or demeaned. The moral of that story reflects what happens when a culture places an inordinate emphasis on educational attainment in the form of a college degree, whether or not the local economy needs all or even most of those graduates, and whether or not the graduates in turn achieve the level of economic opportunity and security they had sought (Zemsky, 1998).

Two images from the team's site visits summarize the tensions surrounding these issues in the Lehigh Valley. The first is what the site team came to call the "vo-tech shuffle"—the morning departure from Emmaus High School of students headed for the Lehigh County Vocational Technical School. Wanting to communicate that the vocational track was as important as the general and college-preparatory tracks, the school district had mandated that vocational students take their general-education courses at their local high schools and their vocational courses at the county's vo-tech institution.

So, vo-tech students in the Emmaus High School District arrived at their home school building each morning, attended classes with students in the other two tracks, and then went their own way—out to the buses waiting to take them to the Lehigh County Vocational Technical School. This shuffle was repeated in the afternoon, with the vo-tech students who had spent the morning at the vo-tech center returning to take their general-education courses. The result? Twice a day, the vo-tech students paraded through the halls of Emmaus, making clear that they were different, going different places to seek different goals.

It was hardly a message that was lost on Emmaus's students, particularly those in the college-preparatory track, who stayed behind. "There go the techers," they would say, making clear that in their world, vo-tech students were those not good enough, not smart enough, not disciplined enough to take the college track. In fact, when asked to describe the typical techer, college-preparatory students resorted to a variety of worn clichés. The techers were like, you know, the cast of the movie *Grease.* They dressed funny, were funky, a little wild, and enviably free.

The second image derives from the team's site visit to the Lehigh County Vocational Technical School itself. Regardless of what the students were like when they boarded the bus, they were almost embarrassingly neat by the time the team met with them in their classes. Many wore uniforms, and they were invariably polite. The hallways were sparkling clean. The entire operation had the look and feel of a military camp—and, indeed, many of the school's instructors had spent time in the military. Students and staff were demonstrably proud of their school and the fact that most graduates found good jobs in the careers for which they were trained. At the same time, the school seemed empty. Despite better marketing and the involvement of the Lehigh Valley business community, enrollments in vo-tech education had not recaptured the ground lost in the 1980s. In the view of too many, both within and outside of the vo-tech environment, VTE continues to be seen as a dumping ground for poorly performing students, those with behavioral problems, and those not academically inclined.

The distance between these two images frames the dilemma facing the Lehigh Valley and, by extension, many formerly industrial communities in the United States that now see their futures more in terms of service and technologically based industries. In the Lehigh Valley, transitions from school to work may not necessarily be so much about transitions as about images of work and the brand of information young people receive and act upon when choosing when and how to invest in their own skills.

SINGAPORE

Singapore remains the very model of a planned economy ordered by market principles and driven by a population that has made competitiveness and a strong work ethic national hallmarks. Its education system is an intriguing blend of Asian sensitivities cast in British molds. Everyone goes to school, where the language of instruction is English, regardless of one's mother tongue. At each educational level, a rigorous testing procedure determines each student's educational pathway. This tracking reaches its apotheosis in the system's advanced secondary schools. The most advantaged track leads to one of the country's ten junior colleges, which are roughly equivalent to the final two years of the college-preparatory track in an elite U.S. high school. Admission to a junior college requires passing a British O-level exam (with the exam books themselves still graded in the United Kingdom). The higher a student scores on his or her O-levels, the greater the probability that he or she will be admitted to Singapore's most prestigious junior college. Almost all junior college graduates proceed to one of Singapore's two universities or to a college or university abroad.

A second path leads to one of the country's several polytechnics, which prepare their students for a host of professions and occupations requiring advanced schooling but not a university degree. Singapore also has developed a university track that runs through the polytechnics and ends at a university. For some students, particularly those good at math and science but not English, this path avoids the pitfalls associated with the O-levels.

Finally, a substantial number of students enroll in Singapore's Institute for Technical Education (ITE)—a multi-institutional system committed to training technical workers and, in the broad British meaning of the word, mechanics. With ITE remaining a third choice for a majority of Singapore's families, the technical training it offers is also seen as a means of acculturating as well as educating the increasing numbers of non-Singaporean workers that the country will continue to admit as it expands the size of its workforce.

No other contrasts in the VTE study were more striking than those between the Lehigh Valley and Singapore. The latter's story was about diversity, about the power of economic and social planning, and about the heady essence of economic competition. In Singapore, globalization is the engine of change—that which makes the island nation an importer rather than an exporter of talent and youth. Importantly, however, both Singapore and the Lehigh Valley share a growing college mania and increasingly attach a stigma to vocational education. The following summary of Singapore's educational system shows some of the key challenges facing those striving to link school and work in the country.

- The Singapore educational system is a traditionally configured enterprise that puts enormous pressure on students. Using the sorting and exam system largely adopted from the British, Singapore has made merit-based testing and tracking its hallmark. Students, schools, and whole segments of the educational system know exactly where they stand on the basis of their test scores. Early on, students understand both what is expected of them and the path they are likely to follow through the educational system and the world of work. The research team was struck by the number of times the students they interviewed said they had "disappointed" someone—themselves, their parents, their school—by not scoring higher on one entrance exam or another. The consequence, they knew, was a lower position in the educational and occupational hierarchy.

- One clear consequence of educational tracking based on standardized testing is substantially lowered expectations for students enrolled in Singapore's ITE. Here, the irony is that Singapore has developed one of the most sophisticated and strategically placed programs for vocational and technical education anywhere in the world. Its new facilities are world-class, and its teaching staff is eager and qualified. The principal motivation for Singapore to participate in the VTE study was its desire to learn how to better position technical education—to make it more important, more a pursuit of status and repute. Singapore did not want ITE to become a dumping ground for the unsuccessful or the recently arrived, although it also understood its social responsibility to reach out to both populations.

- Increasingly, Singapore's educational system has sought ways to offer students a second chance in order to reduce the stigma attached to the system's lower rungs. The Institute for Technical Education has made its upper-end programs a second route to enrollment in a polytechnic and then perhaps a university.
- Even within Singapore's VTE system, strong links do not exist between schooling and work. The Singaporean system has retained the older, established pattern of sending students first to school and then to work. The former experience is expected to provide the skills necessary to succeed in the latter. The socialization to work happens only after one has obtained his or her first full-time job. For those at the top of the system, those bound for a junior college and then a university, there is a curious disjunction between the world of school—in which succeeding is seen as serious work—and the world of employment. For these students, learning about work is postponed until after the completion of an advanced degree. What these students hear is that work does not matter when you are young.

Although the United States is likely to resolve its STW dilemmas by letting market forces shape the outcome, Singapore's commitment to planning and direction suggests that it is likely to seek an articulated solution—a policy that totals up the costs, defines the opportunities, and then prescribes a preferred pattern of action.

SWITZERLAND

Switzerland boasts one of the oldest, most respected apprenticeship systems in the world. For more than 700 years, a majority of young Swiss have entered the workforce through an apprenticeship. As in Germany, the Swiss system represents a formal partnership between industry councils and the states, with the employer picking up a substantial share of the cost in exchange for the labor of the student after he or she becomes productive in the last year of the apprenticeship. And some of the nation's most prestigious jobs—particularly those in the financial sector—have historically been filled by former apprentices who have worked their way up in the organization.

However, Switzerland now finds itself in an awkward position. Having elected not to join the European Union, it is nonetheless an integral part of the European economy, with an increasing number of its major enterprises becoming part of larger multinational corporations. At the same time, the country has become a net importer of workers, first from Turkey and more recently from the former Yugoslavia. What now openly concerns Swiss educators is the prospect that the apprenticeship system will be dominated increasingly by the children of immigrants.

A decade ago, U.S. commentators, analysts, legislators, and even successful presidential candidates celebrated the virtues of a European STW system that stressed societal responsibility, the purposeful linking of schools and employers, and the success of an historic apprenticeship system that guaranteed an educated and skilled labor force. The dominant models for such apprenticeships came from Germany and Switzerland. In the fall of 1998, however, the Swiss apprenticeship system was, if not under assault, at least subject to a renewed set of questions about its effectiveness and hence its future. What Switzerland seemed to be realizing was that it was not immune to the social and economic forces that were reshaping transitions from school to work across the industrialized world. An overview of the country's educational system shows both such vulnerabilities and enduring strengths.

- Within Switzerland, a rising tide of ambition has caused many to equate a university education with social status and economic mobility. What struck most members of the research team were the escalating ambitions of young Swiss and their parents—as well as their sense that good jobs demanded an advanced education.
- Increasingly, economic and educational opportunities are being linked with ethnic identification. This visitor, at least, was struck by how the influx of immigrants into Switzerland is helping to reshape definitions of educational quality and occupational status. Although reluctant to discuss the fact that some employers with highly sought-after apprenticeships are not likely to offer them to the children of recent immigrants, many of those responsible for the system did acknowledge that trouble might lie ahead.
- Switzerland is undergoing an economic restructuring that is redefining the nature of work. One of the more enduring memories of the week in Saint Gallen was a site visit to a major manufacturing firm with a well-articulated and richly supported apprenticeship program. After the formal tour and interviews were completed, the firm made it clear that the skills essential for its future success—one increasingly being shaped by the globalization of its market and the rapid emergence of new technologies—are not those being taught in its apprenticeship program. The firm's leadership knew that it was training workers who would have truly obsolete skills within a decade. This impression was reinforced by the team's visit to a major bank—traditionally the site of one of Switzerland's most prestigious apprenticeships. Even here, managers who themselves were once apprentices talked openly about the fact that they increasingly anticipated hiring university graduates with the financial and money-management skills that modern banking now demands.
- A shifting context is redefining the nature of apprenticeships. In a sense, Switzerland's apprenticeship system is being squeezed from both above and below. Big firms, particularly as they become part of multinational aggregations, are questioning the magnitude of resources they expect to devote to an apprenticeship system that their international partners may neither understand nor appreciate. At the same time, the country's small firms—the traditional backbone of the apprenticeship system—are becoming less able to provide the broad range of experiences that workers in the

future will require. Not surprisingly, the options discussed included both increased time in school and rotating apprenticeships.

In Switzerland, a final question is being asked: How are young Swiss who are preparing for universities likely to learn about work? In the United States, university-bound youth do so by working as teenagers. It is a messy, often unsatisfactory system that somehow gets the job done. Will Switzerland develop a similarly undifferentiated youth labor market? Will firms then turn to university-bound youth as part-time workers instead of offering apprenticeships? Will the introduction of a youth labor market that explicitly includes the country's best and brightest students further accelerate the patterns of ethnic differentiation already present in the Swiss VTE system?

These are tough questions. The good news is that they are being asked by a country with substantial educational assets, an extraordinary tradition of school and employer partnerships, and an economy that understands its dependence on developing a truly skilled workforce.

JAPAN

For most western economists, Japan remains an enigma. Its economy, once relied upon as the engine of Asian development, has languished. Attempts to spur consumer spending through tax and other incentives have largely succeeded in increasing the savings rate without spurring growth. Moreover, the country's banking and insurance industries are deeply troubled—leaving the capacity of Japanese firms to restructure themselves openly questioned both within and outside Japan.

The educational system is in particular turmoil, largely as a result of a demographic downshift that has halved the number of students graduating from high school. The most obvious result is a lessening of demand and hence of competition for places in universities. That shift in turn has raised questions throughout the Japanese educational system. What happens to an educational system based on a culture of competition when decreased demand reduces that competition? If the number of firms promising lifelong employment continues to decline, will Japan develop a youth labor market characterized by job switching, as in the United States? And will the final consequence be a shift from firm-financed on-the-job training to school-supplied training?

The week of intensive interviews in Hamamatsu reinforced those impressions and revealed important new developments.

- There was a noticeable sense that Japanese high-school students are adopting satisfying rather than maximizing strategies. The students and young workers interviewed seemed less tense about the competition for university admission. This impression is to be expected because the declining number of high-school graduates coupled with an excess supply of university and college places meant, again, that competition for entry had reduced significantly. Less expected was the impression that even the very best students interviewed were willing to settle for less-demanding choices.

- For younger workers, the recasting of employment expectations is well under way. Many of the young workers interviewed talked openly and easily about the prospect of not working for the same employer all of their lives. When pushed, the more ambitious of these younger workers stated they were both ready and willing to go in search of better positions with other firms as a way of accelerating their careers.
- The erosion of Japan's once-powerful system of technical education is now complete. Although the vocationally oriented schools that the research team visited remain strong, they were not as interesting as in the past, not as much a viable alternative to the academic-track high schools. Their current strengths lie in their promotion of a sense of community, in their ability to field competitive sports teams, and in their myriad after-school programs that stretch well into the evening hours. Although these institutions have had a long-standing tradition within Japanese secondary schools, it is their cocurricular programs, more than their academic and vocational ones, which give definition to vocationally oriented schools.
- There is an emphasis on the collecting of credentials and certificates on the part of young people. The sense is that one's skills are reflected in the number of special certificates, awards, and other credentials one has to display. It is a radical form of what I have come to call "merit-badge" education (Knight Higher Education Collaborative, 2000), where skills are seen as discrete units whose mastery can be best be demonstrated by passing the appropriate standardized test.
- The link between employment skills and a university education remains uncertain. Most of the students and young workers the research team met understood that their performance in high school and subsequently in university had a powerful impact on the kinds of jobs and careers open to them in the future. Beyond scientific and technical knowledge, however, it was hard to discern what young people thought they would learn at university to succeed at work.

TOWARD A GENERAL PERSPECTIVE

Too often, international studies fail to provide specific advice regarding how to fix what does not work simply because the between-country differences—observed amidst a wealth of comparative data—overwhelm the analyst's ability to distinguish the wheat from the chaff. The VTE study undertaken in Switzerland, Singapore, Japan, and the United States is proving to be an exception to that rule, largely because the research team's approach yielded important commonalities across all four countries. Although none of the specific sites can be said to fully represent the complete range of VTE and STW settings in their respective countries, collectively their experiences suggest a number of common concerns and trends that most policymakers in developed countries are likely to face.

First, what most unites STW and VTE experiences in these four countries can be simply stated: College mania is everywhere. Though coined in the 1970s (Trow, 1974/1994), the term *massification* has increasingly become appropriate to describe the drive for the pursuit of higher education across Europe and those parts of Asia and Latin America with expanding economies and established postsecondary systems. What often accompanies increasing participation rates for postsecondary education are corresponding declines in VTE at the secondary level, less-robust apprenticeship systems, a growing sense that VTE is more suited for the children of foreign workers making their way in a new land, and a potentially disastrous combination of polarized social attitudes and economic returns that widen the gap separating those with and those without a postsecondary education.

In each of the countries examined in this study, college mania is overtaking traditional means of providing secondary-school training that leads to skilled work. In the United States, vocational enrollments in high school have been halved, while an interesting STW movement has stalled. In Switzerland, fundamental doubts are being raised about the efficacy of an apprenticeship system whose upper-level placements were once on a par with those of the country's universities. In Singapore, the competition to pursue university status dominates the educational landscape, while the highly successful ITE worries about whom it is designed to serve. In Japan, a prolonged "baby bust" has substantially altered the competition and preparation for university on the one hand, and has made nonuniversity technical training less viable on the other.

A second commonality is the more ready mixing of school and work experiences beyond the traditional confines of formal apprenticeships. In the United States, the pattern of working while in school is well-established. To non-American observers, it is one of the key traits of the U.S. labor market. As the shift from traditional forms of vocational to postsecondary education gains momentum, observers in Switzerland, Singapore, and Japan worry about how the young people in their countries will learn about work. The answer, it turns out, is that the problem is likely to tend to itself because more and more young people are becoming contingent workers while still in school—even where applicable school rules forbid students from seeking part-time and after-school jobs.

A third common element is a growing realization that jobs are no longer fixed. Increasingly, workers will change occupations as well as jobs over the course of their lifetimes. The occupational swirl that is familiar to most Americans is becoming known to workers everywhere. In part, the globalization of the economy—the birth, death, and rebirth of multinational firms and franchises—is responsible. Yet so is technology, which, after nearly two decades of promises, is now delivering increases in productivity and changing definitions of work.

Finally, what all four national settings of this study give us is a sense that those responsible for education in general and secondary schooling in particular are playing catch-up. In no country did educators or public officials responsible for secondary education brim with confidence. No one was sure that he or she had an answer, let alone that the right questions were being asked. What they wanted was help—in deciding what students should learn, in linking students with work, in explaining to students and their parents that college was not for everyone.

The recasting of education's role in the building and sustaining of robust economies begins, perhaps, with this understanding of just how peripheral the educational professional is becoming. Those directly responsible for the transition from school to work in schools and communities are now learning the need to exhibit less hubris—less attachment to specific models, solutions, and systems—and to initiate more engaged conversations among those who depend on schools to produce employable workers. Each setting visited in the VTE study showed signs that such conversations were beginning: a greater willingness to listen, to avoid the imperative as a form of motivation, and to understand and even accept an important fact. Namely, older, largely linear ways of introducing the young to the world of work are being overwhelmed by a melding that first combines school with work and later blends work, training, and education in dizzying combination.

REFERENCES

Cappelli, P. (1993). *British lessons for school-to-work transition policy in the U.S.* Philadelphia, PA: National Center for the Educational Quality of the Workforce.

Commission on the Skills of the American Workforce. (1990). *America's choice: High skills or low wages!* Rochester, NY: National Center on Education and the Economy.

Hendrick, J. A. (2001). *A community responds to economic change: A case study of the Lehigh Valley.* Unpublished doctoral dissertation, University of Pennsylvania, Philadelphia, PA.

Knight Higher Education Collaborative. (2000, July). The mission and the medium. *Policy Perspectives, 9 (3).*

Metzger, C., Fujita, H., Law, S.-S., Zemsky, R., Berset, J.-E., & Iannozzi, M. (2001). *Different paths, similar pursuits: The economic and personal potential of vocational training and education in an international context.* Saint Gallen, Switzerland: University of Saint Gallen, Institute for the Teaching of Economics.

National Center for Education Statistics. (1997). *Digest of education statistics, 1997.* Washington, DC: U.S. Department of Education.

National Center for Education Statistics. (2001, July). *TIMSS 1995: More about the project.* Retrieved from http://nces.ed.gov/timss/timss95/more.asp#how

Trow, M. (1994). Problems in the transition from elite to mass higher education. In Organisation for Economic Co-Operation and Development (Ed.), *Policy for higher education* (pp. 51–101). Paris: Organisation for Economic Co-Operation and Development. (Original work published 1974.)

Zemsky, R. (1998). Labor, markets, and educational restructuring. *The Annals of the American Academy of Political and Social Science, 559,* 77–90.

Zemsky, R., & Cappelli, P. (Eds.). (1998). The changing educational quality of the workforce. *The Annals of the American Academy of Political and Social Science, 559.*

Zemsky, R., Shapiro, D., Iannozzi, M., Cappelli, P., & Bailey, T. (1998). *The transition from initial education to working life in the United States of America.* Stanford, CA: Stanford University, The National Center for Postsecondary Improvement.

Part IV

Issues, Obstacles, and Opportunities in School-to-Work Programs

10

Developing Work-Based Learning Pedagogies

David Thornton Moore
Katherine L. Hughes

Participation in work-based learning by students and employers nationwide is significant. According to the national evaluation of school-to-work (STW) implementation, more than a quarter of 1998 high-school seniors surveyed in eight states reported having a school-sponsored paid or unpaid work position (Hershey, Silverberg, Haimson, Hudis, & Jackson, 1999). A 1997 national survey found that 39% of private, for-profit business establishments with more than twenty employees were participating in some form of work-based learning, with 20% participating specifically in internships (Cappelli, Shapiro, & Shumanis, 1998). Researchers have attempted to document and measure the benefits of participation in work-based learning to students and to employers (see Stasz & Kaganoff, 1997; Bailey, Hughes, & Barr, 2000). Less attention has been paid, however, to the *processes* of teaching and learning in work-based learning.

This chapter will address the essential issue implied in our title: How can we develop effective teaching methods for work-based learning programs? We will suggest some principles and strategies by which school-based educators can enlarge and deepen their students' work-related learning. First, however, we propose to consider two related questions that stand prior to that more obvious problem, questions any serious educator has to grapple with before turning to specific tactics. The first problem is this: What *is* pedagogy in the context of work-based learning? Second, we should ask this: What is pedagogy *for* in work-based learning? What do we want it to accomplish? Any practical strategy for work-based learning must be founded on answers to those questions. Therefore, we will first identify what educators might think about when they consider pedagogical problems and approaches; then we will propose some alternative ways of defining the basic purposes of pedagogy.

A BROADER DEFINITION OF PEDAGOGY

In the world of schools, we all know roughly what we mean by the term *pedagogy*: a set of strategies and tactics for teaching students, and perhaps, if we wish to get philosophical, some underlying principles about how people learn and what is worth teaching. The basic assumption is that a teacher intends to produce certain kinds of learning through certain kinds of activities: learning about the Civil War through lectures and assigned readings, or about critical readings of *Moby-Dick* through class discussions. But students in work-based learning programs learn not only in the classroom but also in the workplace. Unless teachers are willing to abdicate any responsibility for the educational process in the placement site, we need to define pedagogy in a way that applies to both contexts.

Pedagogy, therefore, encompasses any features of a learner's social experience that shape the way she engages in the creation or use of new kinds of knowledge. Pedagogy is not merely teaching techniques and plans (the lectures, the assignments, the discussions). A broader definition of pedagogy can describe things like how (in what order, by what means, through what interactions with what people in what situations) newcomers encounter and engage various kinds of knowledge. How do participants define and structure knowledge: in rigid categories protected by the powerful or in shifting configurations open to challenge and dispute? Where is knowledge stored: in heads, in computer programs, in books, in stories, or in symbols? Can anyone access the knowledge or is access restricted? How are newcomers introduced to the knowledge: through explicit instruction, through casual observation, or through productive activity? Is their emerging knowledge tested, accredited, and monitored, or can they learn (and think) anything they want without sanctions? The benefit of this conception of pedagogy is that it can help us understand activities in classrooms *and* in workplaces. It gives work-based learning educators a foundation for thinking about two crucial sets of questions: How can I decide where to place a student and determine what she is likely to be able to learn through her experience there? And how can I create activities in the classroom that will enlarge and deepen her experience-based learning, connecting it to her learning back at school?

Pedagogy can be both incidental and intentional. In work-based learning programs, educators should understand how the ongoing practices of the work group in the internship site, organized around productivity needs, shape the way the student-intern encounters and engages different kinds of knowledge. In this form of pedagogy, learning is essentially a byproduct of the work activity, incidental to the core goal of producing something; people make decisions about their activities and resources not specifically so that someone learns something, but so that the work gets done. Those practices look very different across various work organizations. Sometimes, the newcomer is given explicit training in order to take on a substantial task. Sometimes, she is left to her own devices, expected to pick up knowledge as she helps out around the workplace. Other times, she may be consigned to a marginal position performing menial labor and never actually acquire any of the interesting or complex knowledge being used. Part of the educational challenge for work-based learning coordinators is to recognize these naturally occurring features of potential placement sites, and to avoid those organizations where students are likely to be isolated from meaningful knowledge use. (See our previous paper for a framework through which an educator might analyze the situated pedagogy of a particular work context in order to give student-interns better opportunities for learning; Hughes & Moore, 1999.)

There is also the intentional, school-based side of work-based learning pedagogy: the things teachers, counselors, program coordinators, and peers do to enlarge the intern's learning back in the classroom. As we will argue, the school-based pedagogy may well—indeed, should—go beyond the naturally occurring work-based pedagogy in raising questions, generating insights, and building skills. In that sense, the community of practice (Wenger, 1998) in which the intern participates is not simply the workplace, but also the community of learners in the school.

This broader conception of what pedagogy is suggests that what shapes the learning process is not simply the intentional, school-based, teacher-driven activities designed to bring about learning; it is also the texture of work activities and relations in the internship site, as well as the unintended lessons (what used to be called the hidden curriculum) of the school. Wherever and however the student encounters and engages new forms of knowledge use, pedagogy is there. Our purpose in this chapter is to help educators make purposeful and informed decisions about that pedagogy, to develop teaching strategies in both domains, rather than simply let nature—and experience—take their course. That goal is important because, as we have shown elsewhere (see Moore, 1999), pedagogy that happens only incidentally does not always accomplish the claims that work-based learning advocates make for it.

THE PURPOSES OF WORK-BASED LEARNING PEDAGOGY: TWO MODELS

Before outlining a few central principles and features of a well-formed pedagogy for work-based learning, we first wish to make an argument about the purposes of pedagogy for work-based learning. Work-based learning instructors and program designers have a fundamental choice to make about their pedagogical approaches and educational outcomes that has political implications. The teaching method affects not only what the student learns, but also how she becomes a worker, a citizen, a family member—a person.

We see work-based learning practitioners drawing on two alternative models of pedagogy, the first far more often than the second. The two models are surely oversimplified for the purpose of analysis. Moreover, they are not mutually exclusive; one can use both, to some extent. However, educators should be aware of the models and should make an intentional choice, rather than falling by default into one of them. Contrasting them as ideal types draws attention to important elements of the decisions teachers need to make.

We call the first model of work-based learning pedagogy *functionalist*, partly because it has some theoretical connections to the tradition of structural functionalism in sociology, and partly because it rests on the assumption that the basic aim of work-based learning is to make students capable of performing certain functions in the existing economy (see Lave, 1988). The functionalist takes the structure of the workplace—the forms of knowledge, the requisite skills, the social relations of power and action—as given and stable. The teaching premise is that we can identify what students need to know and be able to do in order to function effectively in the workplace, and that we can prepare them for an existing work system. In part, that means teaching them core functional skills, such as the ones described in the literature of the Secretary's Commission on Acquiring Necessary Skills (SCANS, 1991); and in part it means socializing them into habits and values such as punctuality, accountability, and deference to authority. This approach has antecedents in much of the traditional literature on vocational and cooperative education, and in much of the more current discourse on work-based learning (see Urquiola et al., 1997).[1]

The alternative to the functionalist model is the *critical* approach. According to this perspective, one cannot regard work-based learning as learning about work "in general" because work cannot be understood apart from its social context. As Simon, Dippo, and Schenke (1991) state, "all work is organized within historical and contemporary forms and relations of power" (p. 7). Critical pedagogy sees the structures of the workplace as socially constructed rather than given, as contested and potentially (but not necessarily) flawed, and as subject to interrogation and alteration rather than to mere acquiescence. Thus, issues such as workplace hierarchies and employer and employee responsibilities to each other are to be analyzed and debated within their historical, political, and social contexts.

From this perspective, the purpose of work-based learning is not simply to train the neophyte worker, but also to create the conditions and resources through which youth can understand and critique the existing work system and imagine alternatives, penetrate and possibly change the distribution of power and knowledge, and become active participants in the construction of their organizations and cultures. In a program based in the critical perspective, the student certainly develops functional skills and knowledge, but she also steps back from the taken-for-granted assumptions about work and organizations and becomes a constructive participant in work-related activities—and an active learner. This approach, of course, has many precedents: Dewey (1938), Freire (1974), Foucault (1980), Apple (1982), Habermas (1984), Giroux and McLaren (1989); it has been most extensively described by Simon et al. (1991).

In practice, these two models of pedagogy look different in several ways. First, the preparation students get for the field experience varies. In the functionalist approach, the student is essentially told what she will need to know in order to succeed at the worksite, and she is trained in that direction. In the critical approach, the student learns to make sense of her activities in a constructive sense, to question and probe, and to wonder why things are as they are and not some other way. In both models, educators should help the student learn to be an apt observer of the workplace (for example, by using ethnographic methods), but the point of close observation in each is different. In the functionalist approach, the student's observations are meant to help him learn to follow the norms of the workplace. If all the men have short hair and wear ties, the male student should understand to do the same. In the critical approach, close observation of the workplace is data gathering for later discussions in the classroom about such topics as why all the jobs in a hotel's housekeeping department are sex-segregated.

Second, the school-based processing of the ongoing experience takes a different tack. The functionalist teacher encourages the student to fit in, to figure out what she is supposed to know and do. The essential question is: How am I doing in relation to the supervisor's expectations? And those expectations are taken as given. The critical teacher helps the student take charge of her experience, interpret it, and construct her own understanding rather than adopt someone else's. A core question is: What is really going on here, and why? The context and the experience are problematized, and history and social relations are examined. Students in the different approaches come to see themselves differently as workers and as learners, with different senses of agency and possibility.

Finally, the forms of evaluation differ between the approaches. In the functionalist approach, the student is successful if she can demonstrate certain skills, knowledge, and attitudes on standardized measures; and if she is deemed "job ready." From the critical perspective, success is reflected in the complexity and subtlety of the student's understanding of the work system and in her developing identity as a member of the community of practice (Lave & Wenger, 1991; Wenger, 1998).

Again, these two models of work-based learning pedagogy are not mutually exclusive, because a student in a critical program should certainly build useful skills. But it is important for educators to be aware of the dimensions of choice in this domain because the dominant dynamic leans toward the functionalist school, as we found in observations of twenty-five student-interns in five different work-based learning programs.

CRITICAL PEDAGOGY FOR WORK-BASED LEARNING: PRINCIPLES AND EXAMPLES

We believe that there are several strategic principles that underlie a critical pedagogy for work-based learning. The first is that it is important for program coordinators to conduct a learning opportunities analysis of potential placement sites on the basis of the broadened conception of pedagogy that we proposed earlier. In a number of programs, placements seem to be based on the assumption that a knowledge-rich organization will inevitably make for a rich learning environment. But as we have described in other publications (Bailey, Hughes, & Moore, in press; Moore, 1999), the issue is not how much knowledge exists in the organization, but what knowledge use the intern can participate in. A situation may involve many highly skilled people performing highly complex tasks that a student cannot engage meaningfully, so the educational potential may be lost.

Therefore, even before designing the classroom strategies, the program coordinator has to think about how the student's experience in a proposed site will unfold. Will she be able to take part in activities where knowledge is displayed openly, or will she be relegated to a literal or figurative back room and isolated from encounters with practical intelligence? Will she be asked to perform work that requires the use of some kind of challenging information and skill, or will the work be essentially menial and easy to master? Will supervisors and mentors have the time and the inclination to discuss complex issues and processes with her, or will she be left to her own devices or to conversations with her equally isolated peers? These are questions about the naturally occurring pedagogy of the workplace, and they are central to the program coordinator's judgment about the learning potential in the placement site.

Some examples from our study will illustrate the importance of this principle. One student subject worked in the general counsel's office of a large consulting firm. The broad work of the firm was complex: helping other corporations redesign management and work systems in order to improve efficiency and productivity. There were program planners, designers, writers, and organizational development consultants using a huge array of interesting knowledge and skill. Within the general counsel's office, lawyers and paralegals dealt with arcane issues of corporate law, contracts, intellectual property, and so on. But the student was essentially a file clerk, working in a back office, storing and retrieving records. She barely had occasion to read any of the materials, much less witness any of the interactions (such as meetings with clients, court hearings, and strategy sessions) in which the real knowledge in the place was displayed and used. This company was so segmented, so specialized in its division of labor, that the student-intern had virtually no access to its core functions. It was not much of a learning environment, and a program coordinator working from our suggested pedagogical principles might not have chosen to place the student here.

On the other hand, a small veterinary clinic in rural New England turned out to be a stronger choice. Even though the student typically performed tasks that were simple to master and peripheral to the group's function (he fed animals, cleaned up after procedures, and answered phones), at least he had a chance to interact with and observe the veterinarians and their assistants in core events. He watched operations, discussed medical conditions, and even performed lab tests. He felt like part of the community of practice and developed an identity connected to it. This situation afforded the student the kinds of engagement with local knowledge that made it a reasonably sound educational experience. The natural pedagogy in the clinic was adequate for the purposes of the program and the student.

The second principle of pedagogy for work-based learning is that reflection is an indispensable component of the teaching and learning process. The work experience alone is not sufficient to achieve the purposes of well-formed work-based learning. In the absence of a concerted effort to stand back and ask questions about the work and the organization, the student will invariably slip into the native mentality of the worker, the unexamined and taken-for-granted view of the meaning of the experience. Workers, as full participants in the organizational culture, tend to share (and enforce) unspoken assumptions about activities, roles, and values. In order to problematize those assumptions, to foster a critical perspective in the interns, and thus to maximize learning, the instructor must engage them in a process of systematic and extensive reflection.

This argument is supported philosophically by the pragmatist tradition rooted in James (1915/1983) and Dewey (1938), and theoretically in the constructivist psychology of Vygotsky (1978), Piaget (1967), and Bruner (1975); and in the interactionist sociology of Mead (1934) and Blumer (1969). All of these schools of thought have insisted that the learner actively participate in constructing knowledge. The literature on teacher education also emphasizes reflection for teacher-interns (Hatton & Smith, 1995). Moreover, the principle of reflection has been supported empirically by Schön (1990); Boud, Cohen, and Walker (1993); and especially by Eyler and Giles (1999), whose studies of college-level service learning demonstrated convincingly that effects on academic and personal growth were most evident in programs that engaged students in reflection.

The peculiar position of the intern creates a superb opportunity for reflection because she simultaneously occupies two different roles: worker and student. In the former, she is supposed to be competent, able to perform functional tasks; in the latter, she is assumed to need to learn something. The dialectical tension between these two roles generates a powerful dynamic toward trying to make sense of the work, but not simply in the way a new worker does. In a way that the workplace cannot, the school-based program provides a safe haven for asking profound and probing questions and challenging the taken-for-granted nature of the work world. Although some find that effective reflection can occur verbally or nonverbally, alone or through a dyad or within a group (Herbert, 1995), we agree with researchers who believe that reflection is best facilitated through verbal interaction with others (Hatton & Smith, 1995). High-school students in particular need adult guidance. Yet the important point is that without this reflective component, work-based learning becomes more like on-the-job training: useful but hardly transformative. "The critical thing is that experience alone is not necessarily educative—it must be turned into learning by thought" (Herbert, 1995, p. 27).

The case of one intern illustrates the importance of reflection especially well. José, an urban high-school student in a travel and tourism career-academy program, interned during the summer between his junior and senior year in the housekeeping office of a large hotel. He was assigned to work as an assistant to the housekeeping manager, who was responsible for the work of room attendants, housemen, and building engineers. As we discussed in detail in a previous paper (Hughes & Moore, 1999), although many of José's tasks appeared on the surface to be mundane, his position was actually at the hub of a complex system, giving him exposure to a significant array of knowledge about the structure of operations in a large organization. Yet his experience is also a classic case of a functionalist approach to an internship that could have yielded much deeper learning.

Because of the position and tasks he was given, José developed a management perspective on the work and the organization. At least twice during his internship, José was assigned to inspect the hallways of the hotel to make note of stains, broken ice machines, and other problems. He was to report these conditions to the manager, who would then chastise the staff for negligence. On occasion, José was also told by the manager to go to certain floors of the hotel to check up on specific workers. Through these assignments, he came to believe that the workers tended to "slack off" and "whine a lot."

Despite the fact that the manager was using José to help him oversee the other employees, José was still a teenage high-school student-intern. He understood that he was "just a little kid, getting a high position." He perceived, probably correctly, that he was not well-liked by the housekeeping staff. This created a personal conflict for José that was never linked to broader political or sociological themes. When asked in a postinternship interview about whether he usually agreed with the management side of things, he responded in a conflicted way, demonstrating that he was trying to work out these issues on his own:

> Actually I pretty much always did . . . I don't know. I just felt like management material from the beginning. I don't know, just watching the housemen, I am realizing that they . . . they really don't have much to complain about. Their jobs are tough, though. A lot of heavy lifting and stuff. I remember a few times, the manager was talking to the housemen, and they were like wishing that they could trade jobs the whole time.
>
> "Yeah, I'll take your job any day," Mr. ___ was telling them. They were saying, "No, you have a cushy job, just sit in the office the whole time telling us what to do." But I worked with the housemen before. They have a very tough job, but it's all hard labor. But then, management's job, it's all mental.
>
> [Interviewer:] So they both think they have a harder job?
>
> They have harder jobs. They have hard jobs, but different aspects. . . . They're hard jobs in different ways. That's why each side doesn't realize that.

A teacher committed to critical pedagogy might have helped José unpack his thoughts about what it meant to be "management material," about the status hierarchy implied in the term, and about his ambivalence regarding his relations with the working-class housemen in the hotel. She might have encouraged him to examine the power relations in the organization as well as the practical and social meanings of concepts such as "hard work." But José had no such opportunity in his summer experience.

Instead, the work-based learning pedagogy for his program consisted of José's having to write journal entries describing each day's activities and to compose two short papers, one on his satisfaction with the experience and one on his supervisor's career history. There was no school-based internship class or seminar. The journal requirement was particularly mechanical and likely for the purpose of helping school personnel oversee the internship without actually having to visit the worksite. In fact, the journal could be more accurately characterized as a log that kept account of José's daily tasks than as a means of reacting to and reflecting on the experience (Simon et al., 1991). José's entries consisted of short lines such as these:

> I spent the day at the [hotel] in the office. It was really busy. I was given some paper work to do along with answering phones, which never stopped ringing.

José's program was essentially functionalist. He did learn many things about working in a hotel. He could schedule maintenance, respond to customer complaints, and take inventory; his phone skills improved, he learned a bit of management strategy, and he mastered the behavioral demands of a person in his role. These are no small achievements. Yet with a little more adult intervention, he could have learned more deeply from the display of power relations, the division of labor by gender and class, and the union and immigration issues that unfolded in front of him each day on the job. He did not have the opportunity to understand and critique this work system with teachers or other students in a structured way, even though it was clear from our interviews with him that some of these issues troubled him on an inchoate and inarticulate level. This lack of attention to facilitated reflection and lack of connection of José's experiences to topics likely covered in his social studies classes lead to our next points.

Many of the programs that we studied walked the student-interns through the functionalist form of preparation and reflection, examining the strategies and tactics they needed in order to succeed in the organization: being punctual, following directions carefully, looking professional. But almost none of them engaged in what we are describing as critical reflection. Imagine some of the possibilities. For example, a community college student placed in the accounting office of a large advertising firm engaged in a great deal of technical work related to cash flow, expense accounts and payments to vendors; that is, she clearly learned something about the application of accounting methods. Would it not have been interesting, however, for her to have been able to investigate some larger questions about the social functions of advertising, about consumer culture, and about the firm's conception of types of people in terms of market segments? Those issues might seem extraneous to an accountant-in-training, but thinking about them would certainly make her a more reflective professional (Schön, 1990). The questions could also focus on matters closer to the accountant's purview. What priorities and values are reflected in the firm's budget, in where it chooses to spend and save money? What ethical principles apply to the use of expense accounts? These and other considerations would deepen the student's understanding of the meaning of her chosen profession.

A third principle of well-formed pedagogy for work-based learning is that connections to academic knowledge are extremely important but far more complex than the standard rhetoric of "application" implies.[2] That is, it is important to have students explore the intersection between practical experience and classroom theory and skills, but that exploration is not merely a matter of applying concepts to the experience. Some writings about work-based learning (and the text of the School-to-Work Opportunities Act itself) seem to suggest that concepts and skills are neatly transferable between the classroom and the work environment (Office of Technology Assessment, 1995). For instance, writing a business letter at work will help improve a student's English grade, or exposure to corporate organization will lead to understanding of Weber's theory of bureaucracy. In fact, as theorists of situated cognition (Cole, Hood, & McDermott, 1978; Resnick, Levine, & Teasley, 1991; Scribner, 1986) have shown, knowledge is defined and used differently in different domains (such as school and work), and the transfer between them is not automatic or easy.

Therefore, the school-based instructor for work-based learning should engage students in an exploration of the relationship between the two forms of knowledge use, but should not base that exploration on an assumption of one-to-one correspondence. Rather, she should encourage students to deconstruct both the classroom theory and the work-based practices, to probe their underlying structures and assumptions, to look for relations and contradictions, and to inquire about the uses of knowledge in the different arenas. That is, she should help them become critical thinkers about the relationship between school knowledge and work knowledge. That might mean, for example, probing the different techniques and standards used for business writing in the classroom and at work, looking at issues of audience and tone from the twin perspectives of school-like correctness and work-related practicality. Or it might mean critiquing Weber's theory of bureaucracy by trying to apply it to a real-world setting and then investigating the ways in which it does or does not help explain that setting. Koziol and Grubb (1995) recommended assigning students fiction and poems about work to help them analyze and understand different perspectives on the role of work in life. Through literature and their own experiences, students can begin to develop their own sense of the meaning of work.

For example, we conducted observations of a high-school student who interned in the physical therapy (PT) clinic of a hospital, putting patients through the exercises prescribed by the physicians. From a purely academic perspective, he could well have tried to apply textbook physiology and anatomy concepts to his work. Indeed, having the direct experience with people suffering problems with joints, muscles, and nerves might have solidified this knowledge. But the application process, guided effectively by a teacher at school, could have also revealed some interesting features of that knowledge as it is used in practice. He could have learned, first, about the enormous variability of these concepts in real people, about the fact that not everyone's joints function in precisely the same way. More important, he would have had to struggle with the intersection of practice with at least two kinds of academic knowledge: the medical and the psychosocial. That is, in dealing with real people in a real situation, he would have had to think about the ways in which social backgrounds (e.g., ethnic or age differences in the experience of pain or disability) complicate the application of physiological concepts in a PT clinic. This experiential quality would have deepened his understanding of the nature of professional practice.

Our fourth principle of work-based pedagogy is that the teacher's function is not to disseminate already-known information to the students, but to help them construct their own—and to encourage the formation of a community of practice among the students. The teacher does not need to know every detail about the worksites in which the interns are placed; students will learn those things from their supervisors and colleagues. Rather, her job is to foster the spirit of critical discourse (Habermas, 1984) through which the students can learn from one another. She can introduce concepts at appropriate moments, ask probing questions, and show students how to penetrate the assumptions of both academic theories and work-based practices. She will likely need some training for this in order to turn from traditional didacticism and enable the students to develop their own modes of inquiry and their own methods as a community of learners. The students need to learn to treat their own experiences as texts and to share their interpretations of those texts with each other, much as a graduate seminar in literature would discuss *Moby-Dick*.

A corollary of the last point is that this critical pedagogy is the job of the school-based instructor, not of the work-based supervisor. Work-based learning practitioners should probably not expect supervisors or employers to do much in the way of teaching with the interns, at least past the point of showing them how to do their work and telling them how the organization functions. The critical perspective that we call for is not likely to be welcome or useful in the workplace itself—in fact, it could get students into trouble! In one work-based learning program we studied, teachers had student-interns analyzing theories of management, describing the characteristics of an ideal manager, and then comparing their own supervisor's style to this ideal. This is obviously an exercise for the classroom, not the workplace.

First, we do not want to alienate the placement supervisors. The students' first job should be the job—when they are on the job. Second, the students (and even the teachers) may be new at this process and need some practice in conducting critical inquiry before trying it on their colleagues at work. Understanding the situated character of knowledge use is one of the potential benefits of work-based learning programs, and helping students know what is appropriate in school and what is appropriate at work makes them more globally competent.

In other publications (Bailey et al., in press; Hughes & Moore, 1999), we identify and explore some of the more-specific pedagogical tactics used in good work-based learning programs, such as learning plans; keeping journals; concurrent seminars with readings, exercises, and discussions; analytic papers; and evaluation procedures. We will not address these tactics again here. Yet each of them operates in the context of our broader principles: to deepen the students' process of critical reflection on their work experiences, to enhance their ability to examine relationships and activities in order to find underlying assumptions and values, to strengthen their capacity to explore the intersection between academic theory and practical experience, and to foster the creation of a community of practice in which all learn from all. The group process, the dynamic of collaborative inquiry, the realization that everyone has something useful to say about work and ideas—all of this speaks to the importance of the school-based component of work-based learning pedagogies.

PROFESSIONAL DEVELOPMENT FOR WORK-BASED LEARNING EDUCATORS

Whether educators choose functionalist or critical pedagogy for work-based learning programs, they will need professional development because traditional forms of teacher education do not prepare them for this kind of work. The active and contextual nature of work-based learning means that instruction must be different from classroom academic subject instruction. As Herbert (1995) has argued, to bring about truly experiential learning, the students must make more of the decisions on meaning, interpretation, and content, and the teachers must make fewer of these decisions.

But as Hamilton (2000) has pointed out, the increased emphasis nationally on work-based learning has not had a discernible impact on teacher training and certification. Phlegar and Kaufman (1992) suggest that because many work-based learning programs are being newly created, professional development and curriculum development can go hand-in-hand. We agree that deciding what a work-based learning program is for—what we want students to learn—should be accomplished in concert with decisions on pedagogy and professional development. We also contend that what educators wish to foster in the students, both the ability to think critically about work and worker issues and a community of practice that facilitates such reflection and discussion, should first be fostered in the work-based learning instructors.

Researchers and school reformers are increasingly arguing that teachers and other school staff need experiential education themselves (Brown, 2000; Phelps, 1998). A good starting point, frequently mentioned in the literature, is for teachers to visit workplaces. Sargent and Ettinger (1998) have developed guidelines for high-quality internships for educators. Among other things, they recommend that interns develop an action plan for how the internship will be translated into educational practice. An action plan should ask what will change as a result of the internship. Possibilities include new curricular content, strategies for integrating work-based experiences into academic and occupational coursework, and personal growth.

Moreover, the National Center for Research in Vocational Education (NCRVE) designed and piloted a short six-week sabbatical for high-school teachers who wanted to practice contextualized teaching. The teachers spent one week in workplaces, observing tasks and the ways workers were organized and managed. The teachers then designed contextualized learning projects for their students. Despite the short duration of the workplace observations, the teachers benefited in being better able to integrate academic and nonacademic skills in their curricula (Giddens & Stasz, 1999).

Hamilton (2000) has also facilitated and studied teacher training for work-based learning and found that worksite visits can have a significant impact on teachers. One teacher Hamilton worked with said that "he had never trusted business and it had never occurred to him that manufacturers needed employees who could think" (Hamilton, p. 3). In this particular case, the teacher needed to question some of his own preconceptions about the assembly-line nature of manufacturing and the motives of businesspeople. Being able to reflect on these issues with other teachers was valuable.

Indeed, as we noted previously, the literature on teacher education emphasizes the importance of reflection. If the goal is for students to engage in critical reflection, the teachers ought likely to do so as well. Arguments have been made to include questions of ethics, equity, and justice in teacher education (see review in Hatton & Smith, 1995).[3] However, reflection has not necessarily been associated with teaching, which seems more present-oriented (Hatton & Smith, 1995). Teachers likely also lack the time for reflection. As with the student-interns, the opportunity for structured reflection seems important for teachers, particularly those who aim toward contextualized pedagogies. Sargent and Ettinger's (1998) guidelines for educator internships also recommended allotting time for collaborative group debriefing, for discussion of relevant theories and literature, and for individually written reflective narratives.

CONCLUSIONS

Critical pedagogy is not necessarily an easy sell for work-based learning practitioners. In some respects, it seems tangential to the "real" task of making sure that young people are ready for the world of work. It may require a greater degree of teacher training than the mainstream version of work-based learning, and it runs the risk of alienating some potential placements because of what may sound to some like progressive, even left-wing, rhetoric. It implies a more careful and more complex integration of the work experience with the ideas and theories learned in classrooms. Some teachers may also regard the method as too challenging for some students, requiring more analytical and theoretical skills than they can master.

Those cautions may be true, and they may dissuade some educators from adopting this set of principles and practices. But we believe that a truly transformative program must go in this direction. The reason has to do with a final criticism of the critical approach: that it is elitist, a practice that is a luxury of the well-to-do and the privileged. Speaking before a conference of cooperative-education directors, Moore once argued that their primary function was not simply to get youth ready for jobs, but to make them more complete learners, and he was roundly booed. Certainly, finding employment is no small matter, especially for students from working-class and poor families whose connections and cultural capital narrow their career options. Sitting back and reflecting on work, on society, on life—that seems a privilege. It *is* a privilege in our society, but it should not be. Every student, from every background, ought to have that opportunity. If only the already privileged get the chance to engage in this sort of critical inquiry, only they will learn to take charge of their lives and institutions. Limiting this pedagogy to wealthy suburban schools will only reproduce the existing class relations in our society. We believe that students who engage in this sort of critical analysis of their work experience will acquire more skills, write better, think better, and be more employable. But we also believe that the approach fulfills the democratic promise of American schooling because it gives all students, not just the privileged, the opportunity and the ability to understand their worlds more fully and to take charge of their lives. Teaching can have no higher purpose.

NOTES

1. The School-to-Work Opportunities Act (STWOA) was at least partly a response to the changing nature of work and skills requirements of the last two decades. The goal of the legislation, to facilitate "the creation of a universal, high-quality school-to-work transition system that enables youths in the United States to identify and navigate paths to productive and progressively more rewarding roles in the workplace," even has a functionalist tone in that it implies helping youths to fit themselves more effectively into the new economy. The Lewis, Stone, Shipley, and Madzar (1998) analysis of the language of the legislation has found that the problem it is responding to is one of

"subpar" youth, "unable to compete with their counterparts elsewhere in the world" (p. 264).

2. For a further discussion of the connection between work-based learning and academic skills, see Hughes, Moore, and Bailey (1999).

3. In the teacher-education literature, however, critical reflection refers to seeing as problematic the goals and practices of one's own profession, in this case teaching. See the Hatton and Smith review (1995).

REFERENCES

Apple, M. (1982). *Education and power.* Boston: Routledge and Kegan Paul.

Bailey, T., Hughes, K. L., & Barr, T. (2000). Achieving scale and quality in school-to-work internships: Findings from two employer surveys. *Educational Evaluation and Policy Analysis, 22,* 41–64.

Bailey, T., Hughes, K. L., & Moore, D. T. (in press). *Work-based learning and education reform.* Boulder, CO: Westview Press.

Blumer, H. (1969). *Symbolic interactionism.* Englewood Cliffs, NJ: Prentice-Hall.

Boud, D., Cohen, R., & Walker, D. (Eds.). (1993). *Using experience for learning.* Bristol, PA: Society for Research into Higher Education and the Open University.

Brown, B. L. (2000). *Vocational teacher professional development* (Practice Application Brief No. 11). Columbus, OH: Ohio State University, ERIC Clearinghouse on Adult, Career, and Vocational Education.

Bruner, J. (1975). *Beyond the information given.* New York: Basic Books.

Cappelli, P., Shapiro, D., & Shumanis, N. (1998). *Employer participation in school-to-work programs.* Unpublished manuscript, University of Pennsylvania, Philadelphia, National Center on the Educational Quality of the Workforce.

Cole, M., Hood, L., & McDermott, R. P. (1978). *Ecological niche-picking: Ecological invalidity as an axiom of experimental cognitive psychology.* Unpublished manuscript, Rockefeller University, New York City.

Dewey, J. (1938). *Experience and education.* New York: Collier Books.

Eyler, J., & Giles, D. E., Jr. (1999). *Where's the learning in service-learning?* San Francisco: Jossey-Bass.

Foucault, M. (1980). *Power/knowledge: Selected interviews and writings 1972–1977* (C. Gordon et al., Trans.). New York: Pantheon Books.

Freire, P. (1974). *Pedagogy of the oppressed.* New York: Continuum.

Giddens, B., & Stasz, C. (1999). *Context matters: Teaching and learning skills for work* (Centerpoint No. 8). Berkeley, CA: National Center for Research in Vocational Education.

Giroux, H., & McLaren, P. L. (Eds.). (1989). *Critical pedagogy, the state, and cultural struggle.* Albany, NY: State University of New York Press.

Habermas, J. (1984). *The theory of communicative action.* Boston: Beacon Press.

Hamilton, M. A. (2000, September). *Educating teachers and trainers in the United States to foster work-based learning.* Paper presented at the International Conference on Teaching and Learning within Vocational and Occupational Education and Training, Göttingen, Germany.

Hatton, N., & Smith, D. (1995). Reflection in teacher education: Towards definition and implementation. *Teaching & Teacher Education, 11,* 33–49.

Herbert, T. (1995). Experiential learning: A teacher's perspective. In B. Horwood (Ed.), *Experience and the Curriculum* (pp. 19–35). Dubuque, IA: Kendall/Hunt.

Hershey, A. M., Silverberg, M. K., Haimson, J., Hudis, P., & Jackson, R. (1999). *Expanding options for students: Report to Congress on the National Evaluation of School-to-Work Implementation.* Princeton: Mathematica Policy Research, Inc.

Hughes, K. L., & Moore, D. T. (1999). *Pedagogical strategies for work-based learning* (IEE Working Paper No. 12). New York: Columbia University, Teachers College, Institute on Education and the Economy.

Hughes, K. L., Moore, D. T., & Bailey, T. R. (1999). *Work-based learning and academic skills* (IEE Working Paper No. 15). New York: Columbia University, Teachers College, Institute on Education and the Economy.

James, W. (1983). *Talks to teachers and students about psychology.* Cambridge, MA: Harvard University Press. (Original work published 1915.)

Koziol, K., & Grubb, W. N. (1995). Paths not taken: Curriculum integration and the political and moral purposes of schooling. In W. N. Grubb (Ed.), *Education through occupations in American high schools: The Challenges of implementing curriculum integration* (Vol. 2, pp. 115–140). New York: Teachers College Press.

Lave, J. (1988). *Cognition in practice.* New York: Cambridge University Press.

Lave, J., & Wenger, E. (1991). *Situated learning: Legitimate peripheral participation.* New York: Cambridge University Press.

Lewis, T., Stone, J., III, Shipley, W., & Madzar, S. (1998). The transition from school to work: An examination of the literature. *Youth & Society, 29,* 259–292.

Mead, G. (1934). *Mind, self & society from the standpoint of a social behaviorist.* Chicago: University of Chicago Press.

Moore, D. (1999). Behind the wizard's curtain: A challenge to the true believer. *NSEE Quarterly, 25,* pp. 1–4.

Office of Technology Assessment. (1995). *Learning to work: Making the transition from school to work.* Washington, DC: U.S. Government Printing Office.

Phelps, L. A. (1998). Changing work, changing learning: The imperative for teacher learning in workplaces and communities. In L. A. Phelps, V. Hernandez-Gantes, C. Maidl Pribbenow, & T. Sargent (Eds.), *Teacher learning in the workplace and community* (pp. 3–11). Berkeley, CA: National Center for Research in Vocational Education.

Phlegar, J., & Kaufman, J. (1992). *Effective professional development: A guide for youth apprenticeship and work-based learning programs.* Cambridge, MA: Jobs for the Future.

Piaget, J. (1967). *Six psychological studies* (A. Tenzer, Trans.). New York: Random House. (Original work published 1964.)

Resnick, L. B., Levine, J. M., & Teasley, S. D. (Eds.). (1991). *Perspectives on socially shared cognition.* Washington, DC: American Psychological Association.

Sargent, T., & Ettinger, J. (1998). Educator internship programs: Providing a quality learning experience. In L. A. Phelps, V. Hernandez-Gantes, C. Maidl Pribbenow, & T. Sargent (Eds.), *Teacher learning in the workplace and community* (pp. 23–34). Berkeley, CA: National Center for Research in Vocational Education.

Schön, D. (1990). *Educating the reflective practitioner.* San Francisco: Jossey-Bass.

Scribner, S. (1986). Thinking in action: Some characteristics of practical thought. In R. J. Sternberg & R. K. Wagner (Eds.), *Practical intelligence: Nature and origins of competence in the everyday world* (pp. 13–30). New York: Cambridge University Press.

Secretary's Commission on Acquiring Necessary Skills. (1991). *What work requires of schools: A SCANS report for America 2000.* Washington, DC: U.S. Department of Labor.

Simon, R. I., Dippo, D., & Schenke, A. (1991). *Learning work: A critical pedagogy of work education.* New York: Bergin and Garvey.

Stasz, C., & Kaganoff, T. (1997). *Learning how to work: Lessons from three high school programs.* Berkeley, CA: National Center for Research in Vocational Education.

Urquiola, M., Stern, D., Horn, I., Dornsife, C., Chi, B., Williams, L., et al. (1997). *School to work, college and career: A review of policy, practice, and results 1993–1997.* Berkeley, CA: National Center for Research in Vocational Education.

Vygotsky, L. (1978). *Mind in society.* Cambridge, MA: Harvard University Press.

Wenger, E. (1998). *Communities of practice: Learning, meaning, and identity.* Cambridge, England: Cambridge University Press.

11

The Impact of School-to-Work Programs on Minority Youth

Francisco L. Rivera-Batiz

INTRODUCTION

School-to-work (STW) programs seek to integrate school-based learning with work-based learning by fostering linkages between schools and workplaces. Through the combination of curriculum reform with systemic school reform, the STW movement has rapidly grown in the United States since the late 1980s. From career exploration and job immersion to apprenticeships and internships, STW activities have spread rapidly across the country in recent years. This chapter examines differences in the participation of ethnic and racial minorities in STW programs. It also analyzes the impact these programs have had on the schooling and work of racial and ethnic minorities in the U.S.

The difficulties of the transition from school to work in the United States have been under discussion as a policy concern for many years. In his Education Message to Congress in 1968, President Lyndon B. Johnson noted that about 1.5 million young men and women would leave high school and enter the labor force that year. As in previous years, he said, the transition to work for many of them would be very difficult. He concluded: "[T]he irony of this situation is that it has occurred in the country with the most highly developed and the most costly system of education in the world and in a period of unusual prosperity, high employment, and skill shortages" (as cited in Arnow et al., 1968, p. 3).

The situation has not improved since President Johnson's remarks more than thirty years ago. The average unemployment rate of teenagers in 1968 (sixteen to nineteen years old) was 11.6 %, but in August 2000 it was 14.4%, declining from the recession peak of over 20% in 1992 (these and other labor-force statistics below are from Bureau of Labor Statistics, 2001). Because overall unemployment rates in both 1968 and August 2000 were around 4%, the gap between the unemployment experience of youth and the rest of the population has widened since 1968. The situation is worse among minorities. The unemployment rate among black teenagers (sixteen to nineteen years old) was 22.1% in 1968, but it had grown to 27.8% in August 2000, down from a whopping 42% in 1992.

The earning power of the young has also eroded, compounding the difficult unemployment situation. The median weekly earnings of full-time wage and salary workers aged sixteen to twenty-four dropped from $369 in 1985 to $334 in 1998 for men and from $323 to $305 for women (adjusted for inflation, measured in 1998 constant dollars). The incomes of young workers who do not finish high school have also declined in comparison with both high-school and college graduates, as evidenced by rising rates of return for postsecondary education (see Katz & Autor, 1999).

The problematic transition from school to work in the United States has been reflected in the frequent job-hopping of young workers, often referred to as "churning." Studies in the past decade have shown that the average high-school graduate between age eighteen and twenty-seven who did not pursue tertiary education held almost six different jobs and experienced four or more spells of unemployment (Zemsky, Shapiro, Iannozzi, Cappelli, & Bailey, 1998; see also Topel & Ward, 1992). Substantial instability also exists in the transition from school to work, with enrolled high-school students hopping among various part-time jobs and between full-time employment and school.

In aiming chiefly to improve the transition from school to work for American youth, STW programs have followed the vocational-education movement, which has been prominent since the turn of the twentieth century. Evaluations of the success of traditional vocational-education programs, however, have provided sobering results. This is reflected in the following statement from Kantor and Tyack (1982): "[T]he majority of studies have concluded that there is little economic advantage to vocational training, as opposed to nonvocational, at the high school level" (p. 2). The American Association of University Women (1992) shared this view, concluding that "vocational education was originally designed to give work skills to high-school boys who were not planning to attend college. But research indicates that it may not serve either males or females very well in the current environment" (p. 72). These statements are based on a variety of studies that offer sometimes conflicting but ultimately skeptical results on the impact of traditional vocational-education programs on young people's careers (see Cuban, 1982; Desy, Campbell, & Gardner, 1984; Rivera-Batiz, 1995a, 1995b, 1995c, 1998; Schug & Western, 2000). Researchers repeatedly found that lack of collaboration between employers and schools, substitution of basic academic courses for practical job training, and tracking and segregation of students into training for specific, low-skilled jobs caused many vocational programs to offer low-quality education to clients.

Picking up momentum in the 1990s, the STW movement reacted to these deficiencies, redefining the vocational-education movement and offering innovative programs that strengthen the bonds between employers and schools and reintegrate academics with work content (see, for instance, Berryman & Bailey, 1992; Murnane & Levy, 1996). School-to-work links have been fostered by school–employer partnerships; academic curricula with work content offered by employers, apprenticeships and internships; and career academies (see Grubb, 1995; Pauly, Kopp, & Haimson, 1995; Stern, Raby, & Dayton, 1992). In 1994, the movement obtained strong federal support through the School-to-Work Opportunities Act (STWOA), which provided grants to states to implement STW systems. All fifty states have received STW implementation funds and organized local partnerships to create STW systems. In addition, in anticipation of the end of federal funding in 2001, 71% of states instituted programs supporting their STW initiatives (National School-to-Work Office, 2000).

This study uses data collected in the 1997 National Longitudinal Survey of Youth (NLSY97). The survey, sponsored by the U.S. Department of Labor, followed the transition from school to work of 8,984 young people who were between twelve and sixteen years of age in 1996. This chapter uses data currently available from NLSY97, including the initial interviews in 1997 and the first follow-up in 1998. Both black and Hispanic youth were oversampled to ensure adequate sample sizes for analysis. Overall, NLSY97 included 4,096 whites, 2,204 blacks, and 1,771 Hispanics. The remaining participants belonged to Asian, Native American, and other groups whose small sample sizes have not allowed a robust analysis of their situation (for more details on NLSY97, see Center for Human Resource Research, 2000; U.S. Department of Labor, 2000).

The chapter first investigates the differences in the participation in STW programs of the major racial and ethnic groups in the population. Included are a discussion of the variation in participation rates and an analysis of the determinants of this variation. Next, evidence is offered on the effects of STW programs on academic and work experiences of white, black, and Hispanic youth. Finally, conclusions are presented.

INVOLVEMENT OF RACIAL AND ETHNIC MINORITIES IN STW PROGRAMS

The expansion of STW programs in the 1990s has been widely documented. According to the 1996 School Administrator's Survey, sponsored by the National School-to-Work Office, 64.2% of all schools with a twelfth grade offered at least one STW program; in addition, 26% of schools surveyed offered three or more STW programs (see Joyce & Neumark, 2000). The strong involvement of employers in STW programs has contradicted the critics skeptical of this aspect of STW activity. Studies using the National Employer Surveys have found that the percentage of employers participating in formal STW partnerships accelerated in the 1990s. By 1997, 25% of employers surveyed were participating in STW programs and this increased to 37% in 1998 (National

Center on the Educational Quality of the Workforce, 1997; Shapiro, 1998). On the other hand, it also appears that both schools and employers with STW programs have generally adopted the least-intensive forms of work-based learning activities, such as job shadowing and mentoring (Joyce & Neumark, 2000; Shapiro, 1998; Silverberg, 1997).

What has been the involvement of minority youth in STW programs? NLSY97 examined the participation of high-school students in various STW transition programs. Table 11.1 (Center for Human Resource Research, 2000; all tables that follow are derived from NLSY97 data) names and defines these programs. The survey made a distinction between two types of programs: career-major programs, which were defined as including a coherent sequence of courses based upon an occupational goal, and STW-preparatory programs, which included programs that schools have offered to help students prepare for the world of work. As Table 11.1 shows, the latter type included seven

Table 11.1
Types of School-to-Work Transition Programs Examined in NLSY97

Program	Definition
Career Major	A coherent sequence of courses based upon an occupational goal.
School-to-Work Preparatory Programs	Programs that schools offer to help students prepare for the world of work.
Job shadowing	Students following an employee for one or more days to learn about an occupation or industry.
Worksite Visits	Students spending time at a worksite during the school day or after school.
Mentoring	Students being paired with an employee who assesses his or her performance over a period of time, during which the employee helps the student master certain skills and knowledge.
School-Sponsored Enterprise	The production of goods or services by students for sale or use by enterprises, typically involving students in the management of the project.
Cooperative Education	Students alternating or paralleling their academic and vocational studies with a job in a related field.
Tech-Prep	A planned program of study with a defined career focus that links secondary and postsecondary education.
Internship or Apprenticeship	Students working for an employer for a short period to learn about a particular industry or occupation.

different programs, with increasing intensity of the school–work linkages: job shadowing (students follow employees at work for one or more days), worksite visits (students spend some time visiting a worksite during the school day or after school), mentoring (employees oversee the performance of students in their academic work), school-sponsored enterprises (students produce goods and services under the supervision of an enterprise), cooperative education (students alternate academic and vocational studies at school with jobs), tech-prep programs (a comprehensive program of study with a defined career focus linking secondary and postsecondary education is followed), and internships or apprenticeships (students systematically stay at a worksite for a short period).

The involvement of high-school students in these programs is substantial, and it increased sharply between 1997 and 1998. Table 11.2 shows participation rates by race and ethnicity. In 1997, approximately one out of three students in ninth grade or higher had participated in one or more career-major or STW-preparatory programs at the time of the interview. By 1998, close to half of

Table 11.2
Participation of High-School Students Enrolled in Ninth Grade or Higher in Career-Major or STW-Preparatory Programs: 1997–1998

	Non-Hispanic White (%)	Non-Hispanic Black (%)	Hispanic (%)
Participation in Any Career-Major or STW-Preparatory Programs			
At any time up to 1997 interview	32.1	36.2	28.3
At any time up to 1998 interview	47.1	51.2	41.0
Participation in Career-Major Programs			
At any time up to 1997 interview	13.4	18.1	11.8
At any time up to 1998 interview	21.6	29.5	21.4
Participation in STW- Preparatory Programs			
At any time up to 1997 interview	27.4	30.2	24.4
At any time up to 1998 interview	40.5	42.5	33.7

the students had participated in these programs. There were, however, significant differences among the three racial and ethnic groups considered. Non-Hispanic blacks tended to have greater participation rates than both non-Hispanic whites and Hispanics. On the other hand, Hispanics tended to have lower participation rates than other groups. Joyce and Neumark (2000) found this same result using the initial (1997) interviews of NLSY97. I used the follow-up (1998) interviews of NLSY97 to determine that in 1998, 41% of Hispanic teenagers having attained the ninth grade or higher had participated in career-major or STW-preparatory programs, whereas 47.1% among non-Hispanic whites and 51.2% among non-Hispanic blacks had participated.

Table 11.2 also presents data on the participation rates of American youth in the two major types of STW transition program. The racial and ethnic pattern of participation observed for the combination of programs also held for each program type separately. Young black people generally had greater participation rates than other groups, whereas Hispanics had lower rates. Despite the lower participation rate of Hispanics in STW programs in general, there was no evidence that minority youth were being channeled into less-comprehensive and less-intensive STW-preparatory programs than were others.

Moreover, participation in STW programs increased with each grade a student was enrolled in. Using NLSY97 data for 1998, Table 11.3 presents the participation rates first for students in grades nine and ten and second for students who were enrolled in—or had completed—grade twelve. For all ethnic and racial groups considered, STW participation rates rose sharply in high school. For instance, among non-Hispanic black students in ninth and tenth grade, 37.8% participated in one or more career-major or STW-preparatory programs up to the time of interview in 1998. But for students enrolled in or having completed twelfth grade, the rate of participation in one or more STW programs was 66.7%. As Table 11.3 shows, this pattern held also for each type of STW-transition program separately.

An analysis of the participation of high-school students in STW programs on the basis of gender did not produce any major, systematic differences. Actually, the proportion of female students involved in STW programs was slightly higher than that of men.

The STW movement has aimed to improve the transition from school to work for all students, particularly minority students in urban school systems. This goal was incorporated in the School-to-Work Opportunities Act of 1994, which explicitly emphasized the need of STW programs to "increase opportunities for minorities, women, and individuals with disabilities, by enabling individuals to prepare for careers that are not traditional for their race, gender, and disability." The greater participation of black youth in STW programs is therefore not surprising. What is of some concern, however, is the substantially lower participation of Hispanic youth in STW programs. What explains this?

Table 11.3
High-School Student Participation by Grade in Career-Major or STW-Preparatory Programs: 1998

	Non-Hispanic White (%)	Non-Hispanic Black (%)	Hispanic (%)
Participation in any career-major or STW-preparatory programs at any time up to 1998 interview			
Among students in grades 9-10	33.5	37.8	28.0
Among students in (or who completed) grade 12	60.0	66.7	57.5
Participation in career-major programs at any time up to 1998 interview			
Among students in grades 9-10	13.5	20.1	14.0
Among students in (or who completed) grade 12	29.1	40.2	30.6
Participation in STW-preparatory programs at any time up to 1998 interview			
Among students in grades 9-10	27.8	28.7	21.3
Among students in (or who completed) grade 12	53.5	59.8	50.0

To examine the reasons for lower Hispanic involvement in STW programs (a result that held for both men and women), I carried out a multivariate probit analysis that explored how a set of demographic, socioeconomic, and school-based variables affected the probability that a person would participate in career-major and STW-preparatory programs. The variables introduced as possible explanations for participation or nonparticipation in STW programs included (a) a set of characteristics of the student: gender, race and ethnicity, immigrant status, health, grade level, the number of times the student repeated a grade (a rough measure of academic achievement), and the cumulative hours of work since the first job (a measure of labor market interest or attachment); and (b) a set of characteristics of the school or community in which the student resided: residence in a central city, level of discipline in the school, quality of teaching, size of the school, class size, and private or public schooling.

The probit analysis suggested that immigrant status was critical in accounting for the lower rate of participation of Hispanic youth in STW programs. Immigrant status sharply reduced the likelihood of such participation. Indeed, once immigrant status was taken into account, the Hispanic variable in the probit equation lost its power to explain the likelihood of STW participation (see Rivera-Batiz, 2001, for a detailed presentation of these results). Immigrant status affects Hispanics disproportionately more than other groups because a greater share of the Hispanic population is born outside the U.S. As much as 43.2% of the Hispanic youth population in NLSY97 was born outside the United States, but only 3.4% of non-Hispanic whites and 4.5% of blacks were. Table 11.4 shows the average STW-participation rates of Hispanic immigrants and nonimmigrants. Overall, 36.1% of Hispanic immigrant youth had participated in a career-major or STW-preparatory program at any time before the survey interview in 1998. This contrasts with the much higher 47.2% among Hispanic nonimmigrants.

The lower participation of Hispanic immigrant youth in STW programs may be connected to the issue of English proficiency. In the NLSY97 sample, 65% of Hispanic youth lived in households in which the language used was not English. The NLSY97 data set does not currently include measures of the English proficiency of students in the sample (English reading-test results have not yet been released), but it is likely that language constitutes a major factor affecting STW participation in schools. Students with limited English proficiency (LEP) are generally channeled into special-education programs uninte-

Table 11.4
Participation of Hispanic Students Enrolled in Ninth Grade or Higher in Career-Major or STW-Preparatory Programs, by Immigrant Status: 1998

	Hispanic Non-Immigrants (%)	Hispanic Immigrants (%)	Hispanic Overall (%)
Participation in any career-major or STW-preparatory programs at any time up to 1998 interview	47.2	36.1	41.0
Participation in career-major programs at any time up to 1998 interview	22.1	20.5	21.4
Participated in STW- preparatory programs at any time up to 1998 interview	36.8	29.5	33.7

grated with STW programs. This may be temporary, as when students enter one-year immigrant academies, but separation from mainstream curricula may extend longer, as when students are enrolled in long-term bilingual or special-education programs (see Rivera-Batiz, 1995b, 1996a).

Lower participation of LEP students in STW programs may also arise from negative reactions of employers to LEP students, which may encourage these students to avoid or withdraw from STW programs. Although I have no evidence for this connection, there exists a voluminous literature documenting the dire labor-market consequences of LEP (see, for example, Rivera-Batiz, 1991, 1992a, 1992b, 1996b). In programs seeking to foster links between school and work, more research is required on how immigrant status and language affect the involvement of youth in these programs, from both the school and worksite sides.

THE CONSEQUENCES OF STW PROGRAMS FOR MINORITY YOUTH

A substantial amount of research has attempted in recent years to examine the consequences of participation in STW programs for various student outcomes. So far, this evidence is mixed. Some researchers have shown that STW programs have significant impacts on job-related skills and expectations, but have discovered very little or no evidence of effects on academic achievement or performance (Hamilton & Hamilton, 1999; Kemple, Poglinco, & Snipes, 1999; Neumark & Joyce, 2000). Other studies have suggested positive effects of STW programs on both work and academic outcomes (Hanser & Stasz, 1999; Hughes, Bailey, & Mechur, 2001; Westchester Institute for Human Services Research, 2000). For instance, using a sample of 725 high-school students, the Westchester Institute for Human Services Research found that "students who actively participated in STW programs had higher grade point averages, were absent from school less often, failed fewer academic courses, enrolled in more challenging math and science courses, and were more decisive about their career direction than comparable students with little or no STW exposure" (p. 5).

Much existing research showing positive STW impacts, however, cannot establish a causal connection because of the absence of data controlling the characteristics of students before they participate in STW programs. Even the data for the first NLSY97 wave of interviews could not incorporate changes over time. But the 1998 follow-up interviews of the NLSY97 data allow such an analysis. This study uses the 1997 and 1998 interviews of NLSY97 to examine causal relationships, exploring how participation in STW programs in the period between the first and second interviews affected various student outcomes, holding other factors constant. The analysis has been separated on the basis of race and ethnicity.

Impact on Math and Science Courses Taken by High-School Students

The effects of STW programs on the math and science courses taken by high-school students are a key issue because white and minority youth have displayed a huge gap in this regard. For instance, in the NLSY97 sample of high-school seniors or graduates, 26.9% of the white youth population had taken courses in precalculus, calculus, or more advanced math during the year before the 1998 interview. But this figure was only 18.2% among black youth and 16.1% among Hispanics.

By including more math and science courses in their career-oriented curriculum, STW programs may increase the intensity of math and science instruction directly. This is the case argued by Pauly et al. (1995):

> Most of the school-to-work programs examined here apparently induce their students to take more science, math and technical courses than are required for graduation, and more of these courses than they would be likely to take if they were not enrolled in the school-to-work program. For example, the Socorro health academy requires students to take algebra and science courses earlier than many of their regular high-school peers, and pushes them to take additional math and science courses thereafter. (p. 31)

There may be other, indirect—but perhaps as powerful—mechanisms involved. Work-based learning may provide incentives and motivation that stimulate student interest in science and mathematics. As Hughes, Moore, and Bailey (1999) remarked, "activities engaged in at the workplace can be used to bring about a better understanding of knowledge or concepts being taught in the classroom" (p. 8). Heckman (2000) argued that these motivational and incentive effects lie behind the success of the German apprenticeship system:

> [T]he celebrated German Apprenticeship System has been recommended as a model for the U.S. and for many other countries. . . . When stripped to its essentials, the German system differs from the U.S. school system by (1) breaking down the artificial separation between the world of work and the world of learning; (2) giving students and the firms that apprentice them choice among a variety of learning situations; and (3) motivating students to perform well in order to secure the most desirable apprenticeships and motivating many firms to provide valuable training opportunities. (p. 25)

These characteristics of STW programs might enhance the motivation of students to take extra courses, might raise their GPAs, and might provide access to—and interest in—more stimulating and productive career opportunities (see Bishop & Mañe, 2000). As Murnane and Levy (1996) conclude, "Traditional [vocational-education] programs teach students the details of a specific job. The new [STW] programs use the specific jobs to motivate a hidden agenda of mathematics, communication and problem-solving—the New Skills valued throughout the economy" (pp. 122–123).

To measure the intensity of math and science courses taken by high-school students, I used data collected by the 1998 interviews of NLSY97 about the number of courses in math and science subjects completed by students since their interview a year earlier. Because NLSY97 asked questions about the number—and subject—of the introductory and more advanced courses students took, ranging from algebra and biology to calculus and advanced mathematics, an index could be constructed that assigned one point to introductory courses in these fields and additional points to more advanced courses in the fields. The idea was to assess the intensity of effort dedicated by the respondent to the study of science and mathematics. Because basic courses are often required by high-school curriculum standards and do not necessarily reflect a student's enhanced interest in the subject, I assigned greater value to advanced courses taken, which would truly reflect greater effort and desire to learn math and science. General, basic, or vocational math received one point each, and so did general courses in science, including basic courses in biology, chemistry, physics, or other basic science courses. More-advanced courses were assigned greater scores: Elementary algebra or algebra I was assigned two points, geometry three points, intermediate algebra (or algebra II) four points, trigonometry five points, precalculus or advanced algebra six points, calculus seven points, and other advanced mathematics courses eight points. Overall, the value of the index of math and science course intensity ranged from zero (if no math and science courses were taken) to forty-two points (which represented a student who had taken all science courses listed in NLSY97 and the most-advanced mathematics courses).

Table 11.5 compares the scores received by students who had participated in one or more STW programs with the scores of those who had never participated in STW programs. First, the table displays the gaps that exist in math and science courses, taking on the basis of race and ethnicity. Hispanic students had

Table 11.5
Index of Intensity in Math and Science Courses Taken in High School: 1998

	Non-Hispanic White	Non-Hispanic Black	Hispanic
Students in grade 9 or higher who participated in any career-major or STW-preparatory programs at any time up to 1998 interview	6.8	6.5	6.4
Students in grade 9 or higher who *did not* participate in any career-major or STW-preparatory programs at any time up to 1998 interview	6.0	5.4	5.3

the lowest scores, followed by non-Hispanic blacks while non-Hispanic white youth displayed the highest scores.

Table 11.5 also shows that students participating in STW programs had substantially higher scores in the math and science course-taking index. The differences were particularly significant among minorities: For both black and Hispanic youth, students participating in STW programs had indexes of math and science intensity over one point higher than nonparticipating students had. This corresponds to the difference between having taken precalculus and having taken only algebra II and trigonometry.

The major problem of comparisons such as those reported in this table is that a simple correlation of student outcomes with STW participation may break down when influences of other variables are taken into account. For example, as noted earlier, students in later grades tended to have a greater rate of participation in STW programs. As a result, the gaps in math and science course taking determined in Table 11.5 may be purely spurious, resulting from the fact that students who participated in STW programs were more likely to be older students, enrolled in higher grades.

This sample selection-bias problem plagues any evaluation study seeking to compare the performance of students who have participated in a program with that of students who have not participated in it. The characteristics of the two groups must be held constant; otherwise, any measured differential performance may be related to the variation in the characteristics of the two groups and not necessarily to participation in the program. It is essential, then, to carry out a multivariate analysis of the impact of STW programs on student outcomes: that is, an analysis that includes participation in STW programs as an explanatory variable but that holds constant other variables, including for example, grade level.

A multiple regression analysis of the determinants of math and science course taking was carried out; the technical results are presented in Rivera-Batiz (2001). The regression methodology explored how both STW participation and a broad set of background variables—including grade level among them—affected the intensity of the math and science courses taken by students in the NLSY97 sample in 1998 (that is, during the year after their first interview in 1997), as measured by the index discussed earlier. The multivariate analysis allowed me to consider how one specific variable affected course taking while I held constant the characteristics of the individual, the school, and the community. Here, I focus exclusively on describing the impact of STW participation on the math and science course-intensity index, whereas Rivera-Batiz (2001) presents the overall results, considering the effects of other variables.

For non-Hispanic white students, the analysis found no evidence that participation in STW-transition programs increased the intensity of math and science courses taken. However, for minorities, the impact was significant. Participation in STW-transition programs by minority youth at any given time was substantially linked to greater course taking in science and math after participation in such programs. For both non-Hispanic blacks and Hispanic youth, students who participated in STW programs before their first interview in 1997 had approximately one more point on the math and science course-intensity index for courses taken during the year after the 1997 interview. This result was obtained holding other variables constant, including grade level.

Note the causality implied by this analysis: Participation in STW programs before students were interviewed in1997 was strongly linked to greater math and science course taking in the year following participation. In fact, the correlation between participation in STW programs after 1997 on math and science course taking during the same period was also positive, but significantly smaller. This suggests that the mechanism through which STW programs enhance the curriculum of many participants is not just by directly requiring more advanced or comprehensive math and science courses, but also by motivating students to take those courses in the future. This appears to be the case, especially for minority youth.

Impact of STW Participation on Hours Worked

It is to be expected that participation in programs bringing together the worlds of school and work provides students with motivation to enter the world of work. This suggests that students who participate in STW programs should have greater labor-market participation. Are STW programs causing students to work longer hours? This is not an easy question to answer empirically because a simultaneity exists between hours worked and participation in STW programs. If one finds that STW programs are linked to greater hours of work, this may just reflect the fact that the more-intensive employment experience can provide an incentive for students to enroll in STW programs. My analysis, however, disentangled the simultaneity involved in participation in the labor force and participation in STW programs. By utilizing the longitudinal nature of NLSY97, I examined how participation in STW programs before the initial interviews in 1997 was related to hours worked after those interviews during 1998.

Table 11.6 presents the results of this analysis. The outcome variable studied was the number of additional hours that students worked in 1998 over 1997. The first two rows in the table show the average hours worked by students in 1997 and 1998, disaggregated by race and ethnicity. Note first that non-Hispanic white students engaged in substantially more hours of work than non-Hispanic black and Hispanic youth. In 1997, for example, non-Hispanic whites worked an average of 252 hours a year, non-Hispanic blacks 142, and Hispanics 117. These differences in hours worked were related to greater unemployment among minority youth, but further research should be carried out to understand them.

The third row of Table 11.6 shows the additional hours worked in 1998 over 1997. Hours worked in 1998 exceeded those in 1997 for all racial and ethnic

Table 11.6
Impact of Participation in STW Programs on Hours Worked: 1998

	Non-Hispanic White	Non-Hispanic Black	Hispanic
Average hours worked in 1997	252	142	117
Average hours worked in 1998	397	251	276
Additional hours worked in 1998 over 1997	145	109	159
Additional hours worked in 1998 explained by participation in STW-transition programs before the time of interview in 1997	36	45	43

groups considered, with Hispanics working 159 additional hours, non-Hispanic whites 145 additional hours, and non-Hispanic black youth 109 hours. A multiple regression analysis was carried out, relating the increased hours worked to a variety of individual, socioeconomic, school, and community factors. The detailed results of this research are presented in Rivera-Batiz (2001). I focus here on discussing the specific impact of participation in STW programs.

The analysis indicates that participation before 1997 had a significant positive impact on 1998 hours worked. In fact, the methodology utilized allowed me to specify the additional hours worked by students in 1998 associated with participation in any career-major or STW-preparatory programs up to the time of the interview in 1997. The fourth row of Table 11.6 presents the results of this calculation, showing the number of additional hours worked by students in 1998 explained by STW-program participation in previous years. The non-Hispanic black population had the greatest number of hours explained by STW participation, with 45 hours, followed by Hispanics with 43 hours and non-Hispanic whites with 36 hours. These results suggest a clear, positive link between participation in STW programs and subsequent labor-market participation.

Impact on High-School Retention

The previous section provided evidence suggesting that increased hours of work may be linked to participation in STW programs. But could STW programs then be linked to reduced retention, as students drop out to participate in the labor market? Interestingly, some studies have found that STW programs such as career academies have instead increased graduation rates of high-school students. A recent survey found that 91% of school–business partnerships involved in STW programs believe that "STW experiences have led students to stay in school when they otherwise may have dropped out" (National School-to-Work Office, 2000, p. 3). Other studies, however, have been more skeptical, suggesting that by making work more attractive, STW programs have increased the labor-market participation of participants and reduced high-school graduation rates. Research by Crain et al. (1998) has supported the latter point, showing that "comprehensive schools are graduating four students for every three that career magnets graduate. The career magnets' lower graduation rate and higher dropout rate are both of considerable policy importance and are statistically significant" (p. 1).

To examine the impact of STW-program participation on high-school retention, the NLSY97 data set was used to carry out a probit analysis exploring how STW and other background variables influenced the likelihood that a high-school student who last attended tenth grade dropped out before graduation instead of staying in school.

The analysis indicated that with other factors kept constant, participation in STW-transition programs had a significantly negative impact on the likelihood of dropping out of school (the technical results of this analysis are presented in Rivera-Batiz, 2001). This conclusion is consistent with the results linking participation in STW programs to increased intensity of math and science course taking. In fact, one key difference between traditional vocational-education programs and STW-transition programs is that STW programs are intended to stimulate the interests of students in the academic underpinnings of various occupations, which may encourage them to continue their schooling. This result holds despite the fact that participation in STW programs does act to increase hours worked by exposing students to work activities, as was just shown. For the average youth in the study, the dropout-increasing effects that these programs may have through encouraging increased work are more than compensated for by their dropout-reducing effects. When other factors are held constant, students who participate in STW-transition programs have a lower likelihood of dropping out.

CONCLUSIONS

This chapter has examined the causes and consequences of participation in STW-transition programs for minority youth, using the initial 1997 interview and the follow-up 1998 interview of NLSY97 to examine the determinants of participation rates in these programs and the programs' impact on various student outcomes. The following conclusions stand out:

1. The involvement of igh-school students in STW programs has been substantial and has increased sharply between 1997 and 1998. By 1998, close to half of the high-school students sampled in NLSY97 had participated in one of more of these programs. There were significant differences on the basis of race and ethnicity. Non-Hispanic blacks tended to have greater participation rates than both non-Hispanic whites and Hispanics. On the other hand, Hispanics tended to have lower participation rates than other groups.
2. Immigrant status appears critical in accounting for the lower rate of participation of Hispanic youth in STW programs. Immigrant status sharply reduced the likelihood of such participation. Overall, 36.1% of Hispanic immigrant youth had participated in a career major or STW-preparatory program before the interview in 1998. This contrasts with the much higher 47.2% among Hispanic nonimmigrants. Indeed, once immigrant status is taken into account, the Hispanic identifier is no longer negatively related to STW participation.
3. Among the various types of STW-preparatory programs, job shadowing and worksite visits are the most popular. On the other hand, apprenticeships and internships have the lowest participation rates. Hence, the most popular STW programs in place are not the most comprehensive and intensive. On the other hand, there is no evidence in the data analyzed in this chapter that minority youth or women are being channeled into less-comprehensive and less-intensive programs.
4. In terms of the consequences of participation on STW programs for student outcomes, the study considered the effects on math and science course taking, hours worked, and high-school retention. The longitudinal nature of the NLSY97 data set allowed a more robust analysis of the possible causal impacts involved than previous studies have.
5. A math and science course-taking index was constructed showing the number and level of math and science content courses taken by students during the period between the 1997 and 1998 interviews of NLSY97. A set of variables was then selected to explain the differences in this math and science course-intensity index among the youth in the NLSY97 sample. It was found that participation in STW-transition programs undertaken by youth before their first interview in 1997 was substantially linked to greater course taking in science and math in the year after the 1997 interview. This result suggests that STW programs enhance the curriculum experience of many minority participants, not only by requiring them to take more advanced or comprehensive math and science courses, but even more importantly by motivating them to take those courses in the future.
6. A strong link was discovered between participation in STW programs and subsequent labor-market participation. For all ethnic and racial groups, a substantial fraction of the additional hours worked during 1998 could be linked to students' participation in STW programs in earlier years.
7. Participation in career-major and STW-preparatory programs also had a strongly positive impact on high-school retention for all ethnic and racial groups considered. Although STW programs may have a negative impact on retention because they expose students to potential job opportunities, they can also increase retention by stimulating students' interest in pursuing additional academic courses that are connected to those future careers. It was also shown that, other factors held constant,

students in NLSY97 who participated in STW programs had less likelihood of dropping out of school.

REFERENCES

American Association of University Women. (1992). *How schools shortchange girls: A study of findings on girls and education.* New York: Marlowe & Company.

Arnow, P., Harbison, F., Lester, R. A., Michael, B., Nemore, A., & Venn, G. (1968). The transition from school to work: A summary of viewpoints. In *The transition from school to work: A report on the Princeton Manpower Symposium* (pp. 3–19; Industrial Relations Section Report No. 111). Princeton, NJ: Princeton University.

Berryman, S., & Bailey, T. R. (1992). *The double helix of education and the economy.* New York: Columbia University, Teachers College, Institute on Education and the Economy.

Bishop, J., & Mañe, F. (2000, December). *School-to-work in the 1990s: School–employer partnerships and student outcomes.* Paper presented at the National Invitational Conference, "What Do We Know about School-to-Work: Research and Practice," Philadelphia, PA.

Bureau of Labor Statistics. (2001). *Labor force statistics from the Current Population Survey: Employment status of the civilian population by race, sex, age, and Hispanic origin, Table A-2.* Retrieved from http://stats.bls.gov/webapps/legacy/cpsatb2.htm

Center for Human Resource Research. (2000). *NLSY97 user's guide: A guide to the rounds 1 and 2 data of the National Longitudinal Survey of Youth 1997.* Columbus, OH: Ohio State University.

Crain, R. L., Allen, A., Little, J., Sullivan, D., Thaler, R., Quigley D., et al. (1998). *The effects of career magnet schools* (Institute on Education and the Economy Brief No. 22). New York: Columbia University, Teachers College, Institute on Education and the Economy.

Cuban, L. (1982). Enduring resiliency: Enacting and implementing federal vocational education legislation. In H. Kantor & D. Tyack (Eds.), *Work, youth and schooling: Historical perspectives on vocationalism in American education* (pp. 45–78). Stanford, CA: Stanford University Press.

Desy, J., Campbell, P., & Gardner, J. (1984). *High school vocational experiences: In school and in the labor market.* Columbus, OH: National Center for Research in Vocational Education.

Grubb, W. N. (1995). The cunning hand, the cultured mind: Sources of support for curriculum integration. In W. N. Grubb (Ed.), *Education through occupations in American high schools* (pp. 11–25). New York: Teachers College Press.

Hamilton, S., & Hamilton, M. A. (1999). Creating new pathways to adulthood by adapting German apprenticeships in the United States. In W. R. Heinz (Ed.), *From education to work: Cross-national perspectives* (pp. 194–213). Cambridge, England: Cambridge University Press.

Hanser, L., & Stasz, C. (1999). *The effects of enrollment in the transportation career academy program on student outcomes.* Santa Monica, CA: RAND Corporation.

Heckman, J. J. (2000). Policies to foster human capital. *Research in Economics, 54,* 3–56.

Hughes, K. L., Bailey, T. R., & Mechur, M. J. (2001). *School-to-work: Making a difference in education. A research report to America.* New York: Columbia University, Teachers College, Institute on Education and the Economy.

Hughes, K. L., Moore, D. T., & Bailey, T. R. (1999). *Work-based learning and academic skills* (Institute on Education and the Economy Brief No. 27). New York: Columbia University, Teachers College, Institute on Education and the Economy.

Joyce, M., & Neumark, D. (2000). *An introduction to school-to-work programs in the NLSY97: How prevalent are they, and which youths do they serve?* (NBER Working Paper No. 7733). Cambridge, MA: National Bureau of Economic Research.

Kantor, H., & Tyack, D. (1982). Historical perspectives on vocationalism in American education. In H. Kantor & D. Tyack (Eds.), *Work, youth, and schooling: Historical perspectives on vocationalism in American education* (pp. 1–13). Stanford, CA: Stanford University Press.

Katz, L., & Autor, D. (1999). Changes in the wage structure and earnings inequality. In O. Ashenfelter & D. Card (Eds.), *Handbook of Labor Economics: Vol. 3A* (pp. 3309–3415). Amsterdam: North Holland Publishing.

Kemple, J. J., Poglinco, S. M., & Snipes, J. C. (1999). *Career academies: Building career awareness and work-based learning activities through employer participation.* New York: Manpower Demonstration Research Corporation.

Murnane, R. J., & Levy, F. (1996). *Teaching the new basic skills: Principles for educating children to thrive in a changing economy.* New York: The Free Press.

National Center on the Educational Quality of the Workforce. (1997). *Bringing school-to-work to scale: What employers report.* Philadelphia: University of Pennsylvania, Institute for Research on Higher Education.

National School-to-Work Office. (2000). *National good news, facts, and figures: Findings from national evaluations of school-to-work.* Retrieved from www.stw.ed.gov/research/goodfacts2.htm

Neumark, D., & Joyce, M. (2000). *Evaluating school-to-work programs using the NLSY* (NBER Working Paper No. 7719). Cambridge, MA: National Bureau of Economic Research.

Pauly, E., Kopp, H., & Haimson, J. (1995). *Homegrown lessons: Innovative programs linking school to work.* San Francisco, CA: Jossey-Bass.

Rivera-Batiz, F. L. (1991). The effects of literacy on the earnings of Hispanics in the United States. In C. Meléndez, C. Rodríguez, & J. Barry-Figueroa (Eds.), *Hispanics in the labor force* (pp. 53–75). New York: Plenum.

Rivera-Batiz, F. L. (1992a). Quantitative literacy and the likelihood of employment among young adults. *Journal of Human Resources, 27,* 313–328.

Rivera-Batiz, F. L. (1992b). English language proficiency and the earnings of young immigrants in U.S. labor markets. *Policy Studies Review, 11,* 165–175.

Rivera-Batiz, F. L. (1995a). Immigrants and the public school system: The case of New York City. *Forum for Applied Research and Public Policy, 10,* 84–89.

Rivera-Batiz, F. L. (1995b). *The impact of vocational education on racial and ethnic minorities* (ERIC Clearinghouse on Urban Education Digest, EDO-UD-95–5, No. 108). New York: ERIC Clearinghouse on Urban and Minority Education.

Rivera-Batiz, F. L. (1995c). Vocational education, the General Equivalency Diploma and urban and minority populations. *Education and Urban Society, 27,* 313–327.

Rivera-Batiz, F. L. (1996a). *The education of immigrant children: The case of New York*

City (Center for Migration, Ethnicity and Citizenship Working Paper, No. 3). New York: The New School University.

Rivera-Batiz, F. L. (1996b). English language proficiency, quantitative skills, and the economic progress of immigrants. In H. O. Duleep & P. V. Wunnava (Eds.), *Immigrants and immigration policy: Individual skills, family ties, and group identities* (pp. 57–77). Greenwich, CT: JAI Press.

Rivera-Batiz, F. L. (1998). *A profile and analysis of students in vocational training: Literacy skills, demographics, and socioeconomic characteristics.* Berkeley, CA: National Center for Research in Vocational Education.

Rivera-Batiz, F. L. (2001). *The effects of school-to-work programs on minority youth: Evidence from the NLSY97* (Institute for Urban and Minority Education Working Paper). New York: Columbia University, Teachers College.

Schug, M. C., & Western, R. D. (2000, December). *School-to-work: The Wisconsin experience.* Paper presented at the National Invitational Conference, "What Do We Know about School-to-Work: Research and Practice," Philadelphia, PA.

Shapiro, D. (1998). *School-to-work partnerships and employer participation: Evidence on persistence and attrition from the national employer survey* (National Center for Postsecondary Improvement Report No. 2–10). Stanford, CA: Stanford University, School of Education.

Silverberg, M. (1997). *The first national survey of local school-to-work partnerships: Data and summary.* Princeton, NJ: Mathematica Policy Research, Inc.

Stern, D., Raby, M., & Dayton, C. (1992). *Career academies: Partnerships for reconstructing American high schools.* San Francisco, CA: Jossey-Bass.

Topel, R. H., & Ward, M. P. (1992). Job mobility and the careers of young men. *Quarterly Journal of Economics, 107,* 439–80.

U.S. Department of Labor. (2000). *The National Longitudinal Surveys handbook 2000.* Washington, DC: Bureau of Labor Statistics.

Westchester Institute for Human Services Research. (1998). *The balanced view: School to work.* Unpublished manuscript, Westchester Institute for Human Services Research, White Plains, NY.

Zemsky, R., Shapiro, D., Iannozzi, M., Cappelli, P., & Bailey, T. (1998). *The transition from initial education to working life in the United States of America* (National Center for Postsecondary Improvement Project Paper No. 1). Stanford, CA: Stanford University, School of Education.

12

The Impacts of School–Business Partnerships on the Early Labor-Market Success of Students

John H. Bishop
Ferran Mañe

One of the most successful strategies pursued by the school-to-work (STW) movement has been improving communication between schools and employers. At the beginning of the 1980s, most employers hired young workers without paying much attention to student achievement in high school. Even though they were obligated by law to share transcripts with employers when students signed release forms, many high schools were not responding to such requests. For example, in Columbus, Ohio in 1982, Nationwide Insurance sent more than 1,200 requests for transcripts signed by job applicants to high schools and received only ninety-three responses. In other cases, transcripts took so long to arrive that hiring decisions had already been made.

Employers offering the best jobs developed very negative stereotypes of young high-school graduates. Interviewed for a 1990 CBS News special report on educational reform, the personnel director at a large, high-wage company proudly stated, "We don't hire high-school graduates any more; we need *skilled* workers." Recent graduates who were both skilled and disciplined were unable to signal these facts to employers. As a result, recent high-school graduates were effectively frozen out of primary labor-market jobs. They took jobs at low wages in the secondary labor market and hoped that they would be able to establish a record of performance in those jobs that would enable them to get a primary labor-market job sometime later. This meant a long period of churning in the low-wage labor market for everybody.

As a result, young workers with strong basic skills did not earn appreciably more than workers with weak basic skills (Bishop, 1992). Over time, however, those who did a good job were more likely to get further training, promotions, and good recommendations when they moved on, while poor performers were encouraged to leave. Because academic achievement in high school is correlated with job performance (Bishop; Hartigan & Wigdor, 1989), the sorting process resulted in basic skills assessed during high school having a much larger effect on the labor-market success of thirty-year-olds than of nineteen-year-olds, even when contemporaneous measures of completed schooling were held constant (Altonji & Pierret, in press; Farber & Gibbons, 1996).

The long delays before the benefits of academic achievement in high school started accruing sent students the wrong signal. Teenagers knew that college-educated adults had good jobs and lived in large attractive houses, which explains why more than four out of five said they wanted to go to college. They did not know whether the successful adults in their communities took rigorous courses and studied hard in high school. They observed almost no relationship between the academic achievements of their older friends and the quality of their jobs. So it was reasonable for youngsters to conclude that employers reward credentials, not learning. If that was the conclusion they drew, the best strategy for the bulk of students was to study just hard enough to get the diploma and be admitted to college, but no harder. A 1987 survey of a nationally representative sample of tenth graders found that 62% agreed with the statement, "I don't like to do any more school work than I have to" (*Longitudinal Study of American Youth,* question AA37N).

Recognizing these problems, the Labor Secretary's Commission on Workforce Quality and Labor Market Efficiency recommended that "the business community should . . . show through their hiring and promotion decisions that academic achievements will be rewarded" (1989, p. 9). They also recommended that "high school students who excel in science and mathematics should be rewarded with business internships or grants for further study" (p. 11). The school-to-work (STW) movement has made improved communication between schools and employers one of its key goals. The STW movement has brought many employers into schools and involved them with students as mentors and as sponsors of internships, apprenticeships, job shadowing, and cooperative-education experiences. By 1997, participation rates for ninth and tenth graders had reached 12% for job shadowing, 5% for mentoring, 7.3% for cooperative education, and 5% for internships and apprenticeships. Some 12% of students said they had visited a worksite or worked during school hours as part of a STW program (Bishop, Mañe, & Ruiz-Quintanilla, 2000).

This chapter examines the effects of improved signaling of student achievement in high school on the labor market success of recent high-school graduates. The chapter is organized into three sections. In the first section, we reproduce the argument that Bishop put forward in 1985 that better signaling of student achievement to employers would improve the quality of the jobs that recent high-school graduates could obtain and strengthen incentives to learn. In the second section, we analyze longitudinal data on eighth graders in 1988 and attempt to measure the effect of school–employer partnerships on their subsequent success in the labor market, testing the hypotheses put forward in 1985. The final section of the chapter discusses the research and policy implications of the findings.

PREDICTIONS AND HYPOTHESES: THE IMPACTS OF SCHOOL–BUSINESS PARTNERSHIPS AND MINIMUM COMPETENCY EXAMINATIONS ON EARLY LABOR-MARKET SUCCESS OF SCHOOL LEAVERS

In a 1985 report, Bishop argued that "schools can help their graduates avoid unemployment and get better jobs by improving the quality and facilitating the flow of employment-related information available to students and their potential employer." He advocated "close linkages between vocational teachers and local employers who hire their graduates" and "job placement and referral services for all students (not just the vocational students) that are based on long-term relationships of trust with local employers" (pp. 98–100).

The report also suggested that high schools could help students by establishing higher standards in both occupational and academic programs and making sure that employers believed the high standards were real and therefore that the negative stereotypes were false.

These considerations have led us to hypothesize that school–business partnerships (SBPs) and Minimum Competency Exams (MCEs) would improve job opportunities of recent school leavers in three ways. First, by improving student achievement and developing character, they raise worker productivity. Even when this does not immediately increase workers' earnings, the effect of academic achievement on wages grows with time and eventually becomes very large.

A second way that SBPs and MCEs improve job opportunities is by sending a signal to employers that *all* the graduates of a high school meet or exceed their hiring standards. Bringing local employers into the school for presentations or meetings gives school personnel the opportunity to show business partners the school's successful programs and introduce them to outstanding students who might be interested in working at the company in the future.

A third way that SBPs can affect job opportunities is by improving the quality of the information that employers have on the achievements and character of recent high-school graduates. If employers become more able to assess the academic achievement of job applicants, this trait will get more weight in their selection decisions. If character traits such as dependability and honesty get better signaled, these traits will take on more importance. School–business partnerships often result in a school (or specific teachers there) becoming trusted referral sources for local employers (Rosenbaum, 2000). When this occurs, we would expect the school's "better" students to be the greatest beneficiary of the relationship (Rosenbaum, DeLuca, Miller, & Roy, 1999). How would "better" be defined? Probably not by test scores alone. Effort, reliability, and social skills would probably matter even more, but our data set lacks good indicators of these character traits. Grade-point averages reflect effort and reliability as well as test scores, so in our data set, the GPA is probably the best single indicator of whom the referral process would most benefit.

Even if schools recommend and refer only their best noncollege-bound students to high-wage employers, these top students will probably not be the only ones to benefit. Their success at the community's more visible high-wage employers will cast doubt on the negative stereotype that has been hurting all recent graduates. A further benefit is that finding work for some students in the primary labor market reduces competition for the secondary labor market—retail sales and fast food—jobs that are customarily filled by youth. This would make it easier for less-qualified students to find work. Thus, the "best" students might get better jobs while the rest of the students might find it easier to get jobs.

The foregoing logic generates a number of testable predictions. Holding constant socioeconomic status and test scores, GPA, attitudes in eighth grade, whether a student gets a diploma or a Graduate Equivalency Diploma (GED), current and past college attendance, and a complete set of other individual and school characteristics, we predict the following:

- Hypothesis 1. Students with average GPAs will, ceteris paribus, do better in the labor market when they attend high schools that are part of a school–business partnership.
- Hypothesis 2. Rewards for academic achievement will be significantly greater at schools that have established SBPs.

Preliminary support for these hypotheses comes from Rosenbaum, DeLuca, Miller, and Roy's (1999) recent study of who gets job-referral assistance from their high schools and the impact of such assistance on students. They found that students with high test scores were more likely to obtain their first job through a school referral or recommendation. They also found that those who got their first job through a high-school contact or referral earned only slightly more in their first job, but nine years later were being paid 17% more than students who got their first job without the help of their high school.

- Hypothesis 3. Students living in MCE states will be paid more. In most MCE states, transcripts indicate whether the student has passed the MCE but not how the student scored on the MCE test. Consequently, state MCEs may not improve the signaling of academic achievement. We do not know whether the districts with local MCEs are putting MCE scores on the high-school transcript or advertising them in some other way, so it is not clear how local MCEs will influence the tendency of employers to offer the best jobs to the best students.

EMPIRICAL ANALYSIS

Data and Specification

We report on an analysis of restricted data on public-school students from the National Education Longitudinal Study (NELS: 88), a longitudinal data set that followed a nationally representative sample of eighth graders in 1988 through the year 1994. The eighth graders who subsequently dropped out of high school were tested and interviewed in 1992 and 1994, and so are included in the analysis sample.

We created a school–business partnership index by summing "Yes" answers to four questions in the 1992 principals' questionnaire about relationships with the local business community. Table 12.1 presents the exact wording of each question. The mean value for the index across the sample schools is 2.42, and the standard deviation is 1.01.

We expected SBPs to have larger impacts on students with good grades. Consequently, the effects of the partnerships were captured by two variables: the SBP index and an interaction between the SBP index and the student's eighth-grade GPA. The interaction variable was defined as (SBP) × (GPA − 2.91). When we deviate GPA from its mean of 2.91 before constructing the interaction variable, the coefficient for the SBP index becomes an estimate of the impact of SBPs on students who have B to B− averages in eighth grade.

The restricted data identified the state in which each high school is located, and this information was used to construct an indicator variable, *StateMCE,* that was equal to one for students in states that required them to pass a MCE to graduate in 1992 (Alabama, Florida, Georgia, Hawaii, Louisiana, Maryland, Mississippi, Nevada, New Mexico, New Jersey, New York, North Carolina, South Carolina, Tennessee, and Texas) and zero elsewhere. In states that did not have a state MCE, information on local MCEs came from questionnaires completed by the high school principal in 1990 and 1992. In the states with a statewide MCE, local MCE was set equal to zero. The interactions between eighth-grade GPA and the MCE variables were constructed in the same way as for the SBP index.

Models were estimated predicting seven indicators of early labor-market outcomes: earnings in calendar 1993; the total number of months worked in the

Table 12.1
Percentage of Schools Having Different Types of Business Partnerships

Do you have any of the following relationships with your local business community?	% Yes
1. Do employers ask the school to post a listing of job openings?	71.7
2. Do employers ask the school to recommend students for jobs?	88.2
3. School has been adopted by a local business?	40.3
4. A local business sponsors an incentive program in your school?	30.8

twenty-one-month period following high-school graduation; the total number of months unemployed in that period; average monthly earnings; monthly earnings in January–February 1994; the logarithm of the hourly wage rate; and a zero–one variable indicating whether the job is not a service, laborer, or retail sales job. The models predicting these labor-market outcomes included controls for current and past college attendance: a dummy variable for full-time college attendance during the period for which earnings were measured, a dummy for part-time attendance during that period, and the number of semesters of college attendance before the earnings measurement period. Also included were dummies for ever dropping out, obtaining a GED, failing to get either a diploma or a GED, graduating early, and the length of the delay in graduation when graduating late.

Because the outcomes being studied are influenced by a host of other characteristics of the community and the student, we controlled for as many of them as possible in order to increase efficiency and reduce omitted variable bias. Our estimations included controls for a host of student-background characteristics measured in eighth grade: GPA; test scores; whether students took remedial courses; whether they took advanced courses; TV and homework hours; reading for pleasure; whether they were handicapped; family socioeconomic status; a parent-involvement index; family size; family structure; a locus-of-control index; a self-esteem index; hours working for pay during eighth grade (and its square); an index for smoking in eighth grade; dummies for race, ethnicity, and religion; rural, suburban, or urban residence; and ten variables describing the quality of the school. A full description of the variables included in the analysis is available from the authors.

From the principals' questionnaire, we took the following indicators of the quality of the student's secondary school: dummy variables for Catholic schools, for secular private schools, and for schools formed by non-Catholic religious organizations; average teacher salary; pupil-teacher ratio; percentage of students eligible for free lunch; Carnegie units required to graduate; percentage of students who were white; and average enrollment per high-school grade (and its square). Two other measures of the quality of the school attended in tenth grade—the average socioeconomic status and eighth-grade test scores of students at the school—were calculated by averaging student responses for each high school in the NELS: 88 database. In addition, we controlled for the following characteristics of the state: unemployment rate, mean weekly wage in retailing, weekly wage in manufacturing, minimum number of Carnegie units required by the state law, and dummies for four census regions. Our estimations were a decided improvement over the analyses previously conducted using High School and Beyond data because the use of restricted data allowed us to include controls for important variables such as the state unemployment rate and the average earnings in manufacturing and retailing for the state.[1]

Results

Table 12.2 presents the results of our analysis of the capability of partnerships between schools and businesses and high-school graduation test requirements to predict the earnings and employment of high-school graduates and dropouts. Estimated effects of SBPs and networks are given in columns 2 through 5. Estimated effects of State MCEs appear in columns 6 through 9. Local MCE results are given in columns 10 through 13. The first column of each four-column group gives estimated effects for eighth graders with average grades. The coefficient for the interaction with GPA is given in the second column of the group. Predicted effects of the policy on C– students and A students are given in the third and fourth columns of the group. Huber-White standard errors that correct for the clustered sample are given in parentheses underneath the estimated coefficients. The numbers in brackets in the third and fourth column of each four-column group are the *p* value for the null hypothesis that the policy had no effect on C– students and A students, respectively. The statistical significance of each coefficient and of predicted effects is indicated by the number of asterisks to its right or by the plus sign, as indicated in the table.

Figures 12.1 and 12.2 present a visual representation of our model's predictions of the impact of SBPs and state MCEs, respectively, on early labor-market outcomes and how they vary by the student's GPA in eighth grade. The figures are based on analysis of 1994 data on NELS: 88 students who were in the eighth grade in 1988, controlled for attitudes, socioeconomic status, GPA, eighth-grade test scores, and state and high-school characteristics.

The bars in Figure 12.1 represent the predicted effect of a two-unit increase in the SBP index. For the unemployment rate and the probability of getting a good job, the bars represent changes in probability. For earnings, months worked, and hourly wage, the bars represent percentage change from the baseline. Thus, the percentage effect of a two-unit change in the SBP index on the annual earnings of students with B to B– averages is 4.05% ([2 * $108]/$5,330, where $5,330 is the mean annual earnings in the sample). For C– students, the predicted effect is 9.9% ([2 * $264]/$5,330). The asterisks and plus signs above or below a bar indicate the statistical significance of the effect being pictured. Bars that lack these signs describe predicted effects that are not significantly different from zero at the 10% level on a one-tailed test. Because the regressions control for whether students graduated from high school and for whether they attended college, we are measuring the short-run effects of graduation requirements on labor-market success net of effects that operate through the probability of graduating from high school or attending college.

Our first finding is that school–business partnerships significantly reduced unemployment in the two years after leaving high school and significantly increased employment, annual earnings, and hourly wage rates. The quality of the jobs students got after leaving high school also improved significantly. Hypothesis 1, therefore, received strong support.

Table 12.2

Effect of SBPs and MCEs on Employment Outcomes after High School

	Mean (SD)	School–Business P'ships	P'ship x 8th Grade GPA	P'ship for C– Student	P'ship for A Student	State MCE (SMCE)	SMCE x 8th Grade GPA	SMCE on C– Student	SMCE on A Student	Local MCE (LMCE)	LMCE x 8th Grade GPA	LMCE on C– Student	LMCE on A Student	R^2 # Obs.
1993 Annual Earnings	$5,330 (5394)	108* (62)	-130* (77)	264** [.04]	-39 [.67]	476** (190)	264+ (192)	159 [.63]	774*** [.002]	2 (240)	682*** (233)	-816** [.045]	773** [.014]	.2358 8307
Total Months Worked	13.41 (7.45)	.178** (.09)	-.077 (.106)	.27* [.092]	.09 [.53]	.137 (.274)	-.421* (.240)	.64+ [.11]	-.34 [.38]	-.065 (.285)	.73** (.30)	-.94** [.049]	.76* [.074]	.1376 9747
Total Months Unemploy.	1.78 (4.09)	-.13*** (.046)	-.039 (.057)	-.08 [.32]	-.17** [.013]	-.131 (.143)	.022 (.133)	-.157 [.50]	-.106 [.57]	-.018 (.150)	.042 (.162)	.068 [.80]	.029 [.89]	.0591 9747
Average Earnings / Mo.	$528 (505)	3.6 (5.9)	2.1 (6.6)	1.1 [.93]	6.0 [.47]	43.1*** (16.6)	10.9 (15.5)	30 [.27]	55*** [.01]	6.1 (20.4)	26.0 (20.6)	25 [.49]	35 [.49]	.1990 9595
Spr. 1994 Earn. / Mo.	$517 (642)	3.9 (7.6)	4.5 (8.7)	-1.5 [.92]	9.0 [.39]	19.1 (22.4)	18.6 (19.9)	-3.2 [.93]	40.1+ [.16]	-6.3 (25.6)	54.3** (26.7)	-71.5+ [.11]	55.1+ [.12]	.1761 9377
Log. Hourly Wage Rate	1.292 (.556)	.0035 (.0064)	.0088 (.008)	-.007 [.57]	.013+ [.19]	.0027 (.019)	.0066 (.018)	-.005 [.86]	.010 [.71]	.000 (.025)	.061*** (.024)	-.073* [.06]	.069** [.05]	.0874 9696
Good Job [1–0]	.570 (.495)	.096*** (.035)	.068* (.041)	.014 [.76]	.173*** [.008]	.088 (.108)	-.158* (.094)	.278** [.043]	-.09 [.53]	-.013 (.113)	-.221* (.124)	.252+ [.12]	-.263+ [.196]	.0205 4459

Note: Analysis of NELS: 88 data on public high-school students in 1990 interviewed in 1994. The *StateMCE* variable is a 1 for AL, FL, GA, HI, LA, MD, MS, NV, MN, NJ, NY, NC, SC, TN, and TX. Models control for when the respondent got a high-school diploma, whether the respondent was in college full time during spring 1994, whether she was a part-time student in spring 1994, the number of months spent attending college full-time, and months spent attending part time. Models contain a full set of background variables measured in the eighth grade: family socioeconomic status; books in the home; single parent; parents divorced; number of siblings; test scores; GPA in eighth grade; TV hours; homework hours; read-for-fun index; smoking; dummies for gender, ethnicity, religion, handicapped status, in advanced courses, in remedial courses, and central city and rural school location; locus-of-control index; self-esteem index; and hours working for pay. The characteristics of the school the student attended during tenth grade (or had attended prior to dropping out) in the model were private control (three types); teacher salary; percentage student body white; percentage free-lunch eligible; mean eighth-grade test score; mean family socioeconomic status; and enrollment per grade, plus its square. Characteristics of the state controlled were unemployment rate; weekly wages in retailing and manufacturing; and dummies for four census regions, named in the text. Models were not weighted. Numbers in parentheses below the coefficient are Huber-White standard errors that correct for clustering by school. Rows 1 to 6 of the table present linear regression results. Row 7 has the results of a logistic regression. The numbers in brackets in columns 4, 5, 8, 9, 12, and 13 are the p values for a hypothesis test that the SBPs' and MCEs' effects on A students and C– students are significantly different from zero.

+ Statistically significant at 10% level on a one-tailed test.

* Statistically significant at 5% level on a one-tailed test.

** Statistically significant at 5% level on a two-tailed test.

*** Statistically significant at 1% level on a two-tailed test.

Figure 12.1
Effect of a Two-Unit Increase in the SBP Index on Labor-Market Outcomes after High School of Students with Different Grades

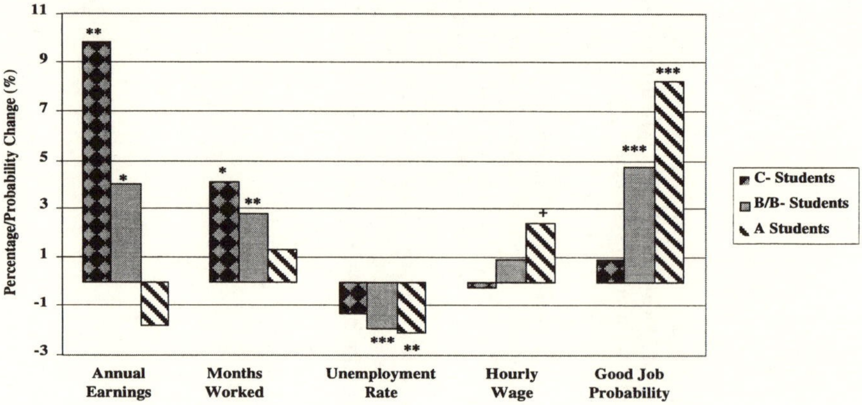

Figure 12.2
Effect of Having a State MCE on Labor-Market Outcomes after High School of Students with Different Grades

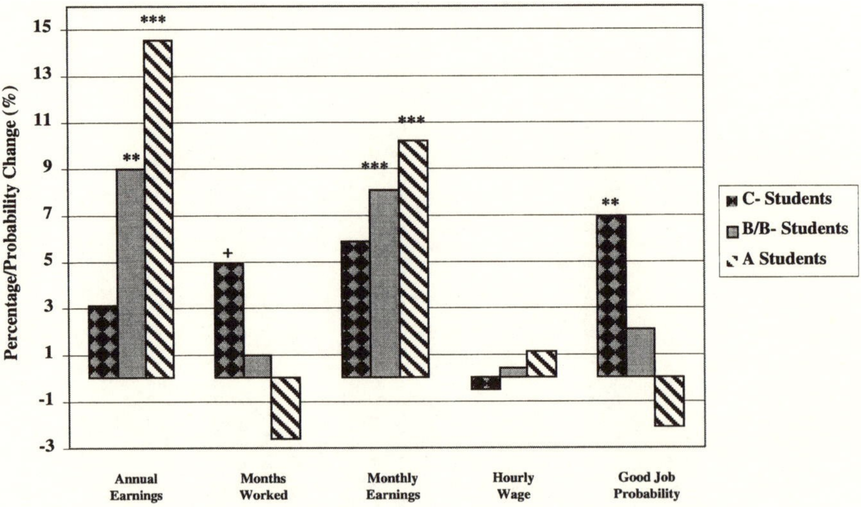

Our second hypothesis, that SBPs would tend to benefit high-GPA students more than low-GPA students, received mixed support. As predicted, the effects of SBPs on unemployment, wage rates, and job quality were significantly larger for high-GPA students. On the other hand, SBPs had larger effects on the months employed and annual earnings of low-GPA students than of high-GPA students. Apparently, SBPs benefit high-and low-GPA students in different ways. For high-GPA students, they improve job quality and lower unemployment. For low-GPA students, job quality does not improve, but employment and earnings increase, partly because unemployment declines but mainly because labor force participation rises. This pattern of results is consistent with the queue model of youth employment put forward at the end of the first section. SBPs appear to help the best (high-GPA) students get better primary labor-market jobs. The exit of these high-GPA students from the secondary labor market may be creating opportunities for low-GPA students to get full-time work that would not have been available to them in the absence of the SBPs.

Our third hypothesis, that Minimum Competency Exams increase wage rates and earnings, received substantial support. Although State MCEs showed no effect on wage rates, they did show significant effects on both annual and monthly earnings of students with average and above-average grades. State MCEs increased the annual earnings of students with average grades by 9% and the earnings of A students by 14%. State MCEs significantly increased employment of students with C– grades, but their estimated impact on annual earnings was only 2.9%, not large enough to be statistically significant.

The effects of local MCEs were different. Local MCEs clearly increased the rewards for the traits that are captured by eighth-grade GPA. The coefficient for the interaction between GPA and a local MCE was significantly positive in the models predicting annual earnings, months employed, hourly wage rate, and monthly earnings in January–February 1994. Our results imply that local MCEs had significant positive effects on the employment, wage rates, and earnings of A students and significant negative effects on the employment, wage rates, and earnings of C– students. They had no effects on students with average grades.

Do School–Business Partnerships Have Negative Side Effects?

Do negative effects on other important student outcomes offset the positive labor-market effects of SBPs? For example, does employer involvement with the school induce some to drop out of high school or to delay graduation? Have partnerships induced students to study harder as intended, or have they distracted the school and students from academic goals? Does the improved access to jobs reduce the number of young people who attend college?

To answer these questions, we estimated models predicting student responses to questions about how hard they were working and direct measures of how much they learned between eighth and twelfth grade. In addition, logit models were estimated that predicted dropping out of high school, getting a GED rather than a regular diploma, taking more time to complete high school, not graduating from high school before 1994, and college attendance.

The estimations found no significant effects of SBPs on most of the outcomes studied. The indexes for working hard and for challenging courses were no different in schools with SBPs. Test-score gains were not significantly different. Dropout rates, overall high-school completion rates (regular diploma plus GED), and college-attendance rates were no different. However, there were two significant differences. First, students in schools with partnerships were less likely to graduate late. Because delays in graduating from high school significantly reduce earnings, this is a very positive outcome. Students from partnership schools were also significantly less likely to get a GED and more likely to get a conventional diploma instead. This too is a very positive outcome because people with regular high-school diplomas earn considerably more than those with GED credentials.

IMPLICATIONS FOR SCHOOL-TO-WORK RESEARCH AND POLICY

STW Program Effectiveness Cannot Be Measured by Comparing STW Participants to Nonparticipating Students at a School

There are two serious problems with such an evaluation methodology: selection bias and leakage of program impacts into the control group (contamination of the control group is an alternate descriptor of the problem). Comparing students at schools that do and do not have STW programs is a better approach. Selection problems can bias school-level analyses, but at least the control-group-contamination problem is avoided.

Effects of School-to-Work Programs Are Not Limited to Those Participating in STW Activities

The school-to-work movement's emphasis on collaborating with local employers is intended to improve employer perceptions of the quality of all of the school's graduates, not just the STW students. Our analysis of NELS: 88 data suggests that this goal may have been achieved. Students from schools with business partnerships and networks experienced less unemployment, were more consistently employed, earned more, and got higher-level jobs. The STW movement's practice of building collaborative networks with local employers may be the most important mechanism by which STW programs help students.

School–Business Partnerships Are a Cost-Effective Strategy for Helping Students

Building such networks takes time and the commitment of school staff. But these direct costs are small when compared to the benefits that students receive.

Our analysis suggests that a two-unit increase in the SBP index was associated with a $216 increase in annual earnings. If a school has 400 ninth graders, and the earnings benefit lasts for just five years, the total earnings benefit of the two-unit increase in collaboration would be $432,000 for each one-year student cohort—much more than ten times what schools of that size would be likely to be spending annually to build and maintain the collaborative network. One particularly attractive aspect of the policy is that no student group appears to be hurt by the policy and all groups are helped in some way. For unemployment, wages, and job quality, benefits are larger for high-GPA students than low-GPA students. For employment and earnings, however, benefits are larger for low-GPA students.

Another attractive feature of SBPs is that one does not have to trade off positive labor-market effects for negative effects on some other front.[2] We tested the hypothesis that SBPs might lower test-score gains, high-school enrollment and completion rates, and college attendance. This hypothesis was rejected in every case. Test-score gains, dropout rates, and college attendance rates were the same. The only significant relationship was with the probability of a delay in graduating from high school and with the proportion of graduates who get the GED credential. Schools with business networks had fewer students delaying their graduation and fewer getting the GED.

NOTES

1. These controls for school characteristics and region may not, however, have been sufficient to avoid omitted-variable bias entirely. States and school districts with SBPs or MCE exams may have differed along unmeasured dimensions having direct effects on labor-market outcomes.

2. By contrast, MCEs increase earnings and college attendance rates, but they also reduce the number of students who get the regular high-school diploma within six years of completing eighth grade. As one might suspect, it is the students who are doing poorly in eighth grade who are most likely to have their graduation delayed or prevented. The positive effects of MCEs go disproportionately to the students whose eighth-grade GPA indicates they are either smarter or trying harder (Bishop, Mañe, Bishop, & Moriarty, 2001).

REFERENCES

Altonji, J., & Pierret, C. (in press). Employer learning and statistical discrimination. *Quarterly Journal of Economics.*

Bishop, J. H. (1985). *Preparing Youth for Employment.* Columbus, OH: National Center for Research in Vocational Education. (ERIC Document Reproduction Service No. ED 254644).

Bishop, J. H. (1992). Impact of academic competencies on wages, unemployment, and job performance. *Carnegie-Rochester Conference Series on Public Policy, 37,* 127–194.

Bishop, J. H., Mañe, F., Bishop, M., & Moriarty, J. (2001). The role of end-of-course exams and minimum competency exams in standards-based reforms. *Brookings Papers on Education Policy, 4,* 267–345.

Bishop, J. H., Mañe, F., & Ruiz-Quintanilla, A. (2000). *Who participates in school-to-work programs: Initial tabulations.* Washington, DC: National School-to-Work Office.

CBS News (Producer). (1990, September 6). America's toughest assignment: solving the education crisis. New York: Author.

Commission on Workforce Quality and Labor Market Efficiency. (1989). *Investing in people: A strategy to address America's workforce crisis.* Washington, DC: Department of Labor.

Farber, H., & Gibbons, R. (1996). Learning and wage dynamics. *Quarterly Journal of Economics, 111,* 1007–47.

Hartigan, J., & Wigdor, A. (Eds.). (1989). *Fairness in employment testing.* Washington, DC: National Academy Press.

Longitudinal study of American youth [Data file]. (1987). Retrieved from Longitudinal Study of American Youth website: http://www.lsay.org.

Rosenbaum, J. E. (2000). Teachers' social construction of employer linkages. *Providing career options to the forgotten half* (Rose Monograph Series, American Sociological Association). New York: Russell Sage Foundation.

Rosenbaum, J. E., DeLuca, S., Miller, S. R., & Roy, K. (1999). *Pathways to work: Short and long-term effects of personal and institutional ties.* Evanston, IL: Northwestern University, Institute of Policy Research.

13

High Schools' Role in College and Workforce Preparation: Do College-for-All Policies Make High School Irrelevant?

James E. Rosenbaum

Despite enormous changes in employment circumstances and college opportunities over the past several decades, young people continue to have work-entry problems. Although a strong labor market reduces unemployment, such a labor market will not last forever, it will not solve employers' skill shortages, and it will not give unskilled youths good jobs, particularly if they lack soft skills that employers do not try to provide through training.

The youth labor market also poses difficulties for employers. Employers complain that high-school graduates have poor basic skills in reading, writing, and mathematics; weaknesses that make them incapable of handling good jobs (Committee for Economic Development, 1985; National Commission on Excellence in Education, 1983). Employers are spending a billion dollars per year to provide basic-skills education for their workers (Eurich, 1985). These problems will become more serious because the number of young people is not increasing while the demand for workers is projected to increase, particularly in jobs requiring the higher skills that many youths lack. As one analyst described the double-edged nature of the problem, "Unless workforce basic skills are raised substantially, and quickly, we shall have more joblessness among the least skilled, accompanied by a chronic shortage of workers with advanced skills" (Howe et al., 1988, p. 2). Many business and labor groups foresee labor-market disruptions for some sectors of the economy. The projected skill shortage suggests that we can no longer afford such serious educational failure, nor can we squander new high-school graduates in long periods of unemployment and aimless job turnover.

This chapter summarizes some of the findings of ten years of research that are reported in full in my recent book, *Beyond College for All* (Rosenbaum, 2001). Based on analysis of national data and on interviews with employers, guidance counselors, vocational teachers, and students, this research has tried to understand the transition from school to work as a system.

Presented here is evidence indicating that high schools have misunderstood work-entry problems by viewing them too narrowly. High schools focus too narrowly on college goals, not job goals; on academic deficiencies, but not other deficiencies; and on students' internal motivation, but not on the external factors that affect their incentives. As a result of this narrow focus, high schools underestimate how many students are work-bound, they prevent some students from developing highly valued noncognitive competencies, and they prevent many students from getting preparation for realistic careers.

Perhaps also as a result of this narrow focus, this chapter explains that students seriously misperceive their incentives, and these misperceptions are encouraged by societal practices. Employers' hiring practices and colleges' open-admissions practices give students the false impression that there are no incentives for high-school effort, when incentives actually exist. The research reported here has found that although students' high-school achievements do not improve *short-term* outcomes, they have large effects on *long-term* outcomes. Although students' school achievements are not rewarded right after high school, they result in major payoffs ten years later. This research has also found payoffs for noncognitive behaviors. Unfortunately, because long-term payoffs are harder to see than short-term ones, students do not see their long-term incentives, but only the lack of short-term incentives. The problem for policy is *not* how to create incentives because they already exist, but rather how to make long-term incentives more visible.

Finally, the chapter examines the procedures other nations use for communicating incentives to youths and shows how such procedures could improve current U.S. reforms. Contacts are a good way to make incentives more visible, and cooperative learning (co-op) and tech-prep reforms help high schools make contacts with employers or colleges. However, problems sometimes arise in tech-prep and co-op reforms, and I discuss these problems and describe procedures that have overcome them in other nations. I also report new findings that indicate how some teachers and employers in the United States also use similar procedures to improve the effectiveness of school–employer contacts, and these practices suggest some ways to improve current reforms.

CURRENT POLICIES VIEW YOUTHS' PROBLEMS TOO NARROWLY

High Schools Focus Too Narrowly on College, Not on Jobs

I begin my analysis by showing the ways policies focus on overly narrow goals. One response to the poor labor market for high-school graduates has been a new policy of encouraging all students to attend college—what I have called "college-for-all" (Rosenbaum, 1998). Without any public decision,

American high schools have quietly adopted this new unofficial policy. High-school guidance counselors used to be gatekeepers; if students were unprepared for college, counselors advised them to plan other careers (Cicourel & Kitsuse, 1963; Rosenbaum, 1976). That has clearly changed. In a recent study, we found that guidance counselors now encourage all students to attend college, regardless of their past records, and they do not warn students if they have poor chances of success (Krei & Rosenbaum, in press; Rosenbaum, Miller, & Krei, 1996). Their new policy has had an impact across the nation. The 1992 National Education Longitudinal Study (NELS: 92) found that 84% of high-school seniors planned to get a two- or four-year college degree. Even students with bad grades, low test scores, and poor high-school attendance planned to complete a college degree.

However, many of these students will be disappointed. Although 84% of seniors expected a degree, only 41.3% of high-school graduates age thirty to thirty-four had a college degree.[1] Similarly, a national study, the High School and Beyond (HS&B) sample, followed high-school seniors ten years after graduation. It found that of seniors who planned to get a college degree, only 37.7% actually completed a degree in the ten years following graduation. For seniors with college plans but poor high-school grades, fewer than 14% completed a degree (Rosenbaum, 1998, 2001). For this 14%, open admissions afforded an extremely helpful second chance. However, an 86% failure rate suggests that the college-for-all approach is usually an unrealistic policy for such students. They need to be told how hard they must work to overcome these odds, and they need to consider fallback options.

The college-for-all policy tends to create serious misconceptions that confuse students and policymakers. The following points need consideration in order to dispel these misconceptions.

- First, many college-bound students are really work-bound. Many students who plan college degrees are almost certain to drop out of college. The HS&B survey suggests that perhaps as many as 31.1% of college entrants got no credits.[2] Moreover, although only 11.7% of students with good high-school grades (A) got zero credits, 52.4% of students with Cs did so (Rosenbaum, 2001). Although they have college plans, such students are really work-bound. They enter the labor market with a high-school diploma as their highest degree (often with no college credits), although they have not planned or prepared to do so.
- In addition, many students in college are not college students. Unprepared students enter college, but they soon drop out. Indeed, 40% of college students take remedial courses that give no college credits (National Center for Education Statistics, 1998), many students take three or more remedial courses (Deil & Rosenbaum, 2000), and increased numbers of remedial courses increase the chances of dropping out of college. Many courses in college buildings are not college courses but remedial courses—high-school level courses that confer no college credits (Deil & Rosenbaum). The students who take these courses are paying college tuition, but they are not taking courses that give college credit.

- Indeed, we find that even after entering college, many students are unclear about requirements (Deil & Rosenbaum, 2000). Although community colleges do a good job of spreading information about their open-admissions policies, they do not disseminate information about remedial courses, dropout rates, or ways that students can anticipate whether they will be taking college-credit courses. To avoid discouraging students, some community colleges avoid telling students that they are in remedial courses or that their courses are not conferring college credit, even after they have taken several such courses.
- Although the labor market does require higher skills than formerly, many good jobs do not require college skills. There has been a large increase in the need for *high-school* level skills: math, reading, and writing skills at a ninth- to eleventh-grade level (Murnane & Levy, 1996). The problem is that more than 40% of high-school seniors lack ninth-grade academic skills (Murnane & Levy). We need to improve youths' skills, but the skills that are needed can be provided in high school. Students do not need college for these skills.

Counselors promoting the college-for-all policy have good intentions. Like all Americans, they are reluctant to discourage students, and they do not want to close off students' options too early. But by withholding information about the requirements for college-credit classes, counselors prevent students from knowing what high-school efforts would prepare them for real college courses and from seeing incentives for high-school effort (Rosenbaum, Miller, & Krei, 1996). Counselors also prevent students from knowing their realistic chances of gaining some college credits and from knowing how much time and tuition it will take before they start getting those credits.

Moreover, counselors should give students information about backup options in good, well-paid careers that do not require college. Such jobs exist in a wide variety of fields, including construction, trades, clerical and administrative support, technical specialties, printing, graphics, financial services, and social services. Unfortunately, few guidance counselors know about such jobs and their requirements (Rosenbaum, 2001). Counselors need training in this area, or else other staff will need to do this advising. Some vocational teachers already help students with poor academic achievement get jobs with career potential (Rosenbaum & Jones, 2000), so their role could be expanded.

The college-for-all focus prevents students from seeing that high-school efforts are required to get some benefit from college, that college is not helpful to all students, that some jobs offer good career prospects, and that high school can help students meet the requirements for better jobs.

Policies Focus Too Narrowly on Academics, Not on Soft Skills

Work-entry reforms have focused too narrowly on academics. Although employers value academic skills, they rate soft skills such as motivation and social skills as their greatest need, far more important than academic skills (Moss & Tilly, 2000; Shapiro & Iannozzi, 1999). In interviews we have conducted, employers stressed attendance, dependability, perseverance, attention to quality, and ability to work with others.

Moreover, young people must learn soft skills before entering the labor market. Although employers sometimes provide training in academic or technical skills, they do not provide training in soft skills. If workers lack these skills—if they are undependable, unmotivated, or get into conflicts—employers do not train them; they fire them. Employers do not believe that they know how to train soft skills (Miller & Rosenbaum, 1997). Similarly, most job-training programs focus on academic or job skills, and the few programs that try to teach motivation find that it is difficult, expensive, and very time-consuming (Herr, Wagner, & Halpern, 1996). If students fail to learn soft skills before entering the labor market, they probably will not be given a chance to learn them later.

High school is the last institution all students attend, so it is the logical place for students to learn how to exert effort and to acquire both soft and academic skills, if they have not already done so. Yet students believe that there is no reason to exert effort in high school. In a survey of more than 2,000 seniors in twelve high schools in cities and suburbs in a large Midwestern metropolitan area, we found that almost 40% of students believed that school effort had little relevance for their future careers (Rosenbaum, 1998). Even many college-bound students believed that high-school efforts were not important, that they could enter college no matter how badly they did in high school (because of open admissions), and that they could wait until college to exert effort. These findings are similar to those of other researchers (Steinberg, 1996). Indeed, in the NELS survey, 31% of high-school sophomores did only one hour of homework a week or less, and teachers reported that 10% of students rarely did homework (DeLuca & Rosenbaum, in press).

Again, we discover a strange discrepancy between societal practices and social needs. Although high schools focus on academic skills, they fail to develop soft skills, which employers value much more than academics, and which must be learned before students enter the labor market. Many employers report that some new workers are absent or late to work several days in the first week on the job, do poor quality work, and talk back to supervisors. Youths have learned that they can get away with these behaviors in high school, so they are surprised when employers fire them. Even more important for high schools than developing academic skills is helping students learn the soft skills that employers require.

Policies Focus Too Narrowly on Student Motivation, Not on Incentives

Policy discussions often focus too exclusively on individuals as the source of motivation problems. We urge students to work harder, we try to increase motivation by redesigning curricula, and we blame teachers for not making students more motivated. However, we rarely take actions to provide incentives or to make them visible to students.

Although researchers discover incentives by doing statistical analyses of what efforts and achievements lead to later payoffs, students do not possess long-term longitudinal data or the means to conduct statistical analyses. To judge from students' unrealistic college goals and their failure to anticipate the importance of high-school grades for college, students are often unaware of the incentives that researchers discover.

If we want students to perceive incentives, we need to provide some means to make this happen. What is missing from many institutional practices is a mechanism for creating and conveying signals that tell students the value of their present actions for achieving desirable career goals. Other countries have linkage mechanisms to produce such signals, and these mechanisms have considerable impact on students' attitudes and behaviors.

In Germany, students are given a variety of desirable goals and clear signals for inferring which goal is appropriate. The German system provides a clear mechanism that makes the relationship between school performance and career outcomes totally obvious to students (Hamilton & Hurrelmann, 1994). Students not bound for college can strive for apprenticeships leading to respected occupations, and students know that school grades are signals of student value that affect selection into apprenticeships. Moreover, after they begin an apprenticeship, the young have clear signals of their productive value. German youths acquire a sense of purpose and confidence from apprenticeship certification that work-bound youths cannot easily get in the U.S. or U.K. (Evans & Heinz, 1994). In a good labor market, young job seekers are highly likely to get jobs, but even in a bad labor market, German youths still know they have qualifications. If unemployed, they feel unlucky but not incompetent.

Similarly, in Japan, noncollege students can get respected occupations, and they know that high-school grades are signals of their chances of getting good jobs. Students know that raising their grades will have clear and certain payoffs in the quality of jobs they get, even if they do not attend college. Work-bound students can look at their grades and infer how well they are doing and what quality of job they are likely to get. If their achievement is too low for their plans, they can see it well in advance, and they know that they must increase their efforts or revise their plans.

In contrast, the U.S. does not provide incentives for most students. American policy does not indicate clear career payoffs for high-school efforts. Indeed, students know that school efforts are unnecessary for their career goals. Colleges with open admissions tell students they can attend, even with poor grades and test scores—a D average is good enough. Students know this, and they infer that they can wait until college to exert effort (Rosenbaum, 1998).

The labor market gives a similar message. Employer hiring practices ignore students' high-school records (Crain, 1984). Indeed, studies have found that nothing in students' high-school records (not grades, test scores, or attendance) has any relationship to employment or earnings just after high school (Bishop, 1993; Griffin, Kalleberg, & Alexander, 1981; Rosenbaum, 2001). Employers report that they do not use high-school grades because high schools do not send out transcripts (Bishop, 1993) and because employers do not think grades are relevant or trustworthy (Rosenbaum & Binder, 1997). Employers assign new high-school graduates to a few undemanding entry jobs with similarly low earnings until they see how the youths do in their workplace. These practices tell students that there are no incentives for high-school efforts.

Thus, unlike German or Japanese students, many American students have no sense that their school achievements matter for their college or job plans. Students do not know whether their goals are realistic, whether they should work harder to attain them, or what actions they can take to improve their chances of attaining what they intend. Although American policy focuses narrowly on students' motivation and makes moral appeals for students to work harder in school, employer practices and college open-admissions practices fail to offer students incentives for effort. As we have seen, these practices tell students that there are no incentives for high-school efforts. We want our students to be motivated in high school, but motivation is irrelevant without incentives. We must offer students incentives for working harder in school.

PROCEDURES FOR MAKING POLICIES MORE EFFECTIVE

Procedures for Showing Students That High-School Evaluations Are Relevant to Career Goals

Students are unlikely to exert effort in high school if they do not see incentives. Contrary to the assumption that incentive systems found in Japan and Germany cannot be implemented in the U.S., we already have such a system, but only for students who aspire to selective colleges that require grades and SAT (or ACT) exams. However, our society does not tell other students what school evaluations will predict their career outcomes.

Although high-school grades have little relationship to short-term outcomes (college admissions or earnings right after high school), they strongly predict important long-term outcomes (Rosenbaum, DeLuca, Miller, & Roy, 1999). Moreover, other high-school behaviors can have similar effects. Earnings and educational attainments are determined by students' soft skills in high school—their attendance, discipline, sociability, and leadership (see Table 13.1). Unfortunately, neither students nor employers realize that these high-school behaviors can predict how well they will do in the labor market. In addition, we found that high schools help some students get jobs, and these students had 17% higher earnings nine years after school than students who got jobs

Table 13.1
Determinants, Including Work Habits and Noncognitive Indicators, of Students' Educational Attainment and 1991 Earnings (Natural Log), Nine Years after the High-School Class Graduation Year

Independent Variable	Years of Education		Natural Log of 1991 Earnings	
	Coefficient	Stand. Err.	Coefficient	Stand. Err.
Socioeconomic status	.581*	(.028)	.099*	(.014)
Female	-.063	(.038)	-.405*	(.019)
Black	.232*	(.068)	.072*	(.035)
Hispanic	.164*	(.061)	.025	(.031)
Northeast region of U.S.	.145*	(.049)	.077*	(.025)
South region of U.S	-.074	(.045)	-.071*	(.023)
West region of U.S	-.406*	(.057)	-.104*	(.029)
Private school	.348*	(.056)	.089*	(.028)
Test	.057*	(.003)	.007*	(.001)
Prepared for class	-.024	(.019)	.003	(.010)
Homework time	.140*	(.014)	.005	(.007)
Attendance	.051*	(.015)	.012	(.008)
Interest in school	.219*	(.045)	-.044	(.023)
Cuts class sometimes	-.017	(.040)	.062*	(.021)
Good discipline	.048*	(.020)	.044*	(.010)
Not socially active	.004	(.019)	-.056*	(.010)
Leader in extracurricular activities	.131*	(.041)	.038	(.021)
Participates in extracurr. activities	.038*	(.009)	.001	(.004)
Grades	.298*	(.018)	.064*	(.009)
Constant	8.059		9.257	
Adj. R^2	40.2%		13.5%	
Signif. F	.0000		.0000	
N	7157		6243	
*p < .05				

through direct applications (see Table 13.2, column 3; cf. Rosenbaum, 2001). Obviously, high schools can help students get good jobs.

In some respects, American society works like Japanese society. In both nations, high-school students with better high-school achievement are more likely to get college degrees and higher earnings. The main difference is that although Japanese students can look at their grades and have some clear ideas of their career prospects and whether they need to work harder to attain their goals, *American society keeps students in the dark*. No one, including employers, seems to realize that high-school grades predict how well students will do in the labor market.

Table 13.2
Three Increasingly Complete Models of Determinants of 1991 Earnings (Natural Log), Nine Years after the High-School Class Graduation Year

Independent Variable	Model 1		Model 2		Model 3	
	Coeff.	Stand. Err.	Coeff.	Stand. Err.	Coeff.	Stand. Err.
Socioeconomic status	.126*	(.020)	.118*	(.021)	.120*	(.021)
Female	-379*	(.025)	-.376*	(.026)	-.372*	(.026)
Black	-.017	(.042)	.035	(.044)	.030	(.044)
Hispanic	.035	(.038)	.030	(.040)	.030	(.039)
Northeast region of U.S.	.146*	(.038)	.111*	(.038)	.110*	(.038)
South region of U.S.	.057	(.033)	.046	(.033)	.048	(.033)
West region of U.S.	.013	(.038)	.011	(.039)	.010	(.039)
General track			-.011	(.030)	-.010	(.030)
Vocational track			.017	(.037)	.011	(.037)
Private school			.084	(.050)	.075	(.050)
Achievement test (x 10^{-2})			.603*	(.182)	.624*	(.182)
PLACEMENT VARIABLES						
Relatives					.086*	(.035)
Friends					-.015	(.033)
Employment service					.084	(.058)
Civil service, union, other					.115*	(.043)
School placement					.170*	(.063)
Constant	9.885		9.588		9.541	
Adj. R^2	7.7%		8.1%		8.5%	
Signif. F	.0000		.0000		.0000	
N = 3,245						
*p < .05						

Procedures for Improving the Quality of Contacts

The problem for policy is not how to create the right incentives, but rather how to make the current incentives more visible. Contacts are a good way to do so. Many reformers have concluded that youths' problems would be improved by helping high schools make contacts with employers or colleges. Two major types of reform are based on such contacts: tech-prep and apprenticeship/co-op programs. As we shall see, these reforms are very promising, but they have difficulty conveying information.

Tech-prep programs create contacts between high schools and community-college programs in specific occupational fields, such as health care and technology. Tech-prep is a promising approach; it is consistent with economic theory, and even critics of other approaches are impressed with the tech-prep idea (Donahoe & Tienda, 2000). By 1990, there were more than 120 tech-prep programs in thirty-three states, and the Carl Perkins Act included funds to encourage the further implementation of this model (Bailey & Merritt, 1993). These programs organize the high-school curriculum in junior and senior years so that it directly meets the prerequisites for certain occupational programs in community colleges and may even provide college credits. Ideally, tech-prep makes a seamless transition between high school and the first course in community college: High-school graduates in these programs are fully prepared to take college courses.

The ideal tech-prep program should reduce some of our concerns about the college-for-all approach because high-school courses in tech-prep are closely synchronized with college programs. Mastery of high-school courses is supposed to allow students to meet the prerequisites for college courses, and performance in high-school courses should provide clear information to students about how well-prepared they are for college. If a program fits those conditions, students will know how prepared they are for college courses. If they do poorly in a high-school course, they will get clear information about a problem that they must repair before they get to college. Tech-prep programs that synchronize high school and college in very strong linkages will address many of the problems that usually arise with a college-for-all approach.

Unfortunately, tech-prep programs do not always match these conditions. Research finds that in many tech-prep programs, students enter college unprepared for college-credit courses, high schools do not provide students with clear signals of what colleges demand or how well individuals meet college requirements, and colleges give their own tests because they do not trust high-school evaluations (Orfield & Paul, 1994).

Tech-prep programs would be helped by improving the way they convey trusted signals of college requirements and students' readiness. Without such signals, students will not see incentives for appropriate achievement, they will not know if they are prepared for college-level courses, and disappointments will occur when they arrive at college.

Youth apprenticeship and co-op programs create contacts between high schools and employers. They attempt to coordinate learning at school and on the job. Both programs try to help students learn academic skills, job skills, and soft skills. Youth apprenticeships are more structured and usually include close supervision and coursework synchronized with the job experience. However, they are very expensive. Although apprenticeships are extensively used in Germany, few American employers are willing to pay for them, and only a few thousand young people are in youth apprenticeships in the entire U.S.

Co-op programs are sometimes viewed as inexpensive youth apprenticeships. They are widely practiced across most American high schools, with about 8% of American high-school juniors and seniors in co-op programs (General Accounting Office, 1991). Co-op usually consists of releasing students from some classes so they can get experience at jobs, which are supposed to provide more training than average jobs.

In practice, co-op programs have shown two kinds of problems. First, if the jobs are not carefully screened, they may be ordinary jobs in the youth labor market that provide little or no learning (e.g., fast food or small retail). Some employers rarely employ co-op participants after graduation. We have interviewed employers who say that they participate in co-op merely for the public-relations benefits and that they would not consider hiring their co-op students.

Second, co-op leads to earnings benefits for students, but only if students take jobs in the same company where they did the co-op program. Research has found that students get no earnings benefit if they take a job in another company (Stern & Stevens, 1992). Although students who complete German apprenticeships get a generalized signal of value trusted by all employers (Hamilton, 1990), students who complete a co-op experience do not get such a signal. Co-op programs have problems in providing relevant, trusted signals that are valued by other employers.

It may seem that this exaggerates the importance of signals. Getting good information is important, one could argue, but surely it is no substitute for good training. Yet that is what the British thought when they set up the expensive Youth Training System to give apprenticeship training to students. They found that the program worked, but not because it provided training. Indeed, program success predicted labor-market failure! Those youths who successfully completed the program were more likely to be labor-market failures than were program dropouts. Looking more closely, researchers found that employers used the program to identify promising workers and immediately shift them to real jobs, rather than wait for them to complete their apprenticeships (Cappelli, 1992). Apparently, information about young workers is sometimes more important than training.

Tech-prep and co-op are promising ideas. They indicate that contacts can improve the transitions from high school to college or work. These programs could be enhanced, however, by improving the way they convey trusted signals of students' readiness and of college and job requirements.

Procedures for Creating Linkage Mechanisms to Convey Relevant and Trusted Signals of Value

Like Germany and Japan, the United States must have some procedures that provide signals of students' value that are relevant and trusted by employers and colleges. I propose several policy actions to improve the transitions to college and employment through better signaling (further reforms are discussed in Rosenbaum, 2001).

To improve students' access to college credit classes, colleges' tests for remedial courses should be made uniform across all colleges in a state and made available to high-school students so they can assess how prepared they are for college courses. In addition, high schools can take two steps to improve students' access to promising jobs.

First, high schools can provide signals of soft skills. Grades already do this. High schools can also provide new evaluations of soft skills such as attendance, discipline, motivation, sociability, and leadership, which predict students' later earnings (see Table 13.1).

Second, high schools need to have trusted relationships with employers. In interviews with 110 vocational teachers, some teachers reported that they have trusted relationships with employers; described actions that they take to create these relationships; and observed that these relationships allow them to place students with good soft skills, even those with poor academic achievement, limited English proficiency, learning disabilities, or other problems (Rosenbaum & Jones, 1995, 2000). The task for reform is to find ways to encourage these relationships and make them more generally available across many teachers in a school.

CONCLUSIONS

In summary, by ignoring goals besides college, ignoring soft skills, and ignoring long-term incentives, employment and educational policy misleads students about societal needs. Indeed, employer hiring practices and college open-admissions practices prevent students from seeing the incentives for high-school effort. There actually are long-term payoffs to good grades and soft skills in high school, but no one sees them. We must develop a mechanism to make these incentives visible and to convey signals that tell students the value of their high-school actions for leading to desirable career goals. If employers and colleges want students to exert more effort in high school, they must help the schools develop relevant and trustworthy evaluations, and they must develop relationships that will reinforce trust. Tech-prep and co-op can do that, but they could be improved. Other nations have developed procedures for fostering such relationships, as have some schools, colleges, and employers in the U.S. We must find ways to introduce these procedures in current reforms to make them more effective.

Many practical steps can be taken.

- State and local policymakers should help counselors and teachers learn about factors predicting college dropout and learn about jobs with good career prospects that do not require college. There actually are long-term payoffs to good grades and soft skills in high school, and policymakers should help school staff to see them.
- High schools should develop evaluations that tell students what actions they can take in high school to improve their future careers. If employers and colleges want students to exert more effort in high school, they must help high schools develop relevant and trustworthy evaluations, and they must develop relationships that reinforce trust.
- College tests for remedial courses should be made uniform and available to high-school students so they can assess how prepared they are for college courses.

- Vocational teachers who have trusted contacts with employers should be supported as a valuable resource for high schools and students.
- Because vocational courses teach valuable soft skills, vocational education should not be dismantled; the college-for-all policy does not justify such dismantling.
- Tech-prep and co-op reforms should be improved to provide more relevant and trusted signals of students' value.

In conclusion, it is encouraging that the underlying conditions are present for accomplishing such reforms. Colleges and the labor market actually do reward grades and other noncognitive behaviors, and some individual teachers and employers have made informal contacts for conveying trusted information. The key is to get institutional actors to recognize this and to produce linkage mechanisms that create and convey relevant and trusted signals of student value. Current tech-prep, co-op, and other linkage activities are the right kinds of approaches, but these contacts must be made more trustworthy if they are to be effective.

NOTES

1. An Associate's or higher degree, according to the U.S. Current Population Survey, March 1998 (National Center for Education Statistics, 1998, Table 9). Similarly, 40.8% of high-school graduates aged twenty-five to twenty-nine have college degrees.

2. That is, if we assume, as Grubb (1995) does, that "no-transcript" students did not stay long enough to have a transcript created. Grubb's inference is supported by our finding that "no-transcript" students have even lower high-school grades than students with zero college credits.

REFERENCES

Bailey, T., & Merritt, D. (1993). *The school-to-work transition project.* New York: Manpower Demonstration Research Corporation.

Bishop, J. (1993). Improving job matches in the U.S. labor market. In M. N. Bailey (Ed.), *Brookings papers on economic activity: Microeconomics* (pp. 335–400). Washington, DC: The Brookings Institution.

Cappelli, P. (1992). *Is the "skills gap" really about attitudes?* (EQW Working Paper No. WP01). Philadelphia: University of Pennsylvania, National Center on the Educational Quality of the Workforce.

Cicourel, A. V., & Kitsuse, J. I. (1963). *The educational decision-makers.* Indianapolis, IN: Bobbs-Merrill.

Committee for Economic Development. (1985). *Investing in our children: Business and the public schools.* New York: Author.

Crain, R. (1984). *The quality of American high school graduates: What personnel officers say and do.* Baltimore: Johns Hopkins University, Center for the Study of Schools.

Deil, R., & Rosenbaum, J. E. (2000, August). *Unintended consequences of stigma-free remediation.* Paper presented at the meeting of the American Sociological Association, Washington, DC.

DeLuca, S., & Rosenbaum, J. E. (in press). Individual agency and the life courses: Do low SES students get less long-term payoff for their school efforts? *Sociological Focus.*

Donahoe, D., & Tienda, M. (2000). The transition from school to work: Is there a crisis? What can be done? In S. Danziger & J. Waldvogel (Eds.), *Securing the future* (pp. 231–263). New York: Russell Sage Foundation.

Eurich, N. P. (1985). *Corporate classrooms: The learning business.* Princeton, NJ: Carnegie Foundation for the Advancement of Teaching.

Evans, K., & Heinz, W. R. (Eds.). (1994). *Becoming adults in England and Germany.* London: Anglo-German Foundation for the Study of Industrial Society.

General Accounting Office. (1991). *Transition from school to work.* Washington, DC: Author.

Griffin, L. J., Kalleberg, A. L., & Alexander, K. L. (1981). Determinants of early labor market entry and attainment: A study of labor market segmentation. *Sociology of Education, 54,* 206–221.

Grubb, W. N. (1995). Response to comment. *Journal of Human Resources, 30,* 222–228.

Hamilton, S. F. (1990). *Apprenticeship for adulthood: Preparing youth for the future.* New York: Free Press.

Hamilton, S. F., & Hurrelmann, K. (1994). The school-to-career transition in Germany and the United States. *Teachers College Record, 96,* 329–344.

Herr, T., Wagner, S., & Halpern, R. (1996). *Making the shoe fit.* Unpublished manuscript. Erikson Institute, Project Match, Chicago.

Howe, H., et al. (1988). *The forgotten half: Pathways to success for America's youth and young families. Final report.* New York: William T. Grant Foundation.

Krei, M., & Rosenbaum, J. E. (in press). Career and college advice to the forgotten half. *Teachers College Record.*

Miller, S. R., & Rosenbaum, J. E. (1997). Hiring in a Hobbesian world: Social infrastructure and employers' use of information. *Work and Occupations, 24,* 498–523.

Moss, P., & Tilly, C. (2000). *Stories employers tell: Race, skill, and hiring in America.* New York: Russell Sage Foundation Press.

Murnane, R. J., & Levy, F. (1996). *Teaching the new basic skills: Principles for educating children to thrive in a changing economy.* New York: The Free Press.

National Center for Education Statistics. (1998). *Digest of education statistics, 1998.* Washington, DC: U.S. Department of Education.

National Commission on Excellence in Education. (1983). *A nation at risk: The imperative educational reform.* Washington, DC: U.S. Government Printing Office.

Orfield, G., & Paul, F. G. (1994). *High hopes, long odds: A major report on Hoosier teens and the American dream.* Indianapolis, IN: The Indiana Youth Institute.

Rosenbaum J. E. (1976). *Making inequality: The hidden curriculum of high school tracking.* New York: Wiley.

Rosenbaum, J. E. (1998). College-for-all: Do students understand what college demands? *Social Psychology of Education, 2,* 55–80.

Rosenbaum, J. E. (2001). *Beyond college for all: Career paths for the forgotten half.* New York: Russell Sage Foundation.

Rosenbaum, J. E., & Binder, A. (1997). Do employers really need more educated youth? *Sociology of Education, 70,* 68–85.

Rosenbaum, J. E., DeLuca, S., Miller, S. R., & Roy, K. (1999). Pathways into work: Short- and long-term effects of personal and institutional ties. *Sociology of Education, 72,* 179–196.

Rosenbaum, J. E., & Jones, S. A. (1995). Creating linkages in the high school-to-work transition: Vocational teachers' networks. In M. T. Hallinan (Ed.), *Restructuring schools: Promises, practices, and policies* (pp. 235–258). New York: Plenum.

Rosenbaum, J. E., & Jones, S. A. (2000). Interactions between high schools and labor markets. In M. T. Hallinan (Ed.), *Handbook of Sociology of Education* (pp. 411–436). New York: Plenum.

Rosenbaum, J. E., Miller, S. R., & Krei, M. (1996). Gatekeeping in an era of more open gates. *American Journal of Education, 104,* 257–79.

Shapiro, D., & Iannozzi, M. (1999). *The benefits to bridging work and school: Results of the 1997 National Employer Survey.* Philadelphia: University of Pennsylvania, National Center for Postsecondary Education.

Steinberg, L. (with Brown, B. B., & Dornbusch, S. M.). (1996). *Beyond the classroom: Why school reform has failed and what parents need to do.* New York: Simon & Schuster.

Stern, D., & Stevens, D. (1992). *Analysis of unemployment insurance data on the relationship between high school cooperative education and subsequent employment.* Washington, DC: U.S. Department of Education, National Assessment of Vocational Education, Office of Educational Research and Improvement.

Part V

The Future of School-to-Work

14

Is the School-to-Work Movement on the Right Track?

Robert I. Lerman

INTRODUCTION

The enactment of the School-to-Work Opportunities Act (STWOA) in 1994 represented one of the fastest transformations of a significant policy idea into national legislation. It was only in the late 1980s and early 1990s that policy analysts and public officials began arguing that the U.S. lacked an effective school-to-work (STW) system to help young people make the transition from school to work and careers. The 1988 William T. Grant Foundation report, *The Forgotten Half,* publicized the labor-market problems facing the majority of the youth cohort not moving on to college and decried the discrepancy between public resources for the college-bound and for those not going to college. In 1990, the Commission on the Skills of the American Workforce expressed concern about the weak skill levels of U.S. workers relative to workers in other advanced countries, attributing the problem partly to the absence of an effective STW system in the U.S. Also in 1990, Stephen Hamilton (in his book *Apprenticeship for Adulthood*) and Hillard Pouncy and I (in *The Public Interest*) called for a youth-apprenticeship system in the U.S.

Policy researchers, foundation officials, and political leaders were taking special interest in European approaches to helping young people move from schools to careers. At a December 1990 conference entitled, "Youth Apprenticeship American Style," the keynote speaker was Governor Bill Clinton of Arkansas. Key educators, including Albert Shanker (president of the American Federation of Teachers) and Herbert Grover (leader of the Chief State School Officers), supported the approach.

In response, the first Bush administration sponsored youth-apprenticeship demonstration projects and proposed the National Youth Apprenticeship Act of 1992. School-to-work initiatives were also developing at state and local levels—in Oregon, Wisconsin, and Arkansas, and in Boston, Rochester, and Tulsa,

Oklahoma. The approach attracted the support of the centrist Democratic Leadership Council and a bipartisan group of political leaders.

The Clinton administration proposed and the Congress enacted the STWOA with large majorities in both houses. The STWOA became law only four to six years after the reports calling for radical change in America's approach to school-to-work transition. The law allocated funding mainly to states so they could create the institutions and reforms. Meanwhile, Congress passed the National Skill Standards Act (NSSA) of 1994 to develop a voluntary national system of skill standards. Although they were separate measures, STWOA and NSSA were complementary. The standards created through the NSSA would give STW programs (including youth apprenticeship) attainable goals and help determine which skills to teach.

So far, the goal of creating a new, effective STW system has gone unrealized. Notwithstanding bipartisan support for STW programs, generous funding to states, and the complementary NSSA, the initiative eventually lost momentum, at least at the federal level. During 1999 and 2000, neither the Clinton administration nor major congressional figures proposed extending the STWOA beyond the 2001 expiration built into the original law. But declining federal interest in STW became evident much earlier. In his 1997 State of the Union message, President Clinton specified ten principles to improve education, but the STW concepts did not even make number ten! Republican interest also waned, despite continuing business support for STW programs. The most effective opposition from the right came from the argument of Phyllis Schlafly and her Eagle Forum that the STWOA turns elementary and high schools into job-training programs, diverting them from their educational mission.

How did this bipartisan effort to help the forgotten half and raise the quality of noncollege careers lose political support? This chapter[1] argues that the STW movement failed to live up to high expectations partly because of the administration's loss of focus on the forgotten half and its emphasis on thin interventions for all students instead of intensive approaches for some. The next two sections describe the motivation for the movement, consider the erosion of this initial vision, and discuss the failure to implement national skill standards. The fourth section examines data on participation in STW activities, especially intensive programs, and analyzes how these findings compare with involvement in secondary vocational-education programs. The fifth section reexamines aspects of the empirical and theoretical case for an apprenticeship-type system. I conclude with recommendations for returning the STW movement to its original goals.

THE POLICY VISION

The primary rationale for the STW movement among policy researchers and politicians in the early 1990s was to improve job-market outcomes for youth not going on to complete a baccalaureate. In their 1992 campaign book, *Putting*

People First, candidates Bill Clinton and Al Gore called for bringing "business, labor, and education leaders together to establish a *national apprenticeship-style program* that offers non-college-bound students valuable skills training, with the promise of good jobs when they graduate" (p. 87). In March 1993, when introducing the National School-to-Work Transition and Youth Apprenticeship Act of 1993, Representative Goodling stated, "Our legislation is designed to provide positive career-related options for these non-college-bound youth—helping them to make successful transitions from high school into the work force, or into further education and training which is directly related to an occupation."

In calling for a new approach to helping noncollege youth, policy researchers emphasized labor-market and educational problems. The declining wages of those with high-school degrees not only meant lower incomes for noncollege workers already employed, but also indicated worsening career prospects for most of today's young people. Demand for skills was increasing rapidly while the educational capacities of young people were stagnant and falling well short of international competitors' performance.

Since the federal report on *A Nation at Risk* in 1983, state and federal policymakers have focused on dealing with educational deficiencies of U.S. students (National Commission on Excellence in Education, 1983). Over the past 15 years, school systems have raised spending per student, lowered class size, increased teacher salaries, encouraged all students to take college-preparatory programs, and required students to meet external standards (Hanushek & Somers, 1999). Payoffs have been mixed, with some reports citing considerable progress and others suggesting only limited gains.[2]

Meanwhile, STW advocates have argued that student motivation is key in improving educational outcomes. Student effort is a critical, often overlooked, input in the educational process (Bishop, 1989). Especially in the high-school years, increasing the number and efficiency of student hours on task has more potential than expanding standard school inputs. Requiring students to meet external standards is one way to motivate them. But so is helping students see the relevance of what they learn for their careers and teaching subjects in a real-world context. School-to-career programs motivate students by using both approaches (Hamilton & Hamilton, 1999).

Disillusionment with federal programs for youth training added to the impetus for STW programs. The youth component of the Job Training Partnership Act and many large-scale youth demonstration projects (including the Youth Incentive Entitlement Pilot Projects and JOBSTART) showed little or no impact on postprogram experiences of disadvantaged youth. Although most training programs for disadvantaged youth looked ineffective, moving away from targeting meant expending too little effort on the neediest individuals. In this context, the STW initiative was a mainstream approach that would indirectly benefit disadvantaged youth.

Perceived weakness in U.S. vocational-education programs led policymakers in several directions. One involved reducing the role of vocational education and encouraging all students toward a college-preparatory concentration instead of a vocational one. Moreover, the movement to integrate academic and vocational education was to add rigor to applied (often viewed as diluted) courses in math, science, and English. Another response was to find alternatives to vocational education that maintained a career focus, including career-academy programs and youth-apprenticeship or internship programs. Although vocational education was appealing enough to induce some potential dropouts to remain in school, consensus held that vocational education had low quality and relevance.[3]

Another concern was high job instability among U.S. youth, who averaged almost nine jobs between the ages of eighteen and thirty-two, including an average of nearly three jobs per worker over the twenty-eight to thirty-two age range. Although some job mobility is part of a productive process of matching workers and employers (Heckman, 1994; Neal, 1999; Topel & Ward, 1992), Holzer and LaLonde (1999) found that early employment instability reduced employment among high-school dropouts in their thirties. Gardecki and Neumark (1998) reported only modest evidence that job stability among young workers contributes to long-term success, but Neumark (1998) concluded that youth job stability raises adult wages.

After witnessing the excellent, career-focused systems operating in some countries, many came to advocate a U.S. system embodying intensive school-to-career components, such as youth apprenticeship. Once such a system became operational, parents, teachers, employers, and students could see career-focused education as a formal sequence of activities embodying high, portable standards and leading to rewarding careers requiring high skills. The system would strengthen career exploration, but it would center on combined school-based and work-based learning (WBL), culminating in an occupational or industry certification.

Advocates of this approach believed the new system would do the following:

- Provide clear pathways and incentives for students, who would gain access to interesting careers and learn that effort in school raises the chances of career and workplace success.
- Use learning in context, including active learning leading to real production.
- Improve the fit between training and careers.
- Channel youth who take jobs into more constructive settings.
- Expose at-risk youth to constructive peers and adult mentors because apprenticeships incorporate a mentoring process, encouraging students to learn more at school and work.

A career-focused system would also do the following:

- Encourage employers to upgrade the skills demanded for entry-level jobs, expand training for workers without a bachelor's degree, and create job ladders. Employers would be more likely to hire young workers attaining recognized skill credentials than young workers attaining only a general high-school diploma.
- Raise incomes of workers lacking a baccalaureate by increasing their productivity, as Germany's apprenticeship system has proven to increase productivity advantages.
- Make training and job placement a formal process in order to raise the stakes for academic excellence and reduce the disadvantage inner-city youth face because of limited access to informal networks.
- Start early to provide clear paths to rewarding careers, which are critical for at-risk youth facing great peer pressure to become involved in crime or have children outside marriage before qualifying for successful careers.

Reformers in the early 1990s hoped the advantages of an intensive STW system would encourage the country to make systemic changes in the U.S. school-to-career transition process.

THE STWOA LEGISLATION AND ITS MIXED MESSAGES

In 1993, as the process of creating a Clinton administration bill unfolded, tensions surfaced over whether to emphasize a youth-apprenticeship system. At least three obstacles stood in the way. Perhaps most important was opposition from unions, especially those important in the registered apprenticeship system. They worried that they would lose control over registered apprenticeship programs and that relatively weak or modest youth-apprenticeship programs would devalue the term "apprenticeship," even for those who had completed registered apprenticeships of high quality.

A second obstacle came from former advocates of youth apprenticeships.[4] They worried that youth apprenticeships would (a) force students to make crucial decisions about careers too early, (b) involve unproductive early tracking, (c) generate opposition from parents resistant to noncollege alternatives for their children, (d) compel students to switch high schools to attain the scale required to justify classes in specific skills, (e) come too soon for students lacking academic preparation for a demanding apprenticeship, and (f) yield too few apprenticeship slots from employers.

A third concern was that too strong a federal vision or mandate would be unworkable in a world of reinventing government and federal–state partnerships. In the event, the federal legislation mandated a range of requirements for receiving money, but they were largely procedural, not substantive. Clear objectives and measurable results got lost amid the multiplicity of goals the bill enunciated.

The preamble to the STWOA began with concerns about youth qualifications, high youth unemployment, and the worsening earnings position of unskilled workers. The next findings discussed the absence of a comprehensive STW system in the U.S., the incoherent existing categorical programs for disadvantaged youth, and the "time-honored apprenticeship concept" that, by integrating theory and training, can engage students' interest, enhance skills, improve work attitudes, and prepare youths for high-skill and high-wage careers.

Still, by the time the bill ultimately became law, the term *youth apprenticeship* was used only to describe how the act would build on promising STW activities, including youth apprenticeship. The act emphasized *career majors* instead of youth apprenticeships. In defining career majors, the STWOA mentioned that these would typically include two years of high school and at least one year of postsecondary education. But this definition linked WBL with career majors only in stating that the majors would integrate classroom learning and WBL. Another link with WBL did appear; the sequence of activities in career majors was to result in a *skill certificate* (in addition to a high-school diploma, GED, or postsecondary degree). This was to be a "portable, industry-recognized credential issued by a School-to-Work Opportunities program under an approved State plan," one certifying that a student had mastered skills at levels at least as challenging as skill standards endorsed by the National Skill Standards Board (NSSB). Thus, while the act did not directly emphasize intensive WBL within career majors, the apparent requirement for a skill certificate provided some encouragement to programs resembling the original youth-apprenticeship vision.

The mandated activities listed under the WBL component (section 103) gave states another outlet for apprenticeship-like initiatives. Included activities were work experience, job training coordinated with school-based learning relevant to career majors and leading to skill certificates, workplace mentoring, and instruction in general workplace competencies and all aspects of the industry. Yet although acceptable plans had to include WBL components, the act allowed states to determine the size and scope of employer-based programs.

More broadly, STWOA shifted the focus from intensive STW by enunciating a large array of goals. On the one hand the act proposed a national framework; portable credentials; the creation of a universal, high-quality STW transition system; and implementation of several types of activities (including career majors). On the other hand, the STWOA promoted the formation of local partnerships, tried to build on state and local capacity, and encouraged states to create statewide STW opportunities systems.

The legislation left some key questions unanswered. Was the focus to be on the forgotten half, on all who lack a bachelor's degree, or on all students, including the college-bound? Was the emphasis on career exploration in elementary schools, on integration of academic and vocational instruction, on promotion of college attendance, or on the "time-honored apprenticeship concept"?

The act envisaged multiple actors playing key roles.[5] If it had emphasized apprenticeship or career majors (with strong work-based components), it would have made sense for employers and workers, including unions and other worker representatives, to drive the process. The legislation authorized governors to place employers in leadership roles, but its multiple goals and requirements for coordination with many education-oriented acts (such as Adult Education, Goals 2000, and the Elementary and Secondary Education Act) made such a designation unlikely.

MISPLACED OR ABSENT FEDERAL PRIORITIES IN IMPLEMENTING THE STWOA

The multiple objectives of the STWOA gave federal and state officials implementing it considerable discretion in determining policy directions. The federal role was significant at the start because of the decision to fund states in stages. Initially, the director of the National School-to-Work Office (administered jointly under the Department of Education and of Labor) could have stressed career majors embodying components of the youth-apprenticeship approach. Instead, the first director, J. D. Hoye, gave priority to ensuring that STW opportunities would reach all students. In using the term "all students" in the STWOA, Congress wanted to make sure that no student was excluded because of race, gender, cultural background, immigrant status, disability, limited English capability, or having dropped out of school. But in public statements, Hoye championed an "all students" concept in which STW programs would be meaningful even to the college-bound. In some states, STW-program officials interpreted this concept as requiring participation by every student, especially in thin activities such as career exploration.

The main concerns about focusing on those not college-bound in STW programs were that participants would be stigmatized as not capable of attaining a bachelor's degree, and that tracking students runs against American notions of egalitarianism. The positive argument for including the college-bound was that all students would benefit from teaching academic concepts along with practical applications and from making WBL part of the curriculum (Goldberger & Kazis, 1995).

Whatever the reasons, the federal STW office did not encourage states to emphasize expanding high-quality careers accessible to students without a bachelor's degree. Most states were led by education officials, not by employers. Most focused on activities only minimally related to intensive career majors or youth apprenticeships, and most exerted considerable effort to engage a wide range of actors. Thin interventions touching many students, such as career exploration and job shadowing, dominated. Other common STW-funded projects were teacher training and summer internships, showing teachers the use of academic skills in work settings, broadening their knowledge of occupations, and stimulating project-based learning.

Another barrier to intensive work-based strategies was the slow development of skill standards by the NSSB. The STWOA mandated that certification required career majors to master skills at levels "at least as challenging as skill standards endorsed by the National Skill Standards Board." Certainly, it made sense to set national or regional skill standards, given the expense involved in creating sound, valid standards and the goal of developing portable, recognized credentials. Unfortunately, the NSSB took an inordinately long time generating these standards and made little effort to integrate them into a school-to-career delivery system. As of 1999, the NSSB had selected voluntary partnerships to define occupational clusters, but none had proposed specific skill standards (Haimson & Hulsey, 1999).

This failure of the NSSB to produce skill standards frustrated the STWOA's provisions for skill certification. Without such standards, each state or community had to develop its own. But doing so would be costly and hinder portability. For standards to be useful, they must certify skills taught in STW programs and demanded by a sizable number of employers. Because of lack of coordination between the NSSB, the National School-to-Work Office, and state STW programs, even a sudden emergence of NSSB-approved standards would do little to promote a new STW system. Skill standards are not self-implementing. Simply developing and publishing standards, even those sanctioned by industry or occupational groups, leaves undone the job of diffusion and practical use.

Despite limited federal encouragement, a few states (notably Wisconsin, Georgia, and Maine) attached high priority to apprenticeships and other intensive WBL approaches. Wisconsin's youth-apprenticeship program, which began before passage of the STWOA, developed the key components required for system change.[6] In light of the NSSB experience, it is striking that Wisconsin state agencies, collaborating with industry and labor groups, have developed about twenty skill standards in fields ranging from the printing and automotive industries to biotechnology and finance. The standards require high-level competencies achieved at the workplace as well as related academic instruction, often delivered through technical colleges. Students are exposed to career exploration and allowed to choose apprenticeships beginning in eleventh grade. At last count, 1,850 Wisconsin high-school students had enrolled in youth apprenticeships. The program has remained small in percentage terms, but the reason seems not to be low student interest or weak employer demand. Indeed, more than 90% of employers reported they would recommend the program to other employers (Phelps & Jin, 1997). Instead, the constraint has been that high schools, subject to local budget limitations, have been unwilling to pay for special courses at technical colleges for large numbers of apprentices.

Certainly, the STWOA spawned much activity aimed at improving links between schools and careers. A recent study of five communities working with Jobs for the Future (JFF) as part of its Benchmark Communities Initiative highlighted efforts of school and other local officials to provide WBL in the context of reforming education as a whole (DeSalvatore, Goldberger, & Steinberg, 2000). These authors pointed to the tension between focusing on vocational programs and the perception that participating students would learn less and not proceed to college. JFF worked with the communities in "positioning school-to-career as a combination of a college-preparatory curriculum with career-relevant learning" (p. 26). Some cities spent much time trying to make pedagogy more project-based and contextual. The authors wrote approvingly of efforts in Boston, North Clackamas (Oregon), and Philadelphia to avoid linking the STW initiatives too closely with vocational education. They cited Louisville and Milwaukee as failing "to transcend the dichotomy between vocational and college-oriented studies" (p. 26), while noting Louisville's success at enhancing vocational education.

In these communities, large numbers of high-school students engaged in substantial WBL. Participation ranged from about 5% of students in Milwaukee and 7% in Boston, to more than 10% in Philadelphia and almost 40% in North Clackamas. The report said little about the types of occupations, skill certification, and actual careers of WBL participants. Although the report's comparisons of participants to nonparticipants in Boston and Philadelphia showed higher attendance, grades, graduation rates, college attendance, and wages for STW participants, evidence for an impact of STW programs is weak, given the absence of reliably constructed comparison groups.

The national evaluation of the STWOA undertaken by Mathematica Policy Research, Inc. (MPR) focused on the eight lead states receiving early grant awards. In their 1999 report to the U.S. Congress, Hershey, Silverberg, Haimson, Hudis, and Jackson of MPR concluded that progress toward the STWOA agenda has been modest. They found that while states created STW partnerships between education and employers and expanded student options, the activities most emphasized have been such low-intensity components as job shadowing, worksite visits, and career-awareness classes. As of spring 1998, about 13% of twelfth graders engaged in a paid or unpaid work experience linked to school, 18% participated in a career-focused school program integrating academic and vocational learning, but only 3% engaged in both. Between 1996 and 1998, participation in career-focused educational programs rose substantially from 10% to 20% among those not expecting to attend college; interestingly, participation also increased from 14% to 19% among those expecting to attend a four-year college.

National evidence on utilization of STW components comes from the Survey of School Administrators linked to the 1997 National Longitudinal Survey of Youth (NLSY97). By 1996, the programs were beginning to emerge. Most schools (64%) offered at least one school-based or work-based activity designated as STW (Neumark & Joyce, 2000). Further, 44% provided at least one work-based activity, defined by Neumark and Joyce as internships, apprenticeships, job shadowing, school-based enterprises, or mentoring. However, only about 14% of schools offered an apprenticeship, 17% offered an internship, and 13% offered a school-based enterprise. Intensive, school-based programs operated at more schools: 33% had tech-prep programs, 33% had cooperative-education programs, and 13% had career majors. Public schools were far more likely to provide STW activities than were private schools. Apprenticeships were most common in suburban schools, schools with high minority enrollments, and schools in the middle with respect to the share of students going to college.

The link between the NLSY97 student self-reported participation and school reports on activities is weak. According to Neumark and Joyce (2000), the share of students stating they participated in an STW activity was almost as high (36% to 38%) in schools not offering STW activities as in schools offering activities. Fewer than 5% of students in the ninth grade or higher reported an apprenticeship or internship. Looking at the characteristics of participants, one finds apprentices more likely to be African American, have parents with no more than a GED or high-school diploma, come from a low-income family, have medium-level grades, and fall in the lower middle group with respect to likelihood of attending college.

Using 1998 data from NLSY97, I tabulated the proportion of eleventh and twelfth graders currently engaged or engaged during the prior year in one of several STW activities. As of the 1998 interview, fewer than 1% of eleventh graders and fewer than 3% of twelfth graders mentioned internships or apprenticeships as their most recent STW activity. However, 10% of eleventh and twelfth graders reported participating in career majors, 8% in tech-prep, 6% in cooperative education, and 4% in another work-based activity linked with schooling. More than 30% of students reported at least one such activity. The intensity of involvement was low, however, as measured by the number of hours over the prior year spent at worksites in school-related programs. Of those reporting involvement in a career major, internship or apprenticeship, tech-prep program, or other work-based program linked with schooling, 38% had no hours in WBL over the prior year, and another 25% participated in WBL for fewer than twenty hours. Only about 20% had engaged in WBL for 100 hours or more.

Moreover, not all of the WBL activity can be attributed to the impact of the STWOA. Cooperative education, internships, and other school-linked work activities have long been part of the U.S. educational system. Although the STWOA stimulated increases in many career-oriented activities, this expansion took place alongside a decline in vocational education. Between 1982 and 1998, vocational-education concentrators dropped from 34% to 25% of high school seniors (Levesque, Lauren, Teitelbaum, Alt, & Librera, 2000).

The STWOA stimulated states and localities to increase school–employer collaborations, which in turn have led to more job shadowing, worksite visits, teacher internships, and student internships or apprenticeships. In some areas, the STWOA helped improve pedagogy through applied learning and integrated academic and vocational education. However, STWOA has fallen far short of creating a new U.S. system for transition from school to careers. STW programs around the country are, if anything, even more varied than before the STWOA. Few portable credentials have been created, let alone implemented to certify student skills with a linked work-based and school-based sequence of education and training. Although some students learned from WBL or career-major experiences, the STWOA failed to open new routes to high-productivity, high-quality careers outside the baccalaureate framework.

HAS THE YOUTH-APPRENTICESHIP APPROACH BECOME OBSOLETE?

The shift from the youth-apprenticeship approach in the U.S. occurred for political and intellectual reasons. Initial political opposition from unions discouraged the administration from emphasizing youth apprenticeship in the STWOA. However, as STW administrators claimed that STWOA's mandate was for all students, and as school districts started requiring career plans and other activities for all students, a new political backlash materialized. The Eagle Forum highlighted mandatory policies in some districts to mobilize vocal opposition to the STW movement generally.[7] Many parents thought it inappropriate to require something for all students before it proved effective for any.

Intellectual opposition focused on the argument that youth apprenticeships reduce opportunity and increase inequality. Unfortunately, these opponents have a misplaced idea of egalitarianism. Equality requires equal opportunity but not a single pathway in which success depends on one's ranking in a single educational hierarchy. Requiring those who are more capable in a less-academic setting to compete only in an academic arena *reduces* equality and can increase frustration.

In its 1998 *Employment Outlook,* the Organisation for Economic Co-Operation and Development (OECD) agreed, arguing that "apprenticeship-type systems work best in giving non-university-bound young people a good start in the labor market" (p. 82). OECD went on to state that "the creation of training opportunities comparable to apprenticeship will be of importance, especially for at-risk youth" (p. 82).

Recent research has renewed the case for an apprenticeship-type system. A cross-country analysis of STW systems by Shavit and Muller (1998) classified countries' programs along three dimensions: (a) *stratification,* separating youth into vocational and academic categories by high-school level; (b) *standardization,* the development of meaningful national or widely accepted standards applicable to all who earn academic or vocational certification; and (c) *vocational specificity,* education and training for a specific occupation.[8] These attributes are often, but not always, found together. Countries ranking high on vocational specificity usually stratify students, but may or may not have high standardization levels. For example, Germany, Denmark, Switzerland, and the Netherlands educate youth in specific fields that provide portable, well-recognized qualifications; in contrast, vocationally specific education has not always led to highly valued qualifications in Australia and the United Kingdom. Shavit and Muller hypothesized that qualifications matter most for careers when educational systems have high standardization, stratification, and vocational specificity. The higher the proportion of youth earning college degrees, the less important educational qualifications become. Finally, high levels of vocational specificity improve the chances of young people finding skilled, blue-collar jobs rather than unskilled jobs.

Their findings corroborated only some of their expectations. Importantly, countries with well-developed, vocationally specific programs provided more opportunities for young people, including low-income youth, to enter skilled careers. No educational alternative effectively substituted for well-developed institutions delivering vocationally specific training. Countries lacking such institutions simply provided fewer good career opportunities for those without a baccalaureate. Second, while stratifying youth into education tracks weakened educational opportunity, it enhanced students' occupational opportunity, fewer dropped out of school into unskilled positions, and fewer failed to acquire at least some marketable qualification. Third, employer-based apprenticeship training (as used in Germany and Switzerland) yielded better outcomes than the school-based vocational approach used in the Netherlands. These findings oppose arguments against vocationally specific approaches heard in the U.S., including concerns about tracking, teaching outdated skills, and diverting students from learning advanced academic skills.

A major argument against even employer-based approaches involving high standards, such as apprenticeship, is that few employers will participate. The logic from human-capital theory is that employers will pay only for training that is specific to the firm and not useful outside it. Training workers for general skills is unprofitable because returns to training accrue entirely to the worker. If the firm employing the worker did not raise wages to match training-induced gains in productivity, the worker trained for general skills could move to another firm and obtain wages equal to her higher level of productivity. But if firms have little incentive to offer general training, will not the type of training they finance—specific training—be too narrow to prepare youth for careers?

In recent years, researchers have challenged aspects of human-capital theory relevant to apprenticeship. Acemoglu and Pischke (1999) offer theoretical and empirical findings, suggesting that employers often do provide general training. Employers may well have an incentive to finance general training in real labor markets because transaction costs, such as matching and search costs, make it difficult for workers to quit jobs and costly for firms to replace employees. These search costs create a potential surplus that can benefit employers and workers when they avoid turnover. Firms can obtain part of this surplus when the productivity gain from added skills rises faster than wages. This wage–productivity gap gives employers an opportunity to earn returns even on general training.

Asymmetric information is one reason why training may raise productivity faster than wages. Firms providing training may know more about its content and value than outside firms. As a result, outside firms may be unwilling to bid up wages of newly trained workers to an amount equal to their productivity. Also, firms are most likely to lay off the lowest-ability workers among those receiving occupational training, and outside firms will recognize this. As Soskice (1994) argues, apprentices leaving companies in which they received training are difficult to screen. High-ability workers will not be able to quit and prove that ability when applying to outside firms. This is another reason why firms providing training can keep highly productive workers without paying the full value of their enhanced productivity. Finally, firms may sponsor training because benefits from general training may increase when workers know the company's goals (specific training). Conversely, the higher the workers' general skills, the more valuable the specific training and the return to employers from investing in specific training.

These theoretical points suggest that employer incentives depend partly on institutional structure: Some structures yield a high-retention, high-training equilibrium; and others do not. Because of asymmetric information, companies not training their own apprentices but attempting to hire from other firms will more likely hire a less-effective, skilled worker. However, the gap between the average ability of internally trained and externally trained workers will depend on the percentage of trained workers who quit. If a large percentage of capable workers receive general training, and only a small proportion quit, then hiring skilled workers from the outside will be risky, and training one's own workers will become attractive. On the contrary, if few firms train, and most workers move frequently from one firm to another, then hiring workers trained elsewhere will be more profitable, and fewer firms will have an incentive to train.

Encouraging a high-training equilibrium is likely to improve outcomes for young workers. One approach is to develop an infrastructure promoting apprenticeship or other types of industry-sponsored occupational training and certification. According to reviews by Paul Ryan (1999, 2001), apprenticeship generates more gains in employment and earnings than both job-training programs and full-time, school-based vocational education.

Overall, on the basis of theoretical and international empirical reasons, apprenticeship-type approaches still make sense. Can the U.S. progress toward such an approach?

NEXT STEPS

Where we go from here depends on the following question: Should a college degree be the only route to a rewarding, high-productivity career? Many jobs involving rewarding careers will require skills best taught outside a college framework. Even with expanded educational opportunities, many students will not complete a four-year degree. Therefore, coordinating increases in skills with employer actions to upgrade jobs and careers can widen noncollege routes to high-skill, high-wage careers.

The Japanese and German approaches constitute two leading examples of institutional success in STW systems (Ryan, 1999). These approaches yield high skills that are rewarded in the job market and affect nearly all youth. Japan relies on schools to sort students and on employers to provide occupational training. Firms recruit from few schools and allow teachers to recommend a few for each job. Because employers rarely reject the recommendations, even students not planning postsecondary education have an incentive to perform well in high school. The knowledge that young entrants will be trainable, coupled with restrictive hiring policies discouraging movement between jobs, gives Japanese firms an incentive to provide serious training.

To Ryan (1999), Germany's mass apprenticeship system lowers youth joblessness and leads to high stocks of workers with intermediate skills vital to the productivity and trade performance of Germany industry. This system builds a young person's employability within a highly motivating framework. Becoming a member of an occupation involves not only earning an occupational qualification but also gaining experience in the field. Work-based learning in a protective environment helps young people establish positive careers.

The key question is not whether an apprenticeship system can work in modern economies but whether national institutions can provide relevant infrastructure. In Germany in the late 1940s and early 1950s, some favored scrapping the traditional apprenticeship system. However, by instituting reforms in the 1960s, Germany, Austria, and Denmark were able to establish firm institutional bases for apprenticeship. Ryan (1999) contrasts these efforts (and those of Japan) to create well-structured transition systems with the succession of poorly funded, targeted youth programs in the U.S. Ryan argues that "the U.K. and the U.S. would be better served by a sustained effort geared to longer-term institutional development than by short-term policy innovation" (p. 450). The U.S. cannot and need not replicate the German system, but a structured system involving effective WBL is within reach.

An important step is to convince enough policymakers to move the country toward a system that not only alters students' learning processes but also yields solid career outlets, especially for students not pursuing a bachelor's degree. Unfortunately, in the mid-1990s, the STWOA implementation strategy produced no significant change in direction toward this broader system. I suggest two initiatives to demonstrate how large and well-designed programs in specific sectors can affect the occupational, earnings, and educational goals of youth. My third suggestion deals with a key bottleneck discussed previously—the lack of portable credentials based on well-designed standards and assessments.

Implement an Industry-Sector Strategy

Attract three to five lead industries, especially national or regional companies, to utilize a school-to-career model for recruiting, initial training, and career development. An industry association or lead companies in an industry would participate in creating standards, verifying skills, working with educators to specify prerequisites, and ensuring delivery of training at school and employer settings. The group would invite schools to participate. As an incentive for school involvement, industries would state that entry-level, career-oriented workers would be hired largely from these programs. These initiatives could be closely evaluated to learn lessons for various STW actors and estimate rates of return and social benefits.

Involve the Government as Employer, Using School-to-Career Approaches

Federal and state governments could designate selected occupation areas for developing internship or apprenticeship models linked to careers. For example, the federal government could work with other employers to develop standards in, say, clerical, administrative, and budgeting areas. The standards would embody school-based and work-based components leading to certification in a broad occupational area. The government would provide two-year internships in these certified programs. The occupational fields would be common in the private and public sectors. Schools would be invited to participate, knowing that the program would widen the range of career and learning choices for their graduates. Currently, the government encourages other employers to involve themselves directly in STW activities, but does not itself provide structured, intensive WBL. Thus, such an initiative could raise the government's credibility with private employers. It could also enhance the quality of government employees while expanding opportunities for young people.

Do More to Promote Regional and National Skill Certification

Although some state and a few local initiatives in this area are taking hold, the development of usable systems of standards and certification lags well behind the pace envisaged in the STWOA. The efforts of NSSB are slow and largely isolated from STW delivery mechanisms. It makes sense to bridge the gaps between active but limited state and local certification activities and the slow and distant federal board. Some states have demonstrated the feasibility of state standards, but these efforts are inherently limited because the scope for economies of scale and portability of credentials is limited. Perhaps a regional approach could work effectively. The National STW Office could document what standards have already been developed and sponsor regional meetings for developing consensus around standards and certification. Research organizations could analyze the relationship between standards across regions and industry clusters, the relationship between standards and the content of higher-education courses, and the impact of standards on employer recruitment and training.

These are modest steps and are by no means meant to be exhaustive. The important point is to rethink goals for the STW movement and to develop a range of incremental strategies to reach them.

NOTES

1. The author thanks the Smith Richardson Foundation for support that made this research possible and Stephanie Riegg for her excellent research assistance.

2. See, for example, Hanushek (1998) and Campbell, Hombo, and Mazzeo (2000).

3. The evidence on training-related placements is mixed. Campbell, Elliot, Hotchkiss, and Laughlin (1987) estimated that 42% of vocational-education graduates worked at jobs using skills they learned in school.

4. In a report copublished in 1995 by Jobs for the Future (JFF) and the American Youth Policy Forum, organizations that were leading proponents of youth-apprenticeship programs, JFF staffers Goldberger and Kazis argued against youth apprenticeships beginning at the high-school level. Although the publication of this study took place two years after the deliberations involving the STWOA, the ideas embodied in the report had already been widely circulated.

5. For example, the state plan had to describe how the state would obtain the active involvement of "employers and other interested parties, such as locally elected officials, secondary schools and postsecondary educational institutions (or related agencies), business associations, industrial extension centers, employees, labor organizations or associations of such organizations, teachers, related services personnel, students, parents, community-based organizations, rehabilitation agencies and organizations, registered apprenticeship agencies, local vocational-educational agencies, vocational student organizations, state or regional cooperative education associations, and human service agencies."

6. Information is based on interviews with officials in the Wisconsin Department of Workforce Development. Also see University of Wisconsin–Madison, Center for Education and Work (2000).

7. See, for example, Holland (1997).

8. Unlike the specific-training construct used by labor economists, in which the training is specific to the firm, the Muller-Shavit concept of specific training is limited to an occupation—and thus the benefits of training may improve the worker's skills outside the firm providing the training.

REFERENCES

Acemoglu, D., & Pischke, J.-S. (1999). Beyond Becker: Training in imperfect labour markets. *Economic Journal, 109,* F112–42.

Bishop, J. (1989). Why the apathy in American high schools? *Educational Researcher, 18,* 6–10.

Campbell, P., Elliot, J., Hotchkiss, L., & Laughlin, S. (1987). *Antecedents of training-related placement.* Columbus, OH: Ohio State University, National Center for Research in Vocational Education.

Campbell, J. R., Hombo, C. M., & Mazzeo, J. (2000). *NAEP 1999 trends in academic progress: Three decades of student performance* (NCES No. 2000–469). Washington, DC: U.S. Department of Education, National Center for Education Statistics.

Clinton, B., & Gore. A. (1992). *Putting people first.* New York: Times Books.

Commission on the Skills of the American Workforce. (1990). *America's choice: High skills or low wages!* Rochester, NY: National Center on Education and the Economy.

DeSalvatore, L., Goldberger, S., & Steinberg, A. (2000). *From innovative programs to systemic educational reform: Lessons from five communities.* Boston: Jobs for the Future.

Gardecki, R., & Neumark, D. (1998). Order from chaos? The effects of early labor market experiences on adult labor market outcomes. *Industrial & Labor Relations Review, 51,* 299–323.

Goldberger, S., & Kazis, R. (1995). *Revitalizing high schools: What the school-to-career movement can contribute.* Washington, DC: American Youth Policy Forum and Jobs for the Future.

Goodling, W. F. (1993, March 23). National School-to-Work and Youth Apprenticeship Act of 1993 [Extension of remarks]. *Congressional Record,* p. E743.

Haimson, J., & Hulsey, L. (1999). *Making joint commitments: Roles of schools, employers, and students in implementing national skill standards. Final report.* Princeton, NJ: Mathematica Policy Research, Inc.

Hamilton, S. F. (1990). *Apprenticeship for adulthood.* New York: Free Press.

Hamilton, S. F., & Hamilton, M. A. (1999). Creating new pathways to adulthood by adapting German apprenticeship in the United States. In W. R. Heinz (Ed.), *From education to work: Cross-national perspectives* (pp. 194–213). New York: Cambridge University Press.

Hanushek, E. (1998). Conclusions and controversies about the effectiveness of school resources. *Federal Reserve Bank of New York Economic Policy Review, 4* (1), 11–27.

Hanushek, E., & Somers, J. A. (1999). *Schooling, inequality, and the impact of government* (NBER Working Paper No. 7450). Cambridge, MA: National Bureau of Economic Research.

Heckman, J. J. (1994). Is job training oversold? *Public Interest, 115,* 91–115.

Hershey, A. M., Silverberg, M. K., Haimson, J., Hudis, P., & Jackson, R. (1999). *Expanding options for students: Report to Congress on the National Evaluation of School-to-Work Implementation.* Princeton, NJ: Mathematica Policy Research, Inc.

Holland, R. (1997, May). What's wrong with school-to-work? *Education Reporter: The Newspaper of Education Rights, 136.* Retrieved from http://www.eagleforum.org/educate/1997/may97/holland.html

Holzer, H. J., & LaLonde, R. (1999). *Job change and job stability among less-skilled young workers* (Institute for Research on Poverty Discussion Paper No. 1191–99). Madison, WI: University of Wisconsin–Madison, Institute for Research on Poverty.

Lerman, R. I., & Pouncy, H. (1990). The compelling case for youth apprenticeships. *The Public Interest, 101,* 62–77.

Levesque, K., Lauren, D., Teitelbaum, P., Alt, M., & Librera, S. (2000). *Vocational education in the United States: Toward the year 2000.* Washington, DC: U.S. Department of Education.

National Commission on Excellence in Education. (1983). *A nation at risk: The imperative for educational reform.* Washington, DC: U.S. Government Printing Office.

Neal, D. (1999). The complexity of job mobility among young men. *Journal of Labor Economics, 17,* 237–261.

Neumark, D. (1998). *Youth labor markets in the U.S.: Shopping around vs. staying put* (NBER Working Paper No. W6581). Cambridge, MA: National Bureau of Economic Research.

Neumark, D., & Joyce, M. (2000). *An introduction to school-to-work programs in the NLSY97: How prevalent are they, and which youths do they serve?* (NBER Working Paper No. W7733). Cambridge, MA: National Bureau of Economic Research.

Organisation for Economic Co-Operation and Development. (1998). *Employment outlook.* Paris: Author.

Phelps, L. A., & Jin, M. (1997). *1997 Wisconsin youth apprenticeship employer survey.* Madison, WI: University of Wisconsin–Madison, Center for Education and Work.

Ryan, P. (1999). The school-to-work transition twenty years on: Issues, evidence and conundrums. In *Preparing youth for the 21st Century: The transition from education to the labour marke*t (pp. 437–458). Paris: Organisation for Economic Co-Operation and Development.

Ryan, P. (2001). The school-to-work transition: A cross-national perspective. *Journal of Economic Literature, 39,* 34–93.

Shavit, Y., & Muller, W. (1998). The institutional embeddedness of the stratification process: A comparative study of qualifications and occupations in thirteen countries. In Y. Shavit & W. Muller (Eds.), *From school to work: A comparative study of educational qualifications and occupational destinations* (pp. 1–48). Oxford, England: Clarendon Press.

Soskice, D. (1994). Reconciling markets and institutions: The German apprenticeship system. L. M. Lynch (Ed.), *Training and the private sector: International comparisons* (pp. 25–60). Chicago: University of Chicago Press.

Topel, R., & Ward, M. (1992). Job mobility and the careers of young men. *Quarterly Journal of Economics, 107,* 439–479.

University of Wisconsin–Madison, Center for Education and Work. (2000). *Students with disabilities in Wisconsin youth apprenticeship programs.* Retrieved from http://www.cew.wisc.edu/cew/ya/default.htm

William T. Grant Foundation Commission on Work, Family, and Citizenship. (1988). *The forgotten half: Pathways to success for America's youth and young families. Final report on Youth and America's Future.* Washington, DC: Author.

15

Career Academies and High-School Reform before, during, and after the School-to-Work Movement

David Stern

High-school students have been the main population of interest for school-to-work (STW) reformers. One of the clearest examples of how to reconfigure high schools to promote STW principles is the career academy. After three decades of development and two decades of evaluation, a major random-assignment study has recently found career academies effective in improving high-school students' performance. This chapter describes the growth and evolution of career academies, reviews evaluation evidence, explains how career academies reflect the aims of the STW movement and other high-school reform movements, and considers future prospects.

WHAT IS A CAREER ACADEMY?

A career academy is a school-within-a-school (SWS) that provides a college-preparatory curriculum with a career-related theme. I coined the term *career academy* in 1992 to encompass three different groups of academies (Stern, Raby, & Dayton, 1992). Career academies are not defined by law except in California, where the state provides them special funding. Nevertheless, researchers at the Manpower Demonstration Research Corporation (MDRC; Kemple & Rock, 1996) have identified three defining features:

- First, career academies are *small learning communities.* An academy comprises a cluster of students sharing some teachers for at least two years and sharing several classes each year. A group of teachers from academic and technical disciplines are scheduled to teach only or mostly academy students, meet regularly, and share in decisions related to administrative policies, curriculum content, and instruction. One faculty member assumes lead responsibility for administrative tasks and usually serves as a liaison between the academy and the principal, other building administrators, district officials, and employer partners.

- Second, academies combine *a college-preparatory curriculum with a career theme.* Examples of common themes are health care, business and finance, communications media, and transportation technology. Academic courses meeting high-school-graduation and college-entrance requirements are linked with technical courses focusing on the academy's field. Teachers sometimes share planning time to coordinate course content and instructional strategies. College and career counseling inform students about options and about planning for employment and further education, which may or may not be related to the academy's career theme.
- Third, academies embody *partnerships with employers.* An advisory group for the academy includes representatives of the local employer community, academy faculty, and school district. Employer representatives advise on curriculum, speak in classes, supervise internships, provide financial or in-kind support, and sometimes mentor individual students.

THE RATIONALE FOR CAREER ACADEMIES AND SIMILAR NEW PATHWAYS

Career academies epitomize what many STW advocates have envisioned for students in high school. Academies are designed to prepare students both for further education and for work. By combining career-related applications with rigorous academics, career academies give students more postgraduation options than if they followed a conventional high-school curriculum.

Traditional vocational education in the United States and elsewhere has been criticized for leaving graduates without sufficient theoretical foundation to continue learning and adapting throughout their working lives. Many students, however, find pure academic education irrelevant or incomprehensible. Combining the two can improve academic performance and develop work-related capabilities simultaneously. If successful, this kind of secondary education may improve students' chances of completing university studies because they will obtain both necessary academic background and better understanding of how schooling relates to desired careers. Having acquired work skills in high school enabling them to earn higher hourly wages, students may find it easier to work their way through college, as most U.S. students do. Students not going directly into postsecondary education after high school can do so later. Those who start college but do not finish will have employment-related knowledge and experience to fall back on.

The rationale for an integrated pathway derives from pervasive trends in the United States and other industrialized countries (for numerical details, see Stern, 1999). First, students are staying in school longer. Most U.S. high-school students aspire—and their parents aspire for them—to complete at least a bachelor's degree. These aspirations stem partly from the facts that university graduates generally find jobs more easily and that those jobs are generally better paid than those found by high-school or two-year-college graduates. Additional earnings associated with a university degree are relatively higher in the United States than in other industrialized countries, and they remained high throughout the 1990s. Conversely, individuals leaving high school without diplomas suffer an increasingly serious disadvantage in the labor market. Career academies and other new pathways are therefore designed to promote high-school completion and preserve the option of attending university for as many students as possible.

At the same time, combining work and school is becoming more common. While labor-force participation of fifteen-to-twenty-four-year-olds has been declining in most industrialized countries, including the United States, the proportion of employed teenagers and young adults who are students has burgeoned. Studies of working students in the United States have found that those working a moderate number of hours actually perform better in school than those not working at all, but performance suffers among students working more than fifteen to twenty hours weekly (Stern & Briggs, in press). School supervision of students' work appears to mitigate negative effects (Stern, Finkelstein, Urquiola, & Cagampang, 1997). Career academies therefore attempt to link students' part-time employment with classroom studies to contribute to educational achievement while still affording students valuable work experience.

Career academies are not the only form of high-school curriculum embodying STW ideas. Career clusters or majors within comprehensive high schools serve similar purposes, as do self-contained career-magnet high schools. However, career academies are distinguished by their durability, definability, and dependability.[1] They have existed longer than other forms of integrated academic-vocational curriculum and are more likely to conform to a clear and consistent definition. Career academies also produce predictable, positive results when replicated in new sites. This chapter therefore confines its attention to career academies as an exemplar of STW reform in high schools.

GROWTH AND EVOLUTION OF CAREER ACADEMIES

In the two decades after their 1969 inception, career academies' growth was steady but gradual. Since 1990, growth in the number of academies has accelerated. Evolution of career academies has been marked by increasing emphasis on preparation for higher education, and more recently by incorporation of academies into strategies for transforming entire high schools.

Only three organized networks provide accurate counts of career academies. In Philadelphia, the nonprofit Philadelphia Academies, Inc., has supported career academies since 1969 and was sponsoring twenty-nine academies in 2000. In California, after two nonprofit-sponsored academies were established in 1981, the state began funding academies in 1985 and was supporting 290 academies in 2000. The nonprofit National Academy Foundation (NAF) has sponsored academies since 1982, and in 2000 was supporting 400 academies in more than thirty states. The total number of academies in these networks grew to about 100 in 1990 and then expanded to more than 700 in 2000.

Beyond these networks, Illinois, Florida, Hawaii, and other states followed California's lead and began funding career academies in the 1990s. Another academy-building network started in 1997 at the Center for Research on the Education of Students Placed at Risk (CRESPAR), which includes career academies as a major component of the Talent Development High School model (LaPoint, Jordan, McPartland, & Towns, 1996). Apart from these organized initiatives, an uncounted number of unaffiliated academies have sprung up across the country. Within California, for example, academies not receiving state funding probably outnumber academies receiving it. Nationwide, the total for academies operating in high schools in 2000 almost certainly exceeded 1,000 and could well have been 2,000 or 3,000.

Until the 1990s, career academies existed only as separate, small units within larger high schools. For example, a career academy might serve 200 students in a school containing 2,000. Since the mid-1990s, however, some schools have converted themselves entirely into groups of career academies or of various small learning communities (SLCs), some of which are career academies. Lee, Ready, and Johnson (1999) conducted an informal national canvass to identify high schools constituted entirely of small learning environments. They identified fifty-five such schools, 80% of which were using career academies as the model. CRESPAR's Talent Development High School is an example; every student in grades 10–12 belongs to a career academy.

Academies began with a focus on dropout-prevention and vocational preparation, but they soon evolved to include preparation for four-year colleges and universities. Philadelphia's first career academy in 1969 was an Electrical Academy at Edison High School, sponsored partly by the Philadelphia Electric Company. The idea was subsequently applied to other fields, including business, automotive, health, environmental technology, law, horticulture, tourism, and aviation. The nonprofit organizations that had mobilized employer support combined in 1982 to what is now called Philadelphia Academies, Inc. Supported by corporate contributions and foundation grants, this organization coordinates and subsidizes academies in Philadelphia, while the city's school district retains jurisdiction and supplies teachers and classrooms. Although Philadelphia's academies began as vocational-training programs, today they send most of their graduates to college.

In 1981, the academy idea was exported from Philadelphia to California, starting with a Computer Academy at Menlo-Atherton High School and an Electronics Academy at Sequoia High School, near Silicon Valley. A series of evaluations demonstrating improved student performance spurred California to pass legislation in 1984 supporting ten replications of the model. Evaluations of these academies also yielded encouraging results, and in 1987 a second state bill was passed that supported approximately forty additional replications. The legislation was renewed in 1993 and 1999, with continued expansion. Career themes are chosen locally, and California academies now represent twenty-five different fields. The California model has formalized student involvement in three academic courses and one career-related course each year in grades 10–12. California has also advanced the notion of preparing students simultaneously for college and careers.

Also in the 1980s, New York City created the first Academies of Finance, sponsored by the American Express Company, which subsequently joined with other companies, now numbering more than 100, to create NAF. The foundation added the travel and tourism field in 1987, public service in 1990, and information technology in 1999. Curriculum, technical support, and professional development for teachers are provided by NAF. The NAF academies usually include only grades 11–12, but some academies, following the Philadelphia and California models, are adding earlier years of high school and more coordination with academic classes. The NAF academies have been college-oriented since their inception.

EFFECTS OF CAREER ACADEMIES ON STUDENT PERFORMANCE

Growing numbers of states, districts, and schools have started career academies because research shows they improve students' performance. This section presents the evidence to date, focusing on quantitative studies of student performance.[2] Individual studies and findings are summarized in Table 15.1.

Several California studies have found that academy students perform better than similar students in the same schools who are individually matched with academy students by demographic characteristics and ninth-grade records of low grades, high absenteeism, and disciplinary problems. An evaluation of the first two academies in California in the early 1980s found that academy students in grades 10 through 12 had better attendance, more credits, higher grades, and more likelihood of graduating than the comparison groups (Reller, 1984; additional citations in Stern, Raby, & Dayton, 1992; see also Raby, 1995). From 1985 through 1988, a similar evaluation of the ten initial state-funded academies in California showed substantial and statistically significant advantages for academy students in attendance, credits toward graduation, GPA, and retention through high school (Dayton, Weisberg, & Stern, 1989; Stern, Dayton, Paik, & Weisberg, 1989).

The California evaluations using individually matched comparison groups also followed students after high-school graduation. Academy graduates were at least as likely to be enrolled in postsecondary education as nonacademy schoolmates one or two years after high school. They also had more hours of paid employment. Stern, Raby, and Dayton (1992) give additional details.

More recently, Maxwell and Rubin (1997) surveyed former high-school students from a large California district one or two years after their graduating year. They found that students from career academies were at least as likely to

Table 15.1
Authors, Dates, Data Sources, and Findings of Studies of the Effects of Career Academies on Academic Performance, High-School Completion, Enrollment in Postsecondary Education, and Employment after High School: Data from 1981 to 1999

Reller, 1984, 1985, 1987. Data collected 1981–1986 on students in two California academies and on matched comparison groups in each school. Follow-up surveys 15 and 27 months after graduation.

Academy students earned more course credits than comparison group. One-year dropout rates 2% to 6% in academies, 10% to 21% in comparison group.

Fifteen months after graduation, academy graduates had higher postsecondary enrollment rate (62%) than comparison group (47%) and higher degree aspirations.

No significant differences between academy and comparison students, 27 months after graduation, in employment status, wages, or hours worked.

Snyder & McMullan, 1987a, 1987b. 1981 sophomores entering business academies in three Philadelphia high schools traced to graduation. Graduates surveyed late 1986 to early 1987 and compared to a random sample of all graduates and to all business-program graduates from those high schools.

Graduation rate (77%) greater than citywide rate for freshmen (67%).

Of business-academy graduates, 18% said school was main activity in 1986–1987, compared to 35% of citywide sample. Of those enrolled, 14% of academy graduates and 43% of citywide sample intended to get bachelor's degrees.

Of business academy graduates, 64% said work was main activity in 1986–1987, in comparison with 42% of citywide sample. Academy graduates employed a larger fraction of time since graduation.

Stern et al., 1988; Stern et al., 1989. Data collected 1985–1990 on students in ten academies funded by state of California and on matched comparison groups in each school.

Academy students overall performed significantly better than comparison groups in attendance, credits earned, average grades, and likelihood of staying in school. Three-year dropout rate for cohort entering 1985 was 7.3% in academies, 14.6% in comparison group.

Academy for Educational Development, 1990. Follow-up of Academy of Finance students who graduated 1984–1989. No comparison group.

Of finance-academy graduates, 89% said they had attended four-year college or university, 58% majored in business or finance, and 67% planned to complete a master's or doctorate.

Stern et al., 1992. Follow-up surveys 10 and 22 months after graduation of graduates from ten state-funded California academies and comparison groups.

1989 and 1990 follow-up surveys found no consistent differences between academy and comparison graduates in postsecondary attendance or degree aspirations.

Follow-up surveys of academy and comparison graduates in 1989 and 1990 showed academy graduates working three more hours per week but no consistent overall difference in hourly earnings.

Table 15.1 (continued)

Hayward & Talmadge, 1995. 1989–92 data from ten different programs using vocational education to promote high-school success. Two of the sites were career academies. Evaluation used random control groups in some sites, nonrandom comparison groups in others, including the academies. Academies showed generally better results than other programs, improving students' attendance, credits, grades, and likelihood of completing high school.
McPartland et al., 1996; McPartland et al., 1998. Reorganization of Baltimore high school in 1995 included creation of four career academies for grades 10–12. Data analyzed from 1993 to 1998. Attendance in first year rose from 71% to 77%, contrasting with districtwide decline from 73% to 70% in grades 9–12. Teacher survey reported much-improved school climate.
Kemple & Snipes, 2000. Ten career academies included in an experimental evaluation since 1993. This is the only evaluation of career academies (or other high-school restructuring strategies) with students randomly assigned to academies and control groups. Academy students earned more course credits and were more likely to have positive developmental experiences. Among students at highest risk, academy students attended school more regularly, earned more course credits, were more likely to participate in extracurricular activities and volunteer projects, and were less likely to be arrested. Dropout rate for the high-risk subgroup was reduced from 32% in the control group to 21% among the career-academy students.
Maxwell & Rubin, 1997, 2000. 1991–1995 school records for three cohorts of students in grades 10–12 in an urban district, including nine career academies. Also a follow-up survey in mid to late 1996. Records show academy students received higher grades. Survey found higher grades increased the likelihood of graduation; result was 92% graduation rate for academy students, 82% for nonacademy. Survey found higher grades for academy students increased their probability of going to college, and two of nine academies gave an added boost to college going, resulting in 52% of former academy students going to 4-year colleges, in comparison with 36% of nonacademy students. Analysis of survey found no significant differences in wages or hours worked between former academy and nonacademy students, but former academy students more often said their high-school program had prepared them well for further education and work.
Elliott et al., 2000. 1994–1996 data from three Junior Reserve Officers Training Corps (JROTC) career academies in large cities were compared with student data from other career academies or magnets in the same or similar schools, on JROTC students not in academies, and on students not in any academy or magnet. Students in career academies or magnets received higher grades, had better attendance, completed more credits, and were less likely to drop out than similar students not in academies.

be enrolled in four-year colleges as students who identified themselves as having been in the high-school academic track. Both career-academy and academic-track graduates had a significantly greater likelihood of enrolling in four-year colleges than graduates classifying themselves as having been in the high-school general track. Yet academy students had lower average scores on sophomore reading tests and were less likely to be native English speakers than general-track students.

Maxwell and Rubin (2000) also analyzed school-district records of academy and nonacademy students. They found that academy students obtained significantly better grades. This was not due to easier grading standards within academies: Maxwell and Rubin found that grades in academy courses were actually *lower* than grades in nonacademy courses in the same subjects.[3] Furthermore, when Maxwell and Rubin divided students into high, middle, and low groups according to tenth-grade math and English test scores, in each group they found academy students obtaining higher grades than nonacademy students. Their higher grades appeared to be the main reason for academy students' higher rate of college attendance.

Maxwell (1999) followed academy and other graduates from the same school district who enrolled at a nearby campus of the state university. She found that academy graduates were more likely to come from high schools with large proportions of low-income minority students. When this was accounted for, academy graduates were less likely to need remedial university coursework, and they were more likely to receive baccalaureates than other graduates from the same district. These findings suggest that academies help low-income students finish both high school and college. They imply that the improvement in high-school graduation rates was not accomplished by lowering academic standards in career academies.

Beyond California, an earlier evaluation of business academies in Philadelphia (Snyder & McMullan, 1987b) found a higher graduation rate than the citywide average, but a lower rate of postsecondary enrollment for academy graduates than for the general student population; no significant differences from graduates of other business programs appeared in employment after graduation. However, an early study of a NAF academy in New York City found high rates of postsecondary enrollment (Academy for Educational Development, 1990). The difference apparently reflects the origin of Philadelphia academies in traditional vocational education and NAF academies in a college-preparatory design. Linnehan (1996) later found that graduates from Philadelphia business academies reported better high-school attendance, which carried forward into less reported absenteeism in jobs after high school. Elliott, Hanser, and Gilroy (2000), analyzing data from three career academies affiliated with the Junior Reserve Officers Training Corps, found positive effects on attendance, credits earned, grades, and the likelihood of staying in high school.

Importance of the MDRC Random-Assignment Study

An unresolved question in these evaluations—even in studies using individually matched comparison groups—was whether positive results for academy students might be attributable to selection. Because students must take initiative to apply to a career academy, academy students may have more motivation, ambition, energy, parental support, or other unmeasured strengths than comparison students. These unmeasured characteristics may have prompted some students' application to career academies and also made them likelier to succeed, whether in academies or not.

The selection issue not only clouds previous career-academy research but also bedevils evaluations of other high-school reforms. For example, numerous studies tested effects of reducing the size of high schools, either by creating separate small schools or by dividing large schools into smaller units. These studies tend to find that students in smaller environments are relatively less alienated, more engaged, more likely to pass courses and accumulate credits toward graduation, and less likely to drop out (Cotton, 1996; Gladden, 1998; Raywid, 1995). However, these patterns may be largely attributable to preexisting differences between students in large and small schools or between students enrolled and not enrolled in small units within larger high schools, and researchers may not measure these differences. For example, students may differ in individual characteristics such as motivation, or in community characteristics such as homogeneity of values. Such differences may make students in small schools or SWSs likelier to succeed even in large schools.

For instance, several frequently cited studies suggest that students in smaller high schools are less likely to drop out (Fetler, 1989; Franklin & Crone, 1992; Howley & Bickel, 1999; Pittman & Haughwout, 1987). Each study compared high schools in a state or national sample at one point in time.[4] The smaller high schools therefore probably included schools in small, close-knit rural communities; magnet high schools or other schools of choice in big cities; and schools located in relatively homogeneous residential enclaves in small cities or metropolitan areas. Characteristics of those communities, such as stronger personal connections and shared values between school staff and parents, may account for the lower dropout rates, and these characteristics were not captured by the simple socioeconomic measures the studies used as statistical controls. The available research, based on comparisons across communities, therefore does not demonstrate that replacing a large high school with smaller high schools would produce lower dropout rates or other desirable results in a given community.[5] Like previous research on career academies, research on small high schools and other kinds of SWSs is suggestive but not conclusive.

The only way to eliminate such uncertainty is the experimental procedure of random assignment. Standard practice in medical research, and sometimes used in classroom-level studies in education, this procedure is very rare in studies of school structure (see Mosteller, Light, & Sachs, 1996). That is why the MDRC study of career academies was so significant. MDRC began its ten-site study in 1993 by creating a list of students applying to the career academy at each site and choosing at random those who would be admitted and those who would not. The latter constituted the control group. Unlike the matched comparison groups in earlier studies, all students in the MDRC control group had initiated application to the academy. They therefore shared the same unmeasured motivation, ambition, or other traits that might characterize the academy student.

The MDRC evaluation results strongly confirmed earlier findings from the matched-comparison studies of career academies. Evaluators found that academy students overall earned more credits toward graduation and were more likely to have positive developmental experiences such as working on a volunteer project. The strongest and most pervasive differences were found among students at highest risk of failure. Among this subgroup, academy students attended school more regularly, earned more credits, were more likely to participate in extracurricular activities and volunteer projects, and were less likely to be arrested. Most consequentially, the dropout rate for the high-risk subgroup fell from 32% in the control group to 21% among the academy students (Kemple & Snipes, 2000). This evidence on career academies' effectiveness is clearer than for any other high-school reform strategy. It provides an unusually solid basis for designing new policies and practices to improve high schools.

Two Issues Raised by the MDRC Study: Test Scores and Schoolwide Effects

Despite positive results, the MDRC study raised two troubling issues, one explicit and the other implicit. The explicit issue concerns test scores. MDRC found that career-academy seniors scored no higher than control-group students on standardized tests in mathematics and language arts (Kemple & Snipes, 2000). Furthermore, previous studies of career academies have not examined effects on standardized test scores. The absence of evidence that academies improve standardized test scores is serious because such tests are sometimes regarded as the best immediate measure of student learning.

However, the long-run benefit of career academies for participating students depends much more on reducing dropout rates than on raising test scores. For instance, the additional earnings associated with completing one more year of high school are estimated to be four to ten times greater than those associated with a grade-equivalent year of test score gain (Levin, 2001), and few if any replicable programs have been able to produce test score gains of that magnitude. Therefore, even if academy students' test scores are no higher than the control group's, career academies still provide substantial benefits by enabling more students to finish high school.

A second issue arising from the MDRC study and previous evaluations of career academies concerns school-wide effects. An academy—or any other program that serves only some of the students in a school—may attract special resources, especially highly committed, energetic, or talented teachers. If so, academy students may gain at the expense of the rest. The MDRC study did examine whether academy teachers were more experienced or better educated than nonacademy counterparts and found no differences on average (Kemple & Rock, 1996). Because teachers were not randomly assigned to academies, however, there may have been unobserved differences in motivation, commitment, or other attributes of good teaching. Furthermore, academy teachers had smaller classes (twenty-four students on average) than nonacademy teachers (26.7). It is possible, therefore, that differences between the performance of academy and nonacademy students were partly attributable to a shift of resources from the rest of the school to the academy.

A related question is whether benefits of career academies can be generalized to a broader student population. The MDRC study was restricted to the subpopulation of students choosing to apply to an academy, in schools where academies served only a small proportion of the student body. What are the effects on student performance of dividing a school into career academies or other kinds of SLCs and of requiring *every* student to choose one? The MDRC study did not answer this question.

The questions of schoolwide effects and of generalizing benefits of academies or similar strategies are important because of the growing conviction that some high schools—particularly large, urban ones—are no longer viable in their traditional form. The next two sections summarize three major contemporary movements to change high schools and review existing evidence on the effects of whole-school reforms.

THE ROLE OF CAREER ACADEMIES IN RECONSTRUCTING AMERICAN HIGH SCHOOLS

American high schools need reconstructing. The proportion of young people completing a regular high-school diploma appears not to have increased since the 1960s,[6] while the economic penalty for not finishing high school has become more severe. I am concerned when I visit high schools and witness the lack of student engagement, even in affluent schools. I am concerned about stubborn achievement gaps between students from different socioeconomic groups.

Such a terse statement of concerns is not a diagnosis of the problems of high schools, and it is not likely to change the mind of anyone believing that American high schools are satisfactory or as good as can be expected. Several sources cited here provide more extensive analysis of high schools' shortcomings and proposals for fixing them (Fine & Somerville, 1998; Grubb, 1995; Sizer, 1984, 1992; Steinberg, 1998; Stern et al., 1992). I will not recapitulate those well-known arguments. Instead, I will describe several movements in which many teachers, administrators, parents, and students are working to change high schools. Their concerns drive much of the change happening in high schools. My review of the evaluation evidence shows that career academies are among the most solid building blocks available for remaking high schools. This is one reason why growth in career academies has accelerated. Another reason is that these reform movements now are including career academies in broader strategies. Three major initiatives incorporating career academies are the STW movement, the Coalition of Essential Schools, and the small-schools movement. Although each initiative emphasizes a distinct set of ideas and practices, career academies share important elements with all three.

School-to-Work

The STW movement (also known as the school-to-career movement) derives its impetus from foundation-sponsored programs in the 1980s, legislation enacted by various states in the early 1990s, and the 1994 federal School-to-Work Opportunities Act (STWOA) that gave the movement its name (Urquiola et al., 1997). Although advocates and participants in the movement espouse different purposes, some central issues were succinctly stated by Olson (1997):

> Today we teach students academic subjects out of context and then are perturbed when they ask, "Why do I have to learn this?" We hire young people without glancing at their high-school transcripts and then wonder why they do not work harder in school. We sequester teens in high schools that are too big for them and then express dismay when they succumb to an adolescent peer culture. We tell young people to attend college to "get a job" but then offer little in the way of career guidance. We convince students that we are preparing them for the "real world" but make their education as removed from the adult society as possible. (p. 27)

School-to-work programs have attempted to make the high-school curriculum more coherent and meaningful for students by creating curricular pathways with career themes. Connections between classroom and work have been reinforced through work-based learning opportunities such as job shadowing and internships. Many STW programs have also sought to articulate high-school courses with studies in two-year or four-year colleges. Despite the name, STW programs usually have *not* been designed to train students for entry-level jobs after high school. Instead, they have attempted to prepare students for postsecondary education while equipping them with work-related knowledge and skill.

Career academies predated the STW movement and exemplified ideas the movement sought to generalize: using career themes to increase curricular coherence, providing forms of workplace experience such as internships to connect classroom learning to the world beyond school, and preparing students for careers requiring postsecondary education. Thus, STWOA explicitly named career academies as one "promising practice" for preparing all students for further education and careers demanding a solid academic foundation. This was the first mention of career academies in federal legislation, and it helped stimulate interest in them.

The High Schools that Work (HSTW) project, which also predated the STW movement and provided some basis for it, is another initiative to which career academies have contributed. Launched in 1987 by the Southern Regional Education Board in thirteen states at twenty-eight sites, HSTW had grown by 2000 to include approximately 1,000 member high schools in twenty-four states. These schools combine challenging academic courses and modern vocational-educational studies to raise the achievement of high-school students not enrolled in college-preparatory courses (Bottoms & Presson, 1995). The HSTW initiative was designed to strengthen vocational programs, abandon the watered-down coursework associated with the general track, and rescue the forgotten students comprising more than half of the population of most high schools (Southern Regional Education Board, 1995). Over time, HSTW has evolved the concept of academic, career, and blended majors containing an academic core and connecting to the world beyond school. Career academies are a natural path to these goals and can be found in many HSTW member schools. Career academies have also been recognized among HSTW best practices (Southern Regional Education Board, 1997).

To broaden awareness of STW principles as a basis for comprehensive high-school reform, the U.S. Department of Education in 1996 began to identify New American High Schools. Additional schools have been recognized subsequently. Principles and practices in these schools have included preparing students for college and careers, learning in the context of a career major or special interest, experiential learning in workplaces or community service, grouping students and teachers in small SWSs, providing support from adult mentors outside of school, and forging links between high schools and post-secondary institutions. Because a number of these schools contain career academies (Visher & Hudis, 1999), academies have gained additional recognition.

The Coalition of Essential Schools

A second major reform movement with widespread influence on American high schools is the Coalition of Essential Schools (CES). In contrast to the more utilitarian and future-oriented emphasis of the STW movement, which has focused on preparing students for college and careers, the fundamental concerns of the CES are to improve intellectual, social, and ethical quality of high-school life for students and teachers. From the work of its founder, Theodore Sizer (1984, 1992), CES has formulated ten common principles: learning to use one's mind well; less is more, depth over coverage; goals apply to all students; personalization of the student–teacher relationship; student as worker, teacher as coach; assessment of student learning through demonstration of mastery; a tone of decency and trust; commitment to the entire school; resources dedicated to teaching and learning; and democracy and equity.

Although a narrow vocationalism would be considered inimical to CES goals, career academies are found in some CES schools, and career-academy education has been endorsed in the coalition's publications. For instance, Cushman, Steinberg, and Riordan (1997) have written the following:

> A career academy promises a meaningful context for students' academic work across disciplines, a culture of high expectations derived from real-world standards, and a structure and opportunity for exploring the world of adults. Ideally, in academic and real-world contexts, students explore and master equivalent sets of intellectual and practical skills. They may apply the analytic methods of different academic disciplines,

for example, to the problems of the health-care system, or they may study the physics of building an electric car. In the process, they also acquire a more real sense of the nature of different work roles than casual observation can provide. They come to appreciate the learning that happens in many work settings. (p. 16)

In Boston, specifically, the authors have observed that "school-to-career pathways or academies tend to attract ambitious students looking for a way to gain the academic background, mentoring, and real-world connections that will help them find a path into and through college to a career" (p. 18).

Their basic design makes career academies likely to fulfill several intellectual and ethical principles espoused by the CES.[7] Career-related themes enhance curricular focus and coherence, encouraging the CES principle of analytical depth. Allowing students to test and deepen their understanding of academic concepts through practical applications and work-based learning in academies promotes the CES principles of engaging students as active "workers" and using demonstrations of authentic mastery to assess learning. The effectiveness of academies in improving the performance of high-risk students demonstrates their compatibility with the CES principle of justice and equity.

Most obviously, the organization of career academies as small learning environments within larger schools enables the formation of personal and caring relationships that the CES considers necessary for good teaching and learning (Meier 1996; Sizer, 1984, 1992). The MDRC evaluation found that students in academies received more personal attention and support from teachers than nonacademy students did (Kemple, 1997). Conchas (1998) found that feelings of affinity created among students in an urban career academy were strong enough to overcome racial and ethnic animosities that caused problems in the rest of the school.

The Small-Schools Movement

The enthusiasm for small schools or SLCs within large schools is shared both by members of the CES and by prominent researchers and educational authorities interested in improving American high schools (Darling-Hammond, 1997; National Association of Secondary School Principals, 1996; Noddings, 1992; Sergiovanni, 1994). Advocates urge creating new small schools and breaking up large schools into self-contained subunits (Fine, 1994; Fine & Somerville, 1998; Oxley, 1989; Raywid, 1995). For example, Fine and Sommerville have observed the following:

Across the country there is a revolution happening within the field of schooling. In urban areas, as well as suburban and rural communities, educators and parents are demanding, creating, and struggling to sustain small, neighborhood-based schools as schools of choice. There is growing literature, both scholarly and popular, that substantiates the positive effects of such small schools. We know that big schools often have harmful effects on many students, teachers, and parents, and that given the right conditions . . . small schools can create an academic climate in which a sense of belonging and rich teaching and learning can flourish. (p. 2)

Congress boosted the small-schools movement by earmarking $45 million in the 2000 Appropriations Act for the Department of Education to fund a new Smaller Learning Communities Program through section 10105 of the Elementary and Secondary Education Act. The intent is to help local school districts "plan, develop, implement, or expand smaller, more personalized learning communities in large high schools" (U.S. Department of Education, 2000, p. 3). The Clinton administration proposed expanding the expenditure for this program to $120 million in fiscal 2001. Meanwhile, the Bill & Melinda Gates Foundation announced $56 million in grants to promote small schools or SLCs within larger schools, especially secondary schools (Gewertz, 2000).

The small-schools movement supports the spread of career academies because these are a significant type of SLC. Some new small schools in their own buildings may organize their curricula around career themes. And when large high schools subdivide into smaller units, some may be career academies.

For example, in 1988, Philadelphia began a massive, multiyear effort to divide its twenty-two comprehensive high schools into SLCs called "charters" (Fine, 1994). The Philadelphia academies, steadily growing since 1969, were regarded as one kind of charter. A study by McMullan, Sipe, and Wolf (1994) found that in 1992–93, out of 7,417 ninth graders enrolled in all charters, 1,214 ninth graders were enrolled in academies. As well-established charters, the academies evidenced curricular coherence and enrollment stability. Although they enrolled a relatively small share of ninth graders who were two or more years over age, repeating ninth grade, or taking more than one-fourth of their courses in special education, the academies enrolled more than the district wide percentage of ninth graders qualifying for compensatory education under Chapter 1 of the Elementary and Secondary Education Act.

In sum, for these high-school reform movements, career academies are one element among multiple strategies. None of these movements would view career academies as a complete strategy for remaking high schools, and neither would I. But all three have used career academies as one component of changes sought.

THE EFFECTS OF TRANSFORMING HIGH SCHOOLS INTO SMALL LEARNING COMMUNITIES

If students and teachers in large high schools are grouped into career academies or other kinds of SWSs, what will be the effects on student performance? The MDRC study evaluated career academies in schools where most students were *not* enrolled in SLCs. That study's results pertained to students who applied to career academies in that context, and the findings cannot be extrapolated to high schools where all students are enrolled in career academies or other small learning environments.

Only a few studies have measured effects on student performance of dividing high schools into smaller subunits. McPartland and his colleagues at CRESPAR (McPartland, Balfanz, Jordan, & Legters, 1998; McPartland, Legters, Jordan, & McDill, 1996; see Table 15.1) have reported the first results of subdividing a high school entirely into career academies in grades 10–12. Patterson High School in Baltimore was reconstituted because "it was one of the two worst high schools in the state of Maryland in 1994" (McPartland et al., 1996, p. 1). For example:

> Small groups of unruly students were constantly roaming the halls and stairways, and repeated faculty efforts to bring order to the building were unsuccessful. Teachers, unable to maintain peace in the halls, retreated to their classrooms where they tried to do their best with the students in their rooms. They kept the doors of their rooms closed, and many papered over their door windows to shut out the outside confusion. (p. 2)

With CRESPAR's assistance, Patterson reorganized into a set of academies: a self-contained SLC with an academic emphasis for ninth graders and four career academies for students in grades 10–12. Results in the first year included better student attendance and a turnaround in teachers' ratings of school climate. Subsequently, students' performance on math proficiency tests also improved (McPartland et al., 1998). These results suggest that career academies can improve performance when they are part of a schoolwide strategy. Given that school's high rates of student turnover, however, it is unclear how far the improvements resulted from changes in the student population, rather than from school reorganization.

Table 15.2 summarizes findings from three other studies done in New York City, Philadelphia, and Chicago, three districts with many students enrolled in small learning environments within large high schools. The results are promising. In New York, Oxley (1990) found small but consistently better academic and social benefits for students in a large high school divided into well-structured small learning environments (houses) than in another large high school with less-tightly-structured houses. In Philadelphia, McMullan et al. (1994) discovered that ninth-grade students in SLCs (the charters discussed previously) earned a larger percentage of credits required for graduation than ninth graders not in charters. After differences between characteristics of charter and noncharter students were adjusted for, the advantage to charter students became quite small—on the order of one-fourth of one yearlong course—but it was still statistically significant.[8] The Chicago study by Wasley et al. (2000) found that students in SWSs had fewer absences, higher grades, and lower one-year dropout rates than students in what were termed "nonsmall" high schools. In "multischools," where all students were in small learning environments, the

Table 15.2
Authors, Dates, Data Sources, and Findings of Studies of the Effects of Dividing Large High Schools into Smaller Subunits: Data from 1988 to 1999

McMullan et al., 1994. Data from Philadelphia's comprehensive high schools during the first five years of the city's charter school program. Analysis focused on comparing charter to noncharter ninth-grade students in the 1992–93 school year (*N* = 7417 and 7765 respectively). The average percentage of necessary credits (for promotion to grade 10) earned by ninth graders in 1992–1993 was 15.3% higher for the average charter student than for the average noncharter student. Using ordinary least squares (OLS) regression to control for differences in student demographics and prior school performance, the difference in average percentage of necessary credits earned was 3.4%. Using two-stage least squares (TSLS), the difference was 4.1%. When the comparison was restricted to charter students who took at least three courses in their home charter, the unadjusted difference was 24.4%, which was reduced to 9.5% after OLS adjustment and 5.8% after TSLS adjustment.
Oxley, 1990. Data on 311 grade 9 and 10 students collected through survey and on-site records from four New York City high schools during the 1988–1989 school year. Compared to students in a large high school without a tightly structured house system, students in another large high school with tightly structured houses showed small but consistent differences: They reported a stronger sense of community, participated in more extracurricular activities, cut fewer classes, earned more credits, and were more likely to be promoted. Results for students in a small school without tightly structured houses were similar to results for the large school with tightly structured houses, except that students in the small school were less likely to report a strong sense of community.
Wasley et al., 2000. School records and survey data from Chicago Public Schools between 1997 and 1999. High-school sample of small schools consisted of 22 schools-within-schools (SWSs) located in eight schools, 27 SWSs located in three multischools (all-SWSs), and three freestanding small schools. Comparison sample was 47 nonsmall high schools that did not contain any SWSs. Hierarchical linear modeling was used to adjust for students' eighth-grade achievement and demographics. Average days absent per semester in nonsmall high schools were 13.56, compared to 9.72 in freestanding small schools, 10.45 in multischools, and 8.09 in SWSs. One-year dropout rate in 1999 from nonsmall high schools was 10.3%, compared to 5.14% from freestanding small schools, 12.26% from multischools, and 6.07% from SWSs. GPA in nonsmall high schools was 1.96, compared to 1.98 in freestanding small schools and 2.11 in SWSs.

absentee rate was lower, but the dropout rate was higher than in nonsmall schools.

These promising results are not conclusive evidence that dividing a high school entirely into small learning environments improves performance. The Philadelphia study combined high schools with all students in charters and high schools with only some in charters. But charters in part-charter schools may have selected students with high motivation or other unmeasured characteristics making them more likely to succeed even if not enrolled in charters. In all-charter schools, some charters may have recruited more-motivated students, but then less-motivated students were enrolled in other charters, so the selection effects canceled out in schoolwide analysis. Including part-charter schools in such analyses, therefore, may not accurately indicate the effects of enrolling students in all-charter schools.

The Chicago study distinguished between part-SWS and all-SWS schools, but found that students in all-SWS multischools did not always perform better. In particular, their one-year dropout rate was high. However, the authors observed that, unlike SWSs located in part-SWSs, "the vast majority of SWSs located in multischools were built around grade levels, not themes" (Wasley et al., 2000, p. 11). The Chicago study, therefore, does not indicate what would happen if entire high schools were divided into career academies or other thematic subschools enrolling students for more than one year.

Because growing numbers of high schools are grouping students and teachers into smaller learning environments, it is important to discover whether this really improves students' performance. For several reasons, benefits of career academies or other SLCs may not generalize when applied schoolwide. A few academies or SLCs within a larger school may recruit students with relatively high motivation, but if all students were enrolled in SLCs, this would be impossible. A single academy or SLC in a larger school may attract relatively innovative and enthusiastic teachers, but if such teachers were in limited supply, their effects would not be generalizable to an all-SLC school.

Even if an academy or SLC in a school with only a few SLCs does not recruit students or teachers with special qualities, the mere fact that students and teachers *choose* the academy or SLC tends to create an esprit de corps that boosts student achievement. If all are told they must join an academy or other SLC, the element of voluntarism may be lost. Naysayers within the SLCs may undermine effectiveness, and rivalries among SLCs may threaten morale (Muncey & McQuillan, 1996).

Further, for career academies or other SLCs requiring active collaboration of employers and the community, expanding to the entire school may overload local capacity to provide internships, service-learning opportunities, or other experiences beyond school. This would dilute the effectiveness of SLCs.

Thus, applying career academies or other SLCs school-wide might reduce their average effects, and the effects might also be inequitably distributed. Student tracking could take a new form. For instance, students in the most advanced classes might gravitate to the same SLC, creating a hierarchical ordering among SLCs. As in traditional forms of tracking, the danger is that students in less-prestigious SLCs would be systematically shortchanged because teachers expected less of them (Mosteller et al., 1996; Oakes, 1985). On the other hand, schools could monitor enrollment trends and intervene to prevent such results. Moreover, the fact that career academies and other thematically defined SLCs recruit those who share common interests could make it easier to ensure that each academy or SLC enrolls students representing a cross section of the entire school.

CONCLUSIONS

In sum, rigorous evaluations have found that individual career academies within larger high schools improve students' academic performance and reduce the number of students dropping out of high school. Approximately 1,500 to 2,000 career academies now operate in American high schools. High schools increasingly group all students and teachers into career academies or other SLCs. Whether subdividing an entire high school into small learning environments improves students' performance and reduces dropout rates is not yet known. This is a principal question on the frontier of knowledge about redesigning American high schools.

As for the STW movement generally, its claim on high-school reformers' attention has diminished since the mid-1990s, as academic standards and accountability have taken higher priority. Prevailing college aspirations among high-school students and their parents has limited the appeal of STW programs since the invention of the unfortunate term *school-to-work. College and careers* probably would have been a more popular term and also more accurate in describing what many STW advocates had in mind.[9] Nevertheless, in many communities, the movement will leave new partnerships between employers and educators. Practices such as career counseling and job shadowing are more widespread than before. Among the legacies of STW, the increased number of career academies may be one of the most valuable and enduring.

NOTES

1. I am indebted to Rob Ivry for this alliterative trinity.

2. Only published results or those about to be published are summarized here. Several unpublished dissertations also contain descriptions and evaluations of academies.

3. Some nonacademy students take academy classes. Academy students also take some nonacademy classes. Therefore, academy students can obtain higher grades than nonacademy students, although average grades are lower in academy classes than in nonacademy classes, if academy students earn higher grades in academy classes, nonacademy classes, or both.

4. Another study (Toenjes, 1989) cited in some reviews does not use individual school data, but makes inferences on the basis of the number of high schools and total student enrollment in each district size category.

5. One study (Gottfredson, 1985) did observe what happened in three schools experiencing major size decreases and in two experiencing major increases because of district reorganization. Dropout rates were not measured, but reports on school safety, drug use, delinquency, and disorder were collected from student and teacher surveys. Results were very mixed. Reports of drug use and delinquency increased in two of the three schools that shrank, and no significant changes in these outcomes occurred in the two schools that grew. On the other hand, teachers' reported feelings of safety improved in one of the three reduced schools and worsened in one of the two increased schools. Students' reports of victimization by other students increased in one of the increased schools, but also in one of the reduced schools.

6. The U.S. Department of Education (National Center for Education Statistics, 1999, Table 104) has shown that the number of high-school graduates each year as a proportion of the seventeen-year-old population peaked at about 77% in the 1960s; then declined during the 1970s and 1980s to about 70% in the 1990s. This decline was more than offset by the increased number of GED certificates awarded each year (Table 107),

so that the proportion of sixteen-to-twenty-four-year-olds not holding either a regular diploma or GED has steadily declined, according to household surveys (Table 108).

7. For a broader discussion of how career-related themes and practical applications can advance the intellectual and academic goals of schooling, see Grubb (1995) and Steinberg (1998).

8. This study also measured how the districtwide policy to create charters within comprehensive high schools affected districtwide student performance in grades 9–12, as measured by attendance, credits earned, and promotion rates. Surprisingly, although the proportion of students enrolled in charters rose steadily from 1988–89 to 1993–94, the trend in most of the performance indicators was an initial rise for the first two or three years, followed by a leveling off or actual decline. The authors suggest that the gains due to charters might have been offset in later years by changes in district policy that moved more over-age middle-school students into high schools and also reduced summer school.

9. I promoted use of this phrase for several years. Belatedly, the Clinton administration finally seemed to have adopted it. An October 13, 2000 White House memorandum on the future of the STW movement was entitled *Preparing American Youth for 21st-Century College and Careers* (White House, 2000). The memo included career academies as one of the "innovative learning strategies" (p. 1) associated with the movement.

REFERENCES

Academy for Educational Development. (1990). *Employment and educational experiences of Academy of Finance graduates*. New York: Author.

Bottoms, G., & Presson, A. (1995). Improving high schools for career-bound youth: Reform through a multistate network. In W. N. Grubb (Ed.), *Education through occupations in American high schools: Vol. 2. The challenges of implementing curriculum integration* (pp. 35–54). New York: Teachers College Press.

Conchas, G. (1998). *Structuring opportunity: Cultural community and Latino high school success*. Unpublished manuscript, University of Michigan, Department of Sociology, Ann Arbor, MI.

Cotton, K. (1996). *Affective and Social Benefits of Small-Scale Schooling* (ERIC Digest No. RC 96–5). Charleston, WV: Clearinghouse on Rural Education and Small Schools. (ERIC Document Reproduction Service No. ED 401 088)

Cushman, K., Steinberg, A., & Riordan, R. (1997). *Connecting school and work as a means to whole-school change*. Providence, RI: Brown University, Coalition of Essential Schools.

Darling-Hammond, L. (1997). *The right to learn: A blueprint for creating schools that work*. San Francisco: Jossey-Bass.

Dayton, C., Weisberg, A., & Stern, D. (1989). *California partnership academies: 1987–88 evaluation report*. Berkeley, CA: University of California, Policy Analysis for California Education.

Elliott, M. N., Hanser, L. M., & Gilroy, C. L. (2000). *Evidence of positive student outcomes in JROTC career academies*. Santa Monica, CA: RAND Corporation.

Fetler, M. (1989). School dropout rates, academic performance, size, and poverty: Correlates of educational reform. *Educational Evaluation and Policy Analysis, 11*, 109–116.

Fine, M. (Ed.). (1994). *Chartering urban school reform: Reflections on public high schools in the midst of change*. New York: Teachers College Press.

Fine, M., & Somerville, J. I. (Eds.). (1998). *Small schools, big imaginations: A creative look at urban public schools*. Chicago: Cross City Campaign for Urban School Reform.

Franklin, B. J., & Crone, L. J. (1992, November). *School accountability: Predictors and indicators of Louisiana school effectiveness*. Paper presented at the meeting of the Mid-South Educational Research Association, Knoxville, TN.

Gewertz, C. (2000, September 13). Gates Foundation awards $56 million for small schools. *Education Week, 20*, p. 14.

Gladden, R. (1998). The small school movement: A review of the literature. In M. Fine & J. I. Somerville (Eds.), *Small schools, big imaginations: A creative look at urban public schools* (pp. 113–137). Chicago: Cross City Campaign for Urban School Reform.

Gottfredson, D. (1985). *School size and school disorder*. Baltimore: Johns Hopkins University, Center for Social Organization of Schools.

Grubb, W. N. (Ed.). (1995). *Education through occupations in American high schools* (Vols. 1–2). New York: Teachers College Press.

Hayward, B., & Talmadge, G. (1995). *Strategies for keeping kids in school*. Washington, DC: U.S. Department of Education.

Howley, C. B., & Bickel, R. (1999). *The Matthew Project: National report*. Albany, OH: Ohio University.

Kemple, J. J. (1997). *Career academies: Communities of support for students and teachers. Emerging findings from a 10-site evaluation*. New York: Manpower Demonstration Research Corporation.

Kemple, J. J., & Rock, J. L. (1996). *Career academies: Early implementation lessons from a 10-site evaluation*. New York: Manpower Demonstration Research Corporation.

Kemple, J. J., & Snipes, J. C. (2000). *Career academies: Impacts on students' engagement and performance in high school*. New York: Manpower Demonstration Research Corporation.

LaPoint, V., Jordan, W., McPartland, J. M., & Towns, D. P. (1996). *The Talent Development High School: Essential components*. Baltimore: Johns Hopkins University and Howard University, Center for Research on the Education of Students Placed at Risk.

Lee, V., Ready, D., & Johnson, D. (1999). *High schools divided into schools-within-schools: Prevalence and design formats*. Ann Arbor, MI: University of Michigan, School of Education.

Levin, H. M. (2001). High-stakes testing and economic productivity. In G. Orfield & C. Edley (Eds.), *Raising standards or raising barriers? Inequality & high-stakes testing in public education* (pp. 39–50). New York: Century Foundation.

Linnehan, F. (1996). Measuring the effectiveness of a career academy program from an employer's perspective. *Educational Evaluation and Policy Analysis, 18*, 73–89.

Maxwell, N. L. (1999). *Step to college: Moving from the high school career academy through the four-year university*. Berkeley, CA: National Center for Research in Vocational Education.

Maxwell, N. L., & Rubin, V. (1997). *The relative impact of a career academy on post-secondary work and education skills in urban, public high schools.* Hayward, CA: California State University, Hayward, School of Business and Economics, The Human Investment Research and Education Center.

Maxwell, N. L., & Rubin, V. (2000). *High school career academies: A pathway to educational reform in urban schools?* Kalamazoo, MI: W.E. Upjohn Institute for Employment Research.

McMullan, B. J., Sipe, C. L., & Wolf, W. C. (1994). *Charters and student achievement: Early evidence from school restructuring in Philadelphia.* Philadelphia: Center for Assessment and Policy Development.

McPartland, J. M., Balfanz, R., Jordan, W., & Legters, N. (1998). Improving climate and achievement in a troubled urban high school through the Talent Development Model. *Journal of Education for Students Placed at Risk, 3,* 337–361.

McPartland, J. M., Legters, N., Jordan, W., & McDill, E. L. (1996). *The Talent Development High School: Early evidence of impact on school climate, attendance, and student promotion.* Baltimore: Johns Hopkins University and Howard University, Center for Research on the Education of Students Placed at Risk.

Meier, D. (1996). *The power of their ideas.* Boston: Beacon Press.

Mosteller, F., Light, R. J., & Sachs, J. A. (1996). Sustained inquiry in education: Lessons in skill grouping and class size. *Harvard Education Review, 66,* 707–842.

Muncey, D. E., & McQuillan, P. J. (1996). *Reform and resistance in schools and classrooms: An ethnographic view of the Coalition of Essential Schools.* New Haven, CT: Yale University Press.

National Association of Secondary School Principals. (1996). *Breaking ranks: Changing an American institution.* Reston, VA: National Association of Secondary School Principals.

National Center for Education Statistics. (1999). *Digest of education statistics, 1999.* Washington, DC: U.S. Department of Education.

Noddings, N. (1992). *The challenge to care in schools: An alternative approach to education.* New York: Teachers College Press.

Oakes, J. (1985). *Keeping track: How schools structure inequality.* New Haven, CT: Yale University Press.

Olson, L. (1997). *The school-to-work revolution.* Reading, MA: Addison-Wesley.

Oxley, D. (1989). Smaller is better: How the house plan can make large high schools less anonymous. *American Educator, 13,* 28–31, 51–52.

Oxley, D. (1990). *An analysis of house systems in New York City neighborhood high schools.* Philadelphia: Temple University Center for Research in Human Development and Education.

Pittman, R. B., & Haughwout, P. (1987). Influence of school size on dropout rate. *Educational Evaluation and Policy Analysis, 9,* 337–343.

Raby, M. (1995). The career academies. In W. N. Grubb (Ed.), *Education through occupations in American high schools: Vol. 1. Approaches to integrating academic and vocational education* (pp. 82–96). New York: Teachers College Press.

Raywid, M. A. (1995). *The subschools/small schools movement—Taking stock.* Madison, WI: Center on Organization and Restructuring of Schools.

Reller, D. (1984). *The Peninsula Academies: Final technical evaluation report.* Palo Alto, CA: The American Institutes for Research.

Reller, D. J. (1985). *The Peninsula Academies, interim evaluation report, 1984–85 school year.* Palo Alto, CA: American Institutes for Research.

Reller, D. J. (1987). *A longitudinal study of the graduates of the Peninsula Academies, final report.* Palo Alto, CA: American Institutes for Research in the Behavioral Sciences.

Sergiovanni, T. J. (1994). *Building community in schools.* San Francisco: Jossey-Bass.

Sizer, T. (1984). *Horace's compromise.* Boston: Houghton Mifflin.

Sizer, T. (1992). *Horace's school: Redesigning the American high school.* Boston: Houghton Mifflin.

Snyder, P., & McMullan, B. J. (1987a). *Allies in education, a profile of Philadelphia high school academies, Philadelphia, Pennsylvania.* Philadelphia: Public/Private Ventures.

Snyder, P., & McMullan, B. J. (1987b). *Allies in education, schools and businesses working together for at-risk youth.* Philadelphia: Public/Private Ventures.

Southern Regional Education Board. (1995). *Charting the progress of education: Annual report, June 1995.* Atlanta, GA: Author.

Southern Regional Education Board. (1997). *1997 outstanding practices.* Atlanta, GA: Author.

Steinberg, A. (1998). *Real learning, real work.* New York & London: Routledge.

Stern, D. (1999). Improving pathways in the United States from high school to college and career. In *Preparing youth for the 21st century: The transition from education to the labour market* (pp. 155–214). Paris: Organisation for Economic Co-Operation and Development.

Stern, D., & Briggs, D. (in press). Does paid employment help or hinder performance in secondary school? Insights from U.S. high school students. *Journal of Education and Work.*

Stern, D., Dayton, C., Paik, I., & Weisberg, A. (1989). Benefits and costs of dropout prevention in a high school program combining academic and vocational education: Third-year results from replications of the California Partnership Academies. *Educational Evaluation and Policy Analysis, 11,* 405–416.

Stern, D., Dayton, C., Paik, I., Weisberg, A., & Evans, J. (1988). Combining academic and vocational courses in an integrated program to reduce high school dropout rates: Second-year results from replications of the California Peninsula Academies. *Educational Evaluation and Policy Analysis, 10,* 161–170.

Stern, D., Finkelstein, N., Urquiola, M., & Cagampang, H. (1997). What difference does it make if school and work are connected? Evidence on co-operative education in the United States. *Economics of Education Review, 16,* 213–226.

Stern, D., Raby, M., & Dayton, C. (1992). *Career academies: Partnerships for reconstructing American high schools.* San Francisco: Jossey-Bass.

Toenjes, L. A. (1989). *Dropout rates in Texas school districts: Influences of school size and ethnic group.* Austin, TX: Texas Center for Educational Research.

Urquiola, M., Stern, D., Horn, I., Dornsife, C., Chi, B., Williams, L., et al. (1997). *School to work, college and career: A review of policy, practice, and results 1993–1997.* Berkeley, CA: National Center for Research in Vocational Education.

U.S. Department of Education. (2000). *Making the case for smaller learning communities.* Washington, DC: Office of Elementary and Secondary Education.

Visher, M. G., & Hudis, P. M. (1999). *Aiming high: Strategies to promote high standards in high schools* (Interim Report, October). Washington, DC: U.S. Department of Education.

Wasley, P. A., Fine, M., Gladden, M., Holland, N. E., King, S. P., Mosak, E., et al. (2000). *Small schools, great strides: A study of new small schools in Chicago.* New York: The Bank Street College of Education.

White House. (2000, October 13). *Memorandum for the heads of executive departments and agencies: Preparing American youth for 21st-century college and careers.* Washington, DC: Author.

16

What's Next for School-to-Career? An Assessment of Progress and Prospects

Richard Kazis
Hilary Pennington

INTRODUCTION

The school-to-career movement[1] is at a critical juncture, after a decade of enthusiasm, experimentation, and progress, and five to six years of moderate federal support. On the one hand, the movement has sparked much activity and progress around the country. The last decade has seen steady growth and maturation in programs seeking to engage and motivate students through contextual learning inside and outside the classroom and through ending the isolation of schools and young people from their communities. In some communities, the school-to-career movement has become important in local efforts to reform high schools and improve the way they prepare youth for their future.

Moreover, a powerful argument can be made that basic school-to-career principles—the innovations in teaching and learning and in the relations between schools and communities that are at its heart—will become common elements of twenty-first-century education. That education will be richer in technology, less classroom-bound, and more focused on what youth will do when faced with new challenges or problems.

At the same time, targeted federal "venture-capital" funding is shrinking and will end a year or two after the 2001 sunsetting of the School-to-Work Opportunities Act (STWOA). Moreover, political support for school-to-career as a discrete national funding stream had almost evaporated by the end of the STWOA funding period.

In this environment, school-to-career advocates and practitioners face difficult questions about how to move forward, building on what is best and learning from early implementation. In 1999, with support from the Charles Stewart Mott Foundation, Jobs for the Future (JFF) undertook a series of conversations and discussions on the question, What's next for school-to-career?[2] This article distills the results of that inquiry.[3] Our assessment is organized around answers to three questions:

1. What did school-to-career proponents in the late 1980s and early 1990s hope to achieve, and how did early debates affect evolution of state and local efforts?
2. What have been the greatest strengths and weaknesses of school-to-career programs, given the implementation experience?
3. Looking ahead, what strategies will promote what has been most successful and appears most promising about school-to-career programs?

CONTEXT: THE RISE OF THE SCHOOL-TO-CAREER MOVEMENT

Factors Driving Interest in the School-to-Career Movement

The school-to-career movement coalesced in the late 1980s and gathered momentum during the early 1990s, propelled by economic and educational concerns and hopes. These included the following:

- concern about the impact of international competition on U.S. economic well-being;
- redefinition of the youth problem to focus not just on the problems of the 25% not completing high school, but also on the 75% not earning a baccalaureate;
- dissatisfaction with the quality of high-school education, particularly its lack of focus and academic rigor; and
- growing demand for higher academic expectations in vocational education.

By the early 1990s, consensus had emerged on a reform agenda that might help more young people succeed in and after high school (Commission on the Skills of the American Workforce, 1990; William T. Grant Foundation Commission on Work, Family, and Citizenship, 1988). The following tenets guided practitioners and policymakers as they experimented with school-to-career strategies.

- *Most young people must be given more help in making a successful transition to adulthood.* For too many young people, our society provides too little preparation and support for success in increasingly complex and demanding work and careers.
- *Any effective solution must address both academic and educational achievement and employment and career prospects.* Preparation needed for success in postsecondary education and in securing a family-supporting job are similar. Schools should provide all young people with a combination of experiences—school-based and work-based, academic and practical—to motivate and help them achieve.

- *This educational strategy demands that schools enter into new relationships with community partners, particularly businesses.* For economic and educational reasons, schools must become less insular and better integrated into the local economic and social fabric. Labor suppliers need to understand more about, and work more closely with, employers who want their graduates. And as Theodore Sizer (1992) suggested, in an information-rich society, learning opportunities exist as much outside as inside classrooms.
- *Reform must be systemic, altering the way school organization and the way major systems—schools, employers, governments—interact and interrelate.* Simply adding programs to existing school responsibilities invites failure. Efforts for change must alter incentives that have led to current school structures and strategies, so that the goal becomes schoolwide and system-wide reforms, not just small, boutique programs.
- *In our national political context, successful reform cannot rely upon a centralized, federal solution.* Our national culture, ideology, and institutions militate against centralized educational or workforce policies. The best the federal government can do in today's context is seed innovation, provide incentives for states and districts to organize efforts differently, and promote effective models and practices. However, underdevelopment of employer and labor organizations will require public- and private-sector initiatives to strengthen local institutions that organize employers and connect schools to their communities.
- *Gradual implementation providing significant flexibility to states and localities will enable schools and their partners to overcome the all-too-familiar cycle of new proposal → initial enthusiasm → eventual collapse.* With a fervor for "reinventing government," school-to-career reformers hoped that a locally driven approach would be more likely to meet local needs and therefore survive longer than typical reform fads.

This consensus formed a foundation for the STWOA, which emerged quickly after the 1992 presidential candidates George Bush and Bill Clinton promised to create a national youth-apprenticeship/school-to-work system. The act passed with little opposition and relative good cheer among Republicans and Democrats. Though modestly funded, it signaled commitment to five years of support for experimentation and development.

Tough Questions and Implementation Choices

Although the broad agreement around defining the school-to-career movement was advantageous for passing legislation, it concealed serious tensions within the movement; permissive legislative language about allowable activities also encouraged conflicting interpretations of priorities and emphases. These unresolved tensions could not long be avoided, however, once states began implementation and local partnerships set priorities for program design and resource allocation.

Implementers had to address numerous complex questions.

- *Who is the school-to-career movement for?* Is this reform for *all* students or for the so-called forgotten half, those young Americans who do not attend college after high school? (See William T. Grant Foundation, 1988.)
- *Which age group should school-to-career programs target?* Is the school-to-career initiative a high-school or a system-wide K–16 initiative? What investment should be made in middle and elementary schools? In two- and four-year colleges?
- *Which school-to-career practices are essential?* Are school-to-career practices primarily about work experience and career exposure? Improved school pedagogy and changes in classroom experiences? Both? Which elements should be implemented first?
- *Which local institutions should school-to-career reform target?* A joint initiative of the Departments of Education and Labor, the STWOA emphasized "connecting activities" linking schools and employers. Is school-to-career a school reform, a way to change employer hiring practices and young people's career prospects, or a combination?
- *Who should manage school-to-career programs?* At state and local levels, how should school-to-career initiatives be governed? Should governance and accountability be community-wide, employer-driven, or school-based? Should school-to-career programs be housed in vocational-education offices, academic instruction offices, or outside the schools?

In 1994, many answers competed for dominance. Some emphasized improving technical education; others eliminating general education; still others preventing dropouts. Some models stressed work experience, others classroom instruction, and some career counseling. Some advocates saw school-to-career programs as a way to improve traditional academic tracks; some saw it as a way to de-track. Some communities focused on what was called building the system, others on creating or adapting a program, and others on offering some school-to-career activity to as many young people as possible as quickly as possible.

Could these competing visions coexist? Some observers argued that school-to-career programs demanded too many concurrent changes; bringing all the interests to the table or implementing all the components of school-to-career initiatives was simply too difficult. Writing soon after passage of the STWOA, one researcher cautioned that as different interests argued for their priorities "to the near exclusion of others" (Grubb, 1994, pp. 53–54), school-to-career advocates risked implementing incomplete reforms unable to deliver on the promise inherent in the fully articulated vision.

In this context, federal venture capital has seeded a decentralized laboratory for experiments with different models for reforming high-school learning and school–community relationships. Lessons are emerging, as is resolution of inherent tensions and design choices "on the ground." We now turn to this assessment of the school-to-career movement's evolution and current standing.

THE SCHOOL-TO-CAREER MOVEMENT TODAY

School-to-career programs are progressing along two tracks. On the one hand, practitioners in many communities are improving learning environments for young people and creating more adult connections for them. On the other hand, the school-to-career movement as a national reform strategy has become barely visible.

What has happened since 1994?

How Federal School-to-Career Funds Have Been Used

Since 1994, the STWOA has appropriated more than $1.7 billion to states and local partnerships (Hershey, Silverberg, Haimson, Hudis, & Jackson, 1999). Because Congress intended annual appropriations to peak midway through the act's life, the largest appropriation was $400 million annually in fiscal years 1997 and 1998. In 2000, Congress authorized $110 million.

Spread across fifty states and more than 15,000 school districts, several hundred million dollars yearly does not go far. A national evaluation estimated spending per district at $25,092 in 1997–98, about $4.32 per elementary and secondary student per year (Hershey et al., 1999; National Center for Education Statistics, 1997).

The lion's share of federal resources has been distributed to states in one-time, four- to five-year grants for regranting to local partnerships (Hershey et al., 1999). States have used remaining funds for developing new relationships among education, workforce training, and economic development; statewide outreach; professional development; new curricula; and other activities.

Local partnerships have had leeway in funds use, provided they could demonstrate support from employers, schools, and other partners. Local school-to-career investments have funded activities such as coordination of student work experiences by school staff, professional development for teachers (including teacher internships in modern workplaces), curriculum development, local labor-market analyses, career-exposure activities, and supplemental support services.

Assessing School-to-Career's Progress

As noted previously, states have used federal funds to create and promote new relationships among agencies, bringing business, school, and government representatives into ongoing planning and deliberations about strategies for improving youth transitions. In some states and communities, these system-building efforts have changed patterns of making policy and of interagency collaboration in lasting ways. One study (Pines & Callahan, 1997) found that states with the most interagency collaboration and joint planning between the workforce and education fields moved that way largely because of federal school-to-career and pre-Workforce Investment Act One-Stop Career Center initiatives.

Moreover, federal funds have supported an impressive variety of innovative and high-quality program models. Some of these initiatives—including many launched before the STWOA—are demonstrating positive outcomes, including improvements in student attendance, rigor of course selection, dropout prevention, college attendance rates, first-job wages, employer engagement, quality of adult relationships, and student satisfaction.

At the same time, implementation has been slow and uneven. The grandest claims of some school-to-career proponents remain unachieved. Some communities invested too much in planning or isolated add-on activities that did not significantly alter academic or work-related learning.

The uneven progress of the school-to-career movement is predictable, given most communities' modest investments, the temptation to spread rather than target resources, the short time for showing results, and the difficulties of implementing a complex reform strategy. Although progress has been impressive in many communities, some efforts have been too small, of too low an intensity, or too laxly implemented to change students' daily experiences significantly.

The research summarized as follows gives hope that the best school-to-career efforts translate into educational and employment gains for young people—and it cautions against ill-conceived, poorly implemented efforts to provide experiences linking school and work.[4]

Employer Engagement

Increased school–employer collaboration has been a particularly successful aspect of school-to-career implementation. About one-fourth of U.S. firms report formal participation in school-to-work partnerships, and one in three report providing work-based learning opportunities (Zemsky, Shapiro, Iannozzi, Cappelli, & Bailey, 1998). Businesses are providing students and teachers with work experiences and participating in curriculum development, promotion and marketing, presentations at schools, and provision of material resources. Businesses and industry associations are bringing industry-valued skill standards and expectations into schools. This growing employer engagement has had positive results:

- *For students.* According to the national evaluation of school-to-career programs, worksite experiences obtained through school, particularly paid positions, are of higher quality than jobs students find on their own. Students access more diverse workplaces and career information, spend more job time in training, and receive more performance feedback (Hershey et al., 1999).
- *For firms.* Employers partnering with schools have more stable youth employment rates, with many fewer of their young workers quitting or being fired (Zemsky et al., 1998).

Local Partnership Formation

The number of partnerships involving schools, employers, postsecondary institutions, organized labor, community-based organizations, and other community interests expanded annually from 1994 to more than 1,000 in 1998. In the thirty-seven states receiving federal implementation funding by fall 1997, more than 90% of high-school-aged students lived in districts covered by local partnerships (Hershey et al., 1999). These collaborations have tended to be led by educators, with strong business involvement and somewhat uneven representation of two- and four-year colleges and organized labor. In many communities, they have increased communication, joint planning, and collaboration among local institutions.

Students Served

The number of secondary-school students receiving an integrated academic and work-related curriculum rose from 700,000 in 1996 to 1,200,000 in 1997. The number participating in work-based learning rose from 280,000 to 470,000 in that period, according to the federal government (Medrich, Ramer, Merola, & Moskovitz, 1998).

School-to-career implementation reflects Congress' intent that programs linking school and work be available to any student, from the low-achieving to the academically talented (Hershey et al., 1999). Participation in comprehensive career-development activities and school-linked workplace activities appears to be as common among high-school seniors enrolled in college-preparatory curricula as among those not enrolled.

School-to-career programs also appear attractive to and beneficial for students who are less likely to continue education past high school, including African Americans. More-intensive programs combining career-related academic courses, work experiences linked to school, and comprehensive career development have tended to attract students from the general and vocational tracks not planning extensive postsecondary education (Hershey et al., 1999). Moreover, the participation rate in academic classes that students perceive as focused on their career interests has increased most among African-American students (Hershey et al., 1999).

Student Satisfaction

Students give high marks to school-to-career activities, particularly those affording them workplace experiences and classes related to their career goals (Hershey et al., 1999).[5] Generally, students are most positive about individualized activities such as job shadowing and school-arranged internships. Some studies have found that school-to-career students consider worksite supervisors and school-to-work coordinators to influence their postsecondary plans more than their teachers (Jobs for the Future & Boston Private Industry Council, 1998).

Postsecondary Educational Attainment

An important benefit of participation in effective school-to-career programs appears to be increased college attendance. Graduates of ProTech, a multiyear school-to-career program in Boston, progress to college at rates higher than those of their peers. Among recent African-American ProTech graduates, 80% enrolled in college the year after high school, while only half of the black students in a comparison group did (Jobs for the Future & Boston Private Industry Council, 1998). Other effective programs show similar results. Graduates of New York City career-magnet high schools, for example, earn at least a third more college credits and are likelier to have chosen a college major the first year or two after graduation than their peers in city comprehensive high schools (Crain et al., 1998).

Academic Performance

Participation in well-designed school-to-career programs appears to increase academic focus and motivation. Studies have found that students in such programs enroll in more college-preparatory courses than peers in the general curriculum, particularly in advanced math and science courses (Committee for Economic Development, 1998; Westchester Institute for Human Services Research, Inc., 1998). Many studies have concluded that participating students have better school attendance than classmates (Hughes, Bailey, & Mechur, 2001). School-to-work program participants also tend to spend more time doing homework, cut fewer classes, and be more challenged by schoolwork (Hughes et al., 2001; Westchester Institute for Human Services Research, Inc., 1998).

In academic achievement, however, school-to-career programs have had difficulty demonstrating clear-cut gains. For example, the ongoing random-assignment study of career academies has found neither positive nor negative effects on students' standardized test scores from career-academy participation (Kemple & Snipes, 2000). Several reasons have been suggested. In some communities, the initial emphasis on securing workplace experiences has prevailed over improving classroom teaching and learning. Reliance on standardized tests as the most significant measure of academic achievement can disadvantage school-to-career programs that are more interdisciplinary and teach to the test less.

Despite limitations of existing research, a coherent story emerges from studies on different school-to-career models and initiatives: Although academic indicators such as test scores are difficult to improve, success in postsecondary admissions and persistence appears greater, as do career-related outcomes such as wages, career direction, and postsecondary planning. Consider this evidence from three very different program models.

ProTech, Boston

Boston's school-to-career system has expanded significantly since the early 1990s. Today, nine high schools and seven middle schools have been designated school-to-career schools as part of a system-wide effort to institutionalize career pathways.

In 1999, 17% of Boston high-school students (2,828 young people) were enrolled in a formal school-to-career pathway, defined as a program lasting at least two years, focusing on a career-related theme, integrating two or more academic subjects yearly, devoting time to career and personal development, and providing a multiyear sequence of worksite experiences integrated with academic learning. Expansion has been rapid in the past three years (from fewer than 600 students enrolled in 1996 to four-and-one-half times as many in 1999). The number of employer partners in ProTech, Boston's most long-standing, well-developed program, rose from 46 in 1995–96 to about 200 in 1997–98. In the 1998–99 school year, more than 1,450 different employers across the district placed school-to-career students.

Research on 107 ProTech graduates from 1993 to 1995 found that these young people were likelier than their local and national peers to graduate from high school, attend postsecondary schools, have jobs, and have jobs paying higher wages. African-American students benefited most from participation.

Wisconsin Youth-Apprenticeship Program

One of the first states to receive a federal school-to-work implementation grant, Wisconsin created a youth-apprenticeship program providing high-school juniors and seniors with 900 hours of supervised worksite learning aligned with a series of academic and technical courses (Phelps, Knox, & Griggs, 1999; Wisconsin Department of Workforce Development, 1999). The state designed the program for students intending to go directly into the workforce, attend college, or both.

Preliminary findings indicate that a youth apprenticeship, although a significant time commitment outside the classroom, does not impede college success. Youth-apprenticeship graduates in the 1994–97 classes who entered technical college were far likelier than other entrants to complete a degree or certificate within three years. Youth apprentices entering the four-year university system stayed in college into the second and third years, at rates comparable to other freshmen in their age cohort.

Wisconsin's youth apprentices have also been able to secure relatively high-wage employment. About 70% of graduates found jobs directly related to their training, a rate much higher than among vocational-program graduates nationwide. These jobs paid a median wage two to three dollars above the median national hourly earnings for youth. Almost two-thirds of graduates combined work and postsecondary education.

Philadelphia's Education for Employment

Results from several studies conducted by the School District of Philadelphia and outside evaluators have indicated measurable gains associated with the city's school-to-career approach, especially its work-based learning program. For example, it was found that participation in that program significantly improved a student's GPA and attendance. These effects were found after controlling for the influence of students' prior grades, attendance, year in school, and school attended (Linnehan, 1998).

In comparisons of all work-based learning students in the eleventh and twelfth grades with their peers city-wide, the district's own data have shown higher attendance, lower dropout rates, and better grades for work-based learning participants. The results are similar for work-based learning students in small learning communities in comprehensive high schools and for peers in the same small learning communities with similar grades and attendance but without work-based learning experiences.

Key Challenges for the School-to-Career Movement Today

If the weakening of the school-to-career initiative as a national reform strategy cannot be attributed to outcomes for students participating in STWOA-funded programs, what has happened?

From our research and experience, we believe four factors have contributed to the current state of affairs:

1. Political realignments.
2. The complexity and ambition of the school-to-career vision.
3. Implementation choices.
4. Conflict between implementation of standards-driven reform and the experiential, outside-the-classroom core of school-to-career programs.

1. *Shifting political realities.* Some observers blame declining support for school-to-career programs on the intense attack from the radical right. The vigorous, orchestrated campaign, led in 1996 and 1997 by Phyllis Schlafly's Eagle Forum, significantly interfered with local innovation and experimentation (Cheney, 1998). It also undercut political enthusiasm in Congress, state legislatures, business leadership, and local school boards.

However, this campaign could not have succeeded had it not coincided with Republican ascendancy in Congress, a political shift that dramatically weakened support for an initiative identified as "the president's school-to-work program." With a five-year life and little support for reauthorization from either Republican or Democratic legislators, the school-to-career initiative seemed a lame duck early in its legislative authorization.

Moreover, when the campaign against the school-to-career movement developed, the administration held back, apparently hoping the furor would die down, as did the Department of Education, which was reluctant to sacrifice momentum in articulating a unified message around improving academic achievement.

Unfortunately, the attack on school-to-career efforts cannot be dismissed as cynical politics. The campaign has resonated with fears of many parents about their children's future: Fears of tracking, narrow careerism, and a reduction of choice for young people struck a chord. Some programs unwittingly provided opponents with ammunition.

2. *The model's complexity and ambition.* Even if the political environment had not changed soon after the passage of the STWOA, the effort faced significant challenges. The school-to-career initiative's strength—its comprehensiveness and emphasis on changes both within schools (difficult enough) and in the relationship of schools and young people to the community and its economic institutions—is also a challenge to rapid, high-quality implementation. In communities where these models have taken hold, years of development and expansion have been necessary. And even the most mature efforts show modest integration of school- and work-based learning.

The complexity of the school-to-career vision has had practical and political costs. Practically, there has been much wheel spinning. Resource, time, and capacity constraints have kept some communities from turning vision into implementation progress. Politically, the complexity of the vision has facilitated critique of poor design and implementation and of the gap between school-to-career rhetoric and its realization.

3. *Implementation choices of school-to-career proponents.* Some school-to-career advocates and practitioners made decisions and took positions that unintentionally weakened both public support and the ability to demonstrate strong results. From our interviews, we identified three factors that appear to have undercut the support for and impact of local efforts.

First, *broad K–12 initiatives have been emphasized at the expense of high-school reforms and links to postsecondary institutions.* Many communities implemented school-to-career as a K–12 initiative. This spread activities thinly across schools. In some districts, the primary focus of activity on elementary grades diluted the potential for school-to-career programs to offer employment connections and figure strongly in high-school reform efforts. Further, the K–12 focus meant that links to postsecondary institutions were frequently underdeveloped—and the potential of two-year colleges as appropriate locations for certain programs linking school and work was overlooked.

Second, *a rush to demonstrate scale and numbers* has predominated. School-to-career legislation had a short lifetime, and results needed to be demonstrated rapidly. Federal officials wanted to show that school-to-career programs could ramp up quickly and have systemic impact. Success was therefore measured in numbers: schools participating, districts with partnerships, employers engaged, and students involved in school-to-career activity. This drive to document expansion made scale, not quality, the primary measure of early success. Research and development on measures that could demonstrate *how* programs affected young people, employers, and teachers received lower priority.

Because of the complexity of design and the rush to show substantial activity, schools and districts tended to implement program elements that were easiest to isolate and deliver, such as job shadowing days or career fairs. This strategy opened the movement to the criticism of "mile-wide, inch-deep" implementation—and made it difficult for programs to demonstrate the academic achievement gains that parents, administrators, and state officials wanted most.

Third, *the laudable goal of providing options for "all students" became a political trap.* The school-to-career movement set itself up for an unwinnable public-relations battle by insisting that school-to-career was for "all students."

The sentiment was right: Experiential learning and active pedagogy are powerful ways for *anyone* to learn, and access to effective school-to-career programs should be available to students with disabilities as well as "typical" students. The best professional schools—business, law, and medical schools—rely on internships and learning outside the classroom. And some of the most effective programs for learning-disabled students involve contextual instruction. Moreover, the all-students goal has highlighted the need for *system building* that might ultimately change the routine organization of learning across schools, districts, and states more effectively than small, boutique *program models.*

But aggressive insistence on universality opened proponents to the criticism that the federal government was *mandating* participation by all students. For how could an initiative be for all students unless required for all? Opponents characterized an effort to ensure high-quality choices for more young people as a government attack on student and parental choice.

4. *The isolation of school-to-career from standards-driven reforms.* During the past decade, the most powerful education reform movement has been state-led efforts to raise academic achievement through higher standards and greater accountability. There is no inherent conflict between the school-to-career movement and this movement. Early in the Clinton administration, Washington saw Goals 2000 and the STWOA as part of the same agenda, although enacted as separate legislative initiatives (Jennings, 1995). As the Committee for Economic Development (CED) wrote in its 1998 policy statement, "High standards are essential, but no guarantee of learning. Students must be motivated to learn, and new instructional strategies are required to reach those young people for whom abstract, passive learning is relatively ineffective. We believe that school-to-career practices can address both these challenges" (p. 16).

But by 1998, the CED was arguing for reversing a trend that frequently pitted advocates of high standards *against* school-to-career programs. States had invested heavily in new academic standards and assessments. With much more limited investment and support and housed typically in vocational-education offices, school-to-career programs took a back seat while states and localities scrambled to respond to demands for quick gains in academic performance.

Two aspects of the standards movement challenge the short-term diffusion of school-to-career instruction and pedagogy: the nature of state assessments and the pressure to teach to the test. For reasons of simplicity, cost, and validity, most states have introduced standardized, core-subject tests that do not incorporate communication, teamwork, and other skills needed for success. State tests focus on what people should *know,* not what they *can do* or, more importantly, *will do* when faced with new situations or problems.

Moreover, pressures on teachers and administrators lead toward teaching to the test and away from risk-taking with nontraditional approaches to curriculum, use of school time, and classroom activities. With limited evidence that work-based or project-based learning can increase test scores, school-to-career advocates have had a hard time defending their reform strategy.

As states begin to assess, fine-tune, or revamp reform tools and systems, opportunities to bring school-to-career strategies back into standards-driven reform will increase, particularly to motivate and structure learning for students in poor-performing schools. However, the current isolation of the school-to-career movement from mainstream educational reform has been particularly costly, both programmatically and politically.

THE FUTURE OF THE SCHOOL-TO-CAREER MOVEMENT: STRATEGIES AND CHALLENGES

The Importance of Taking the Long View

The school-to-career movement is caught in a paradox. Targeted national funding is waning. Yet enthusiasm remains strong in communities that have committed to changing high schools to be more community-connected and to engaging students in more experiential learning. The core principles of the school-to-career movement are powerful, and they are popping up in many different places with different names—or without such "brand names":

- The push toward small, more-personalized learning communities in large comprehensive high schools often focuses on careers (Smith, 1999).
- School–community partnerships grow and deepen in efforts to raise achievement, strengthen after-school programming, and improve regional economic development (Pittman & Irby, 2000).
- Many small, innovative charter high schools are creating curricula- and community-based learning experiences that map to school-to-career principles.
- Service-learning initiatives and community-based arts programs share many of school-to-career's design principles and program components.

The paradox is this: In the short view, there is cause for pessimism about the future of school-to-career programs as promoted and codified in federal legislation. However, in the long view, the picture is quite different.

Knowledge is now available everywhere. The task of schools is to help people develop the skills of analysis, discernment, synthesis, and *use* of knowledge. In an increasingly technological, networked, and entrepreneurial society, schools *must* look outside themselves and prepare students differently. What remains unknown are the pace of change, its institutional form, and what can accelerate evolution toward more community-connected learning systems.

Given current trends, the school-to-career movement's design elements are likely to become more commonplace and less controversial over time, as the economy demands from schools an academically rigorous pedagogy that is active, experiential, and contextual; strong connections to employers and other community resources; better strategies for helping young people make post-secondary choices; and more personalized, less-standardized education.

What is controversial is not these design elements, but how to get from here to there: how to change schools, standards of learning and instruction, routes to career success, and adolescents' daily experiences as they prepare for the future. Also challenging is ensuring that these positive outcomes are not unequally distributed because of class, race, or other accidents of birth.

Shorter Run Optimism Is Also Warranted

Even if we look to the next few years, there are reasons for optimism about the resurgence of school-to-career models and principles. In our research, practitioners and policymakers repeatedly noted the following emerging strategic openings.

Opportunities to Focus on High Schools Will Expand

Districts and states are worried about high schools, where standards-driven reform has been least effective at improving achievement. In many urban high schools, an unacceptably large proportion of students is likely to fail high-stakes tests required for graduation. Even in high schools whose students score well on standardized tests, traditional models appear unable to motivate students and penetrate their alienation and drift.

Alternative high-school models frequently incorporate school-to-career principles and elements: small learning communities, thematic clustering, project-based learning in and outside the classroom, and more individualized attempts to connect with students and their aspirations.

Openings Will Increase for Addressing Youth More Holistically, Not Solely in Terms of Their Intellectual Needs

The school-reform pendulum has swung about as far toward standards and high-stakes assessments as possible. Adolescents have physical, psychological, and other developmental needs that standardized tests cannot measure and that cannot be addressed by improving test scores on one exam. As the pendulum swings back, alternatives that reduce isolation, strengthen social networks, encourage responsibility, and discourage alienation may become more attractive.

Attention Is Increasingly Turning to Postsecondary Retention, Completion, and Quality

One success story of American education is the rapid rise in the percentage of young people entering two- and four-year colleges, now about 65%. However, many new entrants drop out for financial, academic, and other reasons by the end of their first year.

Moreover, postsecondary institutions face a changing competitive environment pitting them against distance-learning and for-profit institutions and forcing them to be more responsive to employers who hire their graduates. Pressures for quality and accountability can create an opening for creative approaches to pedagogy, curricula, and assessing learning that can bring school-to-career principles more quickly into postsecondary institutions.

Employer Interest in Assessing Competencies Will Not Slacken

Employers want to know what people know and, even more, what they can do. Frustration with high-school transcripts and college diplomas runs deep. Particularly in high-tech fields, more employers are creating certifications with labor-market significance. Internet learning technologies will encourage these alternatives and make it more imperative that they be valid. As industry skill standards come on line nationally, employers will explore using them to signal their expectations to schools and faculties. In this context, many employers are experimenting with internships, temporary trial periods, and other ways of getting to know potential workers.

Demographic Trends Will Help Keep Employers Engaged

For as long as the economy stays hot, the combination of a large number of soon-to-retire older workers with a relatively small cohort of young people means that employers are willing to try less-conventional ways to identify potential employees, including novel partnerships with schools and colleges.

But Political Realities Cannot Be Ignored

In 1994, many assumed that reauthorization would be possible five years later. We thought there was a good chance that key principles of school-to-career programs would be integrated into reauthorized Vocational Education, Elementary and Secondary Education, and Workforce Investment Acts. We assumed that states would have had sufficient time and will to create strong school-to-career systems. We believed that Congress and states would look seriously at the lessons of five years of experimentation and support a second generation of improved initiatives.

Now that the STWOA funding has ended, we are far from realizing this scenario. Congress has resisted opportunities to integrate school-to-career endeavors with mainstream education and workforce legislation. Most governors who promoted the school-to-career movement a decade ago have left office. Reauthorization of the STWOA itself is on neither the Republican nor the Democratic agenda.

Nationally, the battle for the school-to-career brand name cannot be won in the short run. Therefore, we propose a strategy that distinguishes between defending the 1994 legislation and aggressively promoting the programs, activities, and outcomes that Congress was trying to encourage. This requires relinquishing the vision of a national school-to-career system in the short run in favor of a longer-term approach to supporting and strengthening effective partnerships, programs, and innovations that can inspire others to embrace school-to-career principles.

SO WHAT'S NEXT?

In 1999, the authors proposed five short-run priorities for the federal Department of Education and of Labor and for states. We argued that government funding and policy should do the following:

1. *Support leading innovators*—programs with demonstrated promise and progress in achieving high-quality outcomes for participating young people.
2. *Focus relentlessly on data and outcomes*—particularly on data demonstrating academic and postsecondary outcomes, including college attendance and completion.
3. *Strengthen partnerships and intermediaries*—through support of employer associations, local consortia, and other networks organizing employers to participate in partnerships and programs.
4. *Reach out to new and potential allies*—particularly institutions and constituencies with school-to-work goals and methods, including innovative postsecondary programs, charter and alternative schools, and after-school programs.
5. *Seed the creation of an independent, nongovernmental resource and documentation center*—or sustain the existing National School-to-Work Learning and Information Center.

These suggestions mapped out high-value investments for the last years of federal school-to-work investments. Some of them have been pursued. At the same time, however, it is clear that preserving and promoting the best of school-to-career practice demands a long-term strategy.

In our view, this strategy should take advantage of the emerging opportunities identified previously and address the perceived and real weaknesses of implementation during the past decade. It must combine elements necessary to "build a field": promoting quality in specific places; documenting and marketing evidence of effectiveness and results; building alliances and influence with other reform efforts; expanding political and public support; identifying material resources; and sustaining an infrastructure for bringing people together and for collecting, analyzing, and disseminating knowledge (see Fine, 1999, on field-building).

Establishing the following five priorities can extend and deepen the work and advance what has been best in the school-to-career movement.

1. Focus on High Schools

Challenges facing high schools, particularly large urban ones, are among the most intractable problems facing education reformers. School-to-career initiatives can point toward different ways of encouraging and motivating academic achievement for young people in their last years of compulsory education (see the National Association of Secondary School Principals' 1996 *Breaking Ranks* report). Emphasizing high schools will enable school-to-career advocates to focus efforts, address a recalcitrant problem, and play to the movement's capability to bridge work and school worlds for young people who are beginning to make important decisions about each.

2. Focus on Postsecondary Institutions and Connections

Increasing postsecondary attendance is at the heart of public-education policy today. Greater school-to-career emphasis on postsecondary institutions can benefit participating students and align school-to-career efforts with an institution that parents value highly. Postsecondary institutions can and should be encouraged to form closer, more creative partnerships with secondary schools to help students transition more successfully. These partnerships could encourage secondary-school students to enroll in postsecondary courses. They could also clarify the roles of high schools and colleges in providing basic and job-specific learning.

Colleges can influence high-school instruction through admissions policies. Public systems in particular can adopt admissions criteria that do not penalize nontraditional courses (as in Wisconsin, Oregon, Colorado, and New Hampshire).

Moreover, colleges and universities are likely to find it worthwhile to introduce school-to-career pedagogies in their programs. Well over 50% of college students work, and the difficulty of balancing work and school is a primary reason for high college-attrition rates. Work-based learning and more motivating pedagogy could provide competitive advantages to entrepreneurial colleges.

3. Promote School-to-Career Principles within Other Reform Movements

Within education and workforce development, several new strategies and initiatives have recently gained momentum. School-to-career advocates should consider carefully which of these developments create opportunities for extending the core principles of the school-to-career movement:

- *The Workforce Investment Act.* Although it was passed in an environment hostile to overt links to school-to-career programs, the bill's youth component provides more opportunities than the Job Training Partnership Act for closer ties between local workforce and education institutions. Local school-to-career partnerships should explore how Workforce Boards and Youth Councils—the governance and planning mechanisms for the act's federally funded public-workforce system—can help sustain collaborative efforts.
- *Charter and other alternative high schools.* Within and outside public schools, charter schools are growing rapidly. Most are elementary and middle schools, but attention to high schools is increasing. Not surprisingly, the high-school models (e.g., career academies) frequently share many elements with school-to-career programs: field-based studies, connections to adults and resources outside schools, and a more personalized, smaller learning environment.
- *The movement for smaller learning communities.* Like the charter movement, efforts to create smaller, more personalized environments for students within large public schools provide opportunities for creating, strengthening, and learning from program designs that embody school-to-career principles.
- *After-school programming.* Improved after-school programming has gained high priority among education policymakers, and funding has been rising steadily. Districts and schools should develop strategies for using the after-school initiative to promote efforts to link schools with community resources.

4. Fund the Local Institutional Base for Long-Term School–Community Partnerships

The pedagogical strengths of school-to-career initiatives—the integration of classroom and external experiences, the projects and performances—can be integrated into mainstream education reform, if a district or state wishes. Professional development resources can be redirected and concentrated; school-improvement funds can be targeted at helping teachers develop curricula; and districts can encourage flexible class schedules, interdisciplinary courses, and out-of-class learning.

What schools cannot do easily do alone is promote and fund the local institutional infrastructure that sustains connections among schools, employers, and other community resources. Federal school-to-career dollars have been used for these connecting activities. Without a funded entity—within the schools or outside them—the day-to-day work of building, maintaining, and developing partnerships that work cannot be accomplished.

We agree with the CED's 1998 policy statement: State or federal governments or both should provide incentive funding to promote innovation and experimentation with different models of staffing and organizing connecting activities. However, other partners should join government in funding these entities. A district's or region's business community, schools, and political institutions must invest time and hard resources in making these connections real and sustainable.

5. Fund Research to Improve Design and Implementation

The school-to-career movement and its proponents have yet to prove sufficiently the power of its instructional strategies. Research on student performance in and following high school is critical if we are to be able to make this case well—and if mainstream education reformers are to recognize school-to-career programs as a viable alternative.

Careful research on postsecondary outcomes—college attendance and persistence, wages and career trajectory—should also be supported. And in the long run, additional achievement measures that capture a broader range of academic and nonacademic skills and competencies than typical standardized assessments will be required.

CONCLUSIONS

In the end, the answer to the question "What's next for school-to-career?" is multifaceted, involving the continued strengthening of practice and strategic policy advocacy at the national level and particularly in the states. We believe the strategies proposed here can advance the school-to-career agenda significantly. They can promote quality and improvement, sustain established state and community efforts that are showing results, and support the school-to-career community while the nation's political and financial capital is evolving. The next few years will not be easy for school-to-career programs, but there are ways to promote the best in past efforts at the federal, state, and local levels, and to position school-to-career principles for emergence and implementation over the long run.

NOTES

1. Language has been an important battleground in defining this reform movement. In the late 1980s, many who were interested in European models of preparing youth for the future advocated the term *youth apprenticeship,* but this was bitterly opposed by organized labor and others. The 1994 federal legislation codified the term *school-to-*

work. Because that seemed to imply that the goal was to move young people in a linear progression through high school into the labor market, the term *school-to-career* came into vogue. We use that term here.

2. In preparing this chapter, we relied on more than 40 conversations with policymakers and practitioners, focus groups with education activists, and frank discussions with leaders from JFF's several networks of practitioners engaged at school and district levels with building strong school-to-career programs. We also relied on Internet debates that JFF initiated in electronic discussion groups, our reading of the evaluation literature, and our firsthand knowledge of programs and ambitious district and state efforts.

3. The authors would like to acknowledge and thank the many individuals who gave generously of their time to be interviewed. We owe a special debt to the leadership group of JFF's Connected Learning Communities, staff at the National School-to-Work Office, and Wendy Puriefoy of the Public Education Network. We also thank Sam Halperin, J. D. Hoye, Rob Ivry, Barbara Kauffman, Bill Spring, Edythe West, Joan Wills, and our colleagues at JFF for careful reading of early drafts. We give final thanks to Christine Sturgis and the Charles Stewart Mott Foundation for their encouragement and support. The original version of this chapter was published by JFF. Funding for this project was provided by the Charles Stewart Mott Foundation.

4. For all the interest in school-to-career programs, only a modest body of well-designed research exists. However, new data are emerging. The national implementation evaluation conducted by Mathematica is useful (see Hershey et al., 1999). Interim results from a random-assignment study of ten career academies nationally, conducted by the Manpower Demonstration Research Corporation, have provided helpful evidence on both outcomes and obstacles, as have independent studies of individual programs (see Kemple & Snipes, 2000; for the most current summary of research evidence on school-to-work outcomes, see Hughes et al., 2001).

5. Female and minority students are likelier than whites to attach high value to their school-to-career experiences (Hershey et al., 1999).

REFERENCES

Cheney, L. (1998, February 3). Limited horizons. *The New York Times*, p. A31.

Commission on the Skills of the American Workforce. (1990). *America's choice: High skills or low wages!* Rochester, NY: National Center on Education and the Economy.

Committee for Economic Development. (1998). *The employer's role in linking school and work.* Washington, DC: Author.

Crain, R. L., Allen, A., Thaler, R., Sullivan, D., Zellman, G. L., Little, J. W., et al. (1998). *The effects of academic career magnet education on high schools and their graduates.* Berkeley, CA: National Center for Research in Vocational Education.

Fine, M. (1999). *Thoughts on field-building: A synthesis of observations.* Washington, DC: Academy for Educational Development.

Grubb, W. N. (1994, August 3). True reform or tired retread? Seven questions to ask about school-to-work programs. *Education Week*, pp. 53–54.

Hershey, A. M., Silverberg, M. K., Haimson, J., Hudis, P., & Jackson, R. (1999). *Expanding options for students: Report to Congress on the National Evaluation of School-to-Work Implementation.* Princeton, NJ: Mathematica Policy Research, Inc.

Hughes, K., Bailey, T., & Mechur, M. (2001). *School-to-work: Making a difference in education. A research report to America.* New York: Columbia University, Teachers College, Institute on Education and the Economy.

Jennings, J. F. (Ed.). (1995). *National issues in education: Elementary and Secondary Education Act.* Bloomington, IN: Phi Delta Kappa International.

Jobs for the Future & Boston Private Industry Council. (1998). *School-to-career initiative demonstrates significant impact on young people.* Boston: Jobs for the Future.

Kemple, J., & Snipes, J. C. (2000). *Career academies: Impacts on students' engagement and performance in high school.* New York: Manpower Demonstration Research Corporation.

Linnehan, F. (1998). Work-based learning (WBL) research—Phase 1. In School District of Philadelphia (Ed.), *School-to-career: Strategies for a quality workforce.* Retrieved from www.phila.k12.pa.us/osess/edforemp/Phila.stc.wbl.results.html

Medrich, E., Ramer, C., Merola, L., & Moskovitz, R. (1998). *School-to-work progress measures: A report to the National School-to-Work Office.* Berkeley, CA: MPR Associates.

National Association of Secondary School Principals. (1996). *Breaking ranks: Changing an American institution.* Washington, DC: Author.

National Center for Education Statistics. (1997). *Digest of education statistics, 1997.* Washington, D.C.: U.S. Department of Education.

Phelps, L. A., Knox, K., & Griggs, L. (1999). *The Wisconsin youth apprentices go to college: Access, persistence and achievement.* Madison, WI: University of Wisconsin–Madison, Center on Education and Work.

Pines, M., & Callahan, J. (1997). *The emerging workforce development system.* Baltimore: Johns Hopkins University, Institute for Policy Studies, Sar Levitan Center for Social Policy Studies.

Pittman, K., & Irby, M. (2000). *Young people continually learning: An overview of the challenges and opportunities for educators.* Washington, DC: Council of Chief State School Officers.

Sizer, T. (1992). *Horace's school: Redesigning the American high school.* Boston: Houghton Mifflin.

Smith, L. (1999, February 17). This is a *nice* private public school. *Education Week,* pp. 50–52.

Westchester Institute for Human Services Research, Inc. (1998, July). New York State's school-to-work initiative demonstrates promising student results. *The STW Reporter, 1* (2), 1–3.

William T. Grant Foundation Commission on Work, Family, and Citizenship. (1988). *The forgotten half: Non-college youth in America. An interim report on the school-to-work transition.* Washington, DC: Author.

Wisconsin Department of Workforce Development. (1999). *Wisconsin youth apprenticeship: Another road to success.* Madison, WI: University of Wisconsin–Madison, Center on Education and Work.

Zemsky, R., Shapiro, D., Iannozzi, M., Cappelli, P., & Bailey, T. (1998). *The transition from initial education to working life in the United States of America.* Stanford, CA: Stanford University, National Center for Postsecondary Improvement.

Index

About the Editors and Contributors

WILLIAM J. STULL is a professor and the chair of economics at Temple University and senior research associate at the Mid-Atlantic Regional Educational Laboratory for Student Success. He has published widely in the areas of urban economics and the economics of education. He is coauthor of two volumes on the Philadelphia regional economy. His most recent research focuses on work-based education. In 1995, he was a visiting scholar at the Federal Reserve Bank of Philadelphia, and he has recently been appointed a member of the Council of Economic Advisors of Philadelphia's mayor, John Street.

NICHOLAS M. SANDERS is a research analyst for quality assurance and evaluation at the Mid-Atlantic Regional Educational Laboratory for Student Success at Temple University. His research and publications have been in the areas of cognition processes, evaluation of moral and citizenship education, school-to-work programs, corporate training, and school privatization. He has been on the educational psychology faculty at the Pennsylvania State University and has coordinated educational research and staff development for educational and business organizations.

JOHN H. BISHOP is an associate professor of Human Resource Studies at Cornell University. He is also executive director of the Educational Excellence Alliance, a consortium of 300 northeastern high schools studying ways to improve school climate and student engagement, and has directed research at the National Center for Research in Vocational Education. His publications include articles on education reform, the impact of business policies on student incentives, and the effectiveness of institutions that match workers and jobs. He has served on various advisory committees related to workforce training.

WILLIAM C. DUNKELBERG is a professor of economics at Temple University, where he has served as dean of the Fox School of Business and Management. He has also served as chief economist for the National Federation of Independent Businesses since 1971. He is a nationally recognized authority on such issues as entrepreneurship and small business, and he has presented expert testimony before the U.S. Congress. He has published extensively, has appeared on national and local news programs, and has served on the boards of many organizations, including the Pennsylvania Council on Economic Education.

BARI ANHALT ERLICHSON is an assistant professor in the department of public policy at Rutgers University. Her research projects include a study of whole-school reform implementation in New Jersey and a multiyear analysis of national education policy. Forthcoming publications on school reform will appear in the *Journal of Education Finance* and *Educational Administration Quarterly.* She served as a poll analyst for NBC news during the 2000 presidential campaign.

ALAN M. HERSHEY is a senior fellow and area leader for welfare studies in the research division of Mathematica Policy Research, Inc. He coordinates national- and state-level studies pertaining to welfare reform, welfare-to-work programs, and associated policies and services. He is the project director and principal investigator for the five-year evaluation of school-to-work implementation sponsored by the U.S. Department of Education. He has published extensively on school-to-work systems and tech-prep programs.

KATHERINE L. HUGHES is a senior research associate at the Institute on Education and the Economy (IEE), Teachers College, Columbia University. She has taught sociology at New York University and Columbia University. At IEE, she has directed and conducted field research on school-to-work programs and vocational high-school reform. Her many publications on school-to-work programs include a book with Thomas R. Bailey and David Thornton Moore, *Work-Based Learning and Education Reform* (in press). Her current efforts include an evaluation of the National Academy Foundation's Career Academy program.

RICHARD KAZIS is the senior vice president of Jobs for the Future, leading the organization's policy and research efforts. He directed its multi-site initiative on school-to-career models and has directed many projects helping high-school students connect with employers and other community resources more effectively. He has published many books, reports, and articles on issues of work and learning for disadvantaged populations. A former teacher at an alternative high school for returning dropouts, he serves on the boards of the Institute for Local Self-Reliance and the Brookline Foundation.

MICHAEL A. LEEDS is an associate professor of economics at Temple University, and has been director of the honors program in the Fox School of Business at Temple since 1994. He has published in the areas of labor, applied microeconomics, and the economics of sports. He is the coauthor of a new textbook on the last subject, *The Economics of Sports* (2002). He has served as executive director of the American Economic Association Summer Minorities Program.

ROBERT I. LERMAN is the director of the Labor and Social Policy Center at the Urban Institute and is a professor of economics at American University. He has conducted research and published in the areas of welfare, income inequality, family structure, and youth employment. He coauthored a 1990 article on youth apprenticeship in *The Public Interest* that influenced the debate over school-to-work programs. As a staff economist for the Congressional Joint Economic Committee, he worked on national employment and training reform.

FERRAN MAÑE is an assistant professor at the Rovira I Virgili University in Spain. He has been a visiting fellow at Essex University in England and at Cornell University. He has published articles and book chapters on vocational education, worker training and productivity, and the effects of technological change on educational and occupational structures. He is currently involved in research projects examining changes in the demand for skilled workers and the school-to-work transition in the United States.

DAVID THORNTON MOORE is the associate dean of the Gallatin School of Individualized Study at New York University. An educational anthropologist, he specializes in studies of learning in the workplace. His earlier research on an experience-based high-school program was published in *Harvard Educational Review, Anthropology and Education Quarterly,* and *Experiential Education.* A former Kellogg National Leadership Fellow, he has investigated quality-of-work-life issues in Scandinavia, Africa, China, Australia, and the United States.

LEONARD I. NAKAMURA is an economic advisor in the Research Department of the Federal Reserve Bank of Philadelphia. He has published articles and books on financial and monetary economics, economic measurement, and energy use. Most recently, he has been applying and extending Joseph Schumpeter's theory of creative destruction to analyze the new economy. His other research projects include Argentine financial history and bank monitoring of troubled borrowers.

HILARY PENNINGTON is the vice chairman, chief executive officer, and cofounder of Jobs for the Future. She has overseen the organization's extensive and nationally influential research and policy agenda in the areas of economic change, youth transitions, and workforce development. She has published extensively in journals, including the *Harvard Business Review* and the *Boston Globe*, and she has appeared on national and regional television and radio. A member of several national task forces and organizational boards, she has been co-chair of the Presidential Advisory Committee on Expanding Training Opportunities.

FRANCISCO L. RIVERA-BATIZ is an associate professor of economics at Columbia University and of economics and education at Teachers College at Columbia. Among his many books, monographs, and articles on the economics of education are *A Profile and Analysis of Students in Vocational Training: Literacy Skills, Demographics, and Socioeconomic Characteristics* and *Reinventing Urban Education*. He has served as an advisor to the New York City Board of Education and the Council of Education of the Commonwealth of Puerto Rico.

MARK ROHLAND is an editor and writer at the Center for Research in Human Development and Education at Temple University. Trained in American literature, he has published articles on Thomas Pynchon and Alice Walker. He has edited books and monographs on labor economics, educational productivity, and the sociology of medicine. His commentary has appeared in the *Philadelphia Inquirer.*

JAMES E. ROSENBAUM is professor of sociology, education, and social policy at Northwestern University. His studies of work, education, and housing opportunities have been published extensively. He is the author of *Beyond College-for-All: Career Paths for the Forgotten Half* (2001). A new project, Employers' Interactions with Community Colleges and Proprietary Schools, compares institutional practices and explores school–employer communication. His research, described frequently in the media, has influenced national policies.

MARK C. SCHUG is director of the University of Wisconsin–Milwaukee Center for Economic Education. He has taught at the middle-school, high-school, and college levels, and won teaching awards from the University of Wisconsin and the Minnesota Council on Economic Education. He edited *The Senior Economist* for many years and has coauthored eight national curriculum programs as well as *Economics: Choices & Challenges*, a high-school economics text. He has conducted training programs for teachers throughout the United States.

DAVID STERN is a professor of education at the University of California, Berkeley. He has directed the National Center for Research in Vocational Education and been principal administrator in the Center for Educational Research and Innovation at the Organization for Economic Cooperation and Development. His extensive research and publications have focused on the relationship between education and work and on resource allocation in schools. He is the lead author of *School to Work: Research on Programs in the United States.*

RICHARD D. WESTERN is an associate professor (retired) and a lecturer (currently) in the Department of Curriculum and Instruction at the University of Wisconsin–Milwaukee, where he directed the teacher-education program for secondary-school English and served as department chair. He has published extensively on the teaching of English and on education policy in Wisconsin. Involved in editorial work for several years, he has served as editor of *Metropolitan Education* and as associate editor of the *Journal of Teacher Education* and other publications.

ELIZABETH WHEATON is pursuing a Ph.D. in economics at Temple University and holds an M.S. in international business and trade from Grambling State University. She has presented papers at conferences, including the International Atlantic Economic Conference. She is interested in the field of labor economics with specialization in child-labor issues.

ROBERT ZEMSKY is founding director of the University of Pennsylvania's Institute for Research on Higher Education, a major national public policy center. He also serves as a senior scholar in the National Center for Postsecondary Improvement, leading the project focusing on the employability and educational attainment of college students and graduates. With Peter Cappelli, he edited *The Changing Educational Quality of the Workforce,* and his publications include reports on the school-to-work transition and international workforce training. He plays a major role in the Six-Nation Project on Global Education for the 21st Century, sponsored in the United States by Penn's Graduate School of Education.